YANKEE
Blues

YANKEE
Blues

*Musical Culture and
American Identity*

MACDONALD SMITH MOORE

*Indiana
University
Press*

BLOOMINGTON

Library of Congress Cataloging in Publication Data

Moore, MacDonald Smith.
Yankee blues.

Bibliography: p.
Includes index.
1. Music—United States—History and criticism.
I. Title.
ML200.M75   1985   781.773   83-49407
ISBN 0-253-36803-0
1 2 3 4 5   89 88 87 86 85

For
Deborah,
Mordecai, and Mikhael

For Puritan and Transcendentalist alike, autobiography and spiritual biography fused in the process of writing "our" New World history. And for both of them, auto-American-biography meant simultaneously a total assertion of the self, a jeremiad against the misdirected progress of the "dead" present, and an act of prophecy which guaranteed the future by celebrating the regenerate "Americanus." The closing scene of Mather's Life of Winthrop—where the venerated Davidic ruler addresses the tribes of the American Israel—is transparently a private wish-fulfillment. It is properly balanced by the biography's opening quotation: *"Quincunque venti erunt, art nostra certe non aberit"*—"Whatever winds may blow, our art will surely never pass away."

    —Sacvan Bercovitch, *The Puritan Origins of the American Self*

There can be no society which does not feel the need of upholding and reaffirming at regular intervals the collective sentiments and the collective ideas which make its unity and its personality. Now this moral remaking cannot be achieved except by the means of reunions, assemblies and meetings where the individuals, being closely united to one another, reaffirm in common their common sentiments. . . . If we find a little difficulty today in imagining what these feasts and ceremonies of the future could consist in, it is because we are going through a stage of transition and moral mediocrity. . . . In a word, the old gods are growing old or already dead, and others are not yet born. . . . But this state of incertitude and confusing agitation cannot last forever. A day will come when our societies will know again those hours of creative effervescence, in the course of which new ideas arise and new formulae are found which serve for a while as a guide to humanity. . . . There are no gospels which are immortal, but neither is there any reason for believing that humanity is incapable of inventing new ones.

    —Emile Durkheim, *Elementary Forms of Religious Life*

Music is our myth of the inner life—a young, vital, and meaningful myth. . . .

    —Susanne K. Langer, *Philosophy in a New Key*

CONTENTS

PART ONE

New England's Musical Mission

I

1. The Nervous Burden   10

2. Redemptive Culture   44

PART TWO

Ethnic Dissonance

65

3. Jazz and the Asphalt Jungle   73

   Ragged Prelude / 74
   Bête Noire / 82
   White Rebels and the New Negro / 92
   Motor Music / 105

4. The Distorted Mirror   109

   Europe Crowns Jazz / 111
   Modernism: Errant Symbols / 119

5. Passing the Torch   128

   The Jewish Nexus / 130
   The Great White Hope / 160

Epilogue / 169
Notes / 172
Bibliography / 198
Index / 208

ILLUSTRATIONS

Charles Ives   20
Daniel Gregory Mason   25
Charles Ives and his daughter   30
Carl Ruggles   41
The Original Dixieland Jazz Band   84
Carl Van Vechten   97
John Hammond and friends   102
Ken Johnson and Bessie Dudley   105
Louis Armstrong and his band   113
Duke Ellington   114
George Gershwin   138
Aaron Copland   142
Serge Koussevitzky, Aaron Copland, and Leonard Bernstein   148
Ernest Bloch   159
Roy Harris   162

PART ONE

New England's Musical Mission

"If men define situations as real, they are real in their consequences," wrote the sociologist W. I. Thomas. Thomas's observation illuminates an important truth about symbolic social groups: they are landmarks on the social topography, coordinates with which society triangulates its consciousness of order and meaning and its sense of collective personality. Symbolic groups exist because people believe in them. Their effects are real. A symbolic group may profoundly shape its members' identities even though it would not otherwise decisively determine the possibilities that life offers them.

In the United States, race serves as a key common denominator defining symbolic groups. For roughly the first third of this century, Americans used the word *race* in its various forms to designate virtually any group of people—family, clan, nation, the brotherhood of all mankind—even when no blood continuity could possibly be maintained. Simultaneously it served as a public euphemism in discussions of the American "color problem." Context was everything in such a situation. Since World War II, the word has been used in a sharply narrowed sense, even though dictionaries have not generally kept pace with the precipitous change in usage. *Race*, in the United States today, means color. Both *racism* and *racialism* are strongly pejorative. The newly narrowed base of usage is no better than the old vagueness. In each instance a conceptual problem is aggravated by a linguistic inadequacy. *Ethnicity* has been seized upon to fill the public euphemism gap, among both scholars and the general public. Its elasticity covers many conceptual embarrassments. Behind the pseudoanthropology of traditional "racial" distinctions lives the conviction that people actually perceive reality in ways unique to their "own kind," and hence arrive at standards of truth, beauty, and morality idiosyncratic to their group. Racial theory is rooted in the belief that the spirit of a people is distinctive. Such symbolic group definition is an interactive ritual, but with frequent imbalances of power.[1]

Symbolic groups are concrete correlatives of a class of "collective representations," as the great sociologist Emile Durkheim called socially defined categories of understanding. These symbolic reference groups of society embody points of the cultural compass. Usually they represent clusters of traits about which much of society has deeply ambivalent feelings. Indeed, the tensions of their internal ambiguities powerfully hold people's imaginations. The core ambiguities of symbolic groups are most cogently expressed through metaphors. Metaphor lends ambiguity the allure of paradox. Because it is preoccupied with metaphorical exploration and manipulation, artistic culture serves as a highly public arena for the confirmation, the modification, even the occasional transformation of these collective representations. Plato banned poets from his utopian state because he believed they could recast ideal reality, distorting the true order of things. A post-Enlightenment cult of culture treats art as a sacred activity, artists as "unacknowledged legislators," keepers of the collective consciousness. If artistic culture is a kind of civil religion, the qualifications of its "elect" are of artistic and civil interest to the entire society.

This book studies how cultural debate manipulates the root metaphors of symbolic groups in the United States, and how this discussion impinges upon cultural criticism. The controversy within American musical culture between the world wars reveals this metaphorical dialectic as an intricate drama. Yankee composers defined their civic selves in terms of a cultural mission. In the 1920s their vision of redemptive culture became the matrix for a generational battle that turned increasingly on racial issues. The arena of musical culture provided a forum for a complex courtship of desires, antipathies, dreams, and fears. Formally trained musicians and a variety of critics and laymen contested characteristics attributed to the culture of Yankees, Negroes, and Jews in a metaphorical struggle to define the essential nature of America, its past meaning, and its future identity.[2] Yet debates over America's music did not merely mirror the larger dialectic of ideological, regional, and ethnic antagonisms. Rather, musical culture came to be regarded as a renascent American civil religion. This belief in the religious potential of musical culture can be traced, in its modern American formulation, to the generation of native composers born in the 1870s.

Yankee composers pursued a dual mission. They conducted an errand into the wilderness of the twentieth century to manifest New England's right to speak for America. And they campaigned for Matthew Arnold's Victorian vision of culture as "sweetness and light," as a religious force capable of formulating principles of individual and social value. Thus, they elided their Yankee and Victorian callings into a prophetic religious ideology, believing that a nation scuttling pell-mell into the twentieth century needed to affirm a unique consciousness. They hoped to herald America's glorious future by sublimating in music the spiritual heritage of New England. Yet as mature men, they faced public apathy and rejection by younger composers. A "conflict of generations" pitted modernist "sons" against Yankee "fathers" unwilling to embrace the anarchic present. Because Yankee composers had managed to link music in the United States with issues of American identity, music criticism became a primary locus of national cultural conflict in the 1920s. Through metaphors of musical valuation, Americans struggled to define and rank the key symbolic groups in American society of the twentieth century: Yankees, Negroes, and Jews.

The Yankee composers constituted a particularly self-conscious segment of a symbolic group trying to assert its centrality to the national destiny. All born within four years of the American centennial, the centennial composers were united by a common sense of tradition and destiny. Typically of old Anglo-American stock, nominal Congregationalists in religion, they received their educations at Harvard or Yale. These composers included Arthur Farwell (1872), Edward Burlingame Hill (1872), Daniel Gregory Mason (1873), Charles Ives (1874), Carl Ruggles (1876), John Alden Carpenter (1876), and David Stanley Smith (1877). Yankees by regional affiliation and sense of destiny, the centennial composers adopted a genteel lifestyle while challenging the assertion that therefore they were effeminate, unattached idealists. By virtue of the world view they shared with such an English missionary to the middle class as Matthew Arnold, they were humanist Victorians, devoted to culture as a civil religion capable of ordering a distracted national moral consciousness.

The centennial generation was the third group of Yankee composers to share similar backgrounds and aspirations. The New England school, extending from the 1760s to 1820, included such figures as Daniel Read, William Billings, Justin Morgan, Andrew Law, and Jeremiah Ingalls. The second Yankee school, active in the late nineteenth and early twentieth centuries, began with John Knowles Paine, its musical patriarch, and included George Chadwick, Mrs. H. H. A. Beach, Arthur Foote, Theodore Parker, Arthur Whiting, and possibly the romanticist Edward MacDowell. The centennial composers followed this second generation and comprised the academic musical establishment in the 1920s. Hill, Mason, and Smith headed the music departments of Harvard, Columbia, and Yale respectively.

Conflict between the centennial Yankees and the younger generation of composers born from 1895 to 1900 strengthened the older men's sense of the tradition that bound them together.[3] A diverse group, the younger men included few Yankees.[4] As Mason and his peers distinguished themselves from the younger generation, they increasingly referred to their Yankee tradition in terms of an Anglo-Saxon heritage. They believed that this "racial" inheritance had sired a neighborly sense of moral community peculiar to old New England, and they worried that theirs was the last generation of composers to retain a semblance of ethnic unity. The diversity of the younger generation encouraged the Yankees to define themselves by what they were not: not recent immigrants, neither Catholics nor Jews, seldom enthusiasts of the emergent ethnic, industrial, urban America, not

Southerners, and surely not Negroes. But Puritan family roots and identification allowed the centennial composers to easily assimilate midwesterners such as Farwell, Carpenter, and Smith into the Yankee family.

Daniel Gregory Mason best represents the mainstream experiences and outlook of the centennial composers.[5] Descended from the country's most illustrious musical family, Mason rooted his concern for the social and spiritual potential of music in his family's Yankee lineage. Mason's education strengthened the lessons of his heritage.[6] He attended Harvard as a matter of course and learned there to approach music not as a secular skill but as a key element of humanistic culture. He dedicated his life to musical culture, through critical writing, teaching, and composing. During the 1920s and 1930s, Mason figured importantly in the American musical establishment. In his time he was the most widely read American author of critical essays and books on music.[7] As professor and chairman of the music department at Columbia University, his opinions commanded respect. He composed a large body of well-crafted, moderately conservative works that were performed by the most renowned ensembles in the United States. Yet characteristic though he is of his more successful peers, by himself Mason cannot examplify the range of the Yankee composers.

Charles Ives provides a useful contrast to Mason. Son of a talented and quirky bandmaster, Ives was torn all his life between his conviction that some classical music represented a creative moral order of religious dimensions, and his fear that genteel culture, including much classical music, might be terminally infected by a debilitating effeminacy. Ives failed to accommodate himself to the requirements of the musical culture taught at Yale and controlled by genteel patronage. He responded by dividing his life: he pursued success and public fulfillment through business; in private he struggled to create a manly, spiritual music. He melded dissonances, experimental rhythms, innovative timbres, and vernacular tunes into a singular style that stretched the limits of "classically" defined music. Ives's idiosyncratic music was deliberately tough. His eclectic "modernism" sprang from his impulse to strengthen and democratize culture.

The concept of "modernism" suffers from categorical flatulence as it expands to accommodate naturalists, dadaists, cubists, nèoromantics, expressionists, precisionists, realists, futurists, and even a cantankerous Yankee eclectic. This bloated "modernism" excludes only those whose art, lifestyle, and world view are all conservative. Perhaps Ives's idiosyncratic eclecticism legitimates his inclusion under the broad aegis of "modernism." But by no means was Ives an avant-garde composer, a purveyor of radical expressionism or radical materialism as a weapon against cultural responsibility. True, the conservative establishment shunned him, and eventually several young modernists lionized him. But while Ives valued their appreciation and the individuals who befriended him, he considered the bohemian avant-garde effeminate and spiritually bankrupt—a killing Victorian damnation. Nor would Ives have been sympathetic to the "system builders" among European modernists.[8]

Because of his profound ambivalence toward the culture of classical music, Ives provides an excellent test of generalizations about the views of centennial Yankees. The extent to which his experiences and beliefs approached Mason's norm serves as a measure of how Yankee composers perceived their calling.

Through culture, the centennial composers asserted the rebirth of a specifically American self-consciousness out of the germinal Puritan errand into the wilderness. Men as different as Mason and Ives shaped their lives to the mold of "auto-American-biography," as the literary historian Sacvan Bercovitch has called the mode of the American errand. From their sense of being chosen instruments of God-in-history, Puritans evolved a vision of spiritually ordered community that, stripped of its specifically Christian formulation, became the Yankee's religion of Americanism. But as politicians, industrialists, revivalists, reformers, poets, and novelists all appropriated the symbolism of redemptive America to identify their own interests with a transcendent national destiny, Yankees found themselves no longer caretakers of their own tradition.[9] Yankee composers felt increasingly isolated from the sources of political and economic power, from the pulse of national life in general. They found it difficult to extol an individualistic, boundless, and rootless progressivism, as Emerson had done, in the face of evidence that such Americanism fed a materialistic society with little use for the values Yankees represented. Through culture they sought to reestablish their vision of an essentialist American faith that would delineate not merely a horizontal democratic order but a vertical order of transcendental values.

As "unacknowledged legislators," the centennial composers discovered their calling to sensitize Americans to a moral ether whose steady breeze could fill the vacuum of social life, imparting an existential sense of direction to human activity. Their task was to recapture for a modern age the moral ether of innocence that the novelist Henry James felt blowing through Hawthorne's prose. "The cold, bright air of New England . . . looks young," wrote James, "the light of the sun seems fresh and innocent, as if it knew as yet but few of the secrets of the world and none of the weariness of shining."[10] Only in the realm of art did a spiritual wind still blow unsullied. Through an art with sources in New England's traditions, culture would restore for Americans the experience of religious order, like a fresh sea breeze.[11] In his ideal of music as the key to redemptive culture, the Yankee composer combined Emerson's New England mission with Arnold's Victorian mission. Great music served the spiritual and civic responsibilities of culture.[12] Great Yankee music would help America know its best self. At the core of the centennial composers' redemptive culture lay their aesthetic of identity.

The Yankee aesthetic of identity drew upon the commonplaces of Victorian assumptions about music as an art. Yankee composers are different as Mason and Ives synthesized remarkably congruent theories. They balanced the claims of formalism and functionalism and held both in uneasy symbiosis with a mediating idealist and imaginative naturalism. Though proud that music was the most formally pure art, they distrusted the claims of hermetic formalism. They argued that music's abstract purity made it uniquely able to reflect forms of spiritual reality instead of the profane material existence of modern life. Likewise, they deemed music the perfect medium through which the heroic artist communicated spiritual order to his fellow citizens. Yankee composers hoped that music would sublimate an essential American spirit. Artists sensitive to the roots of national consciousness might create in their works the most fundamental grammar of identity, a standard of American value.

Unlike romantics, who characteristically worshipped art, the Victorian Yankee composer worshipped culture.[13] Art gives wings to culture but must be tethered against Icarus-like expressionism. Culture harnesses art to tradition, justifying each in terms of the other. As these Yankees distrusted hermetic formalism, they also shunned a narrow interest in art traditions as such. In the spirit of Arnold, who called on culture to "preserve the best that has been thought and written," and in the spirit of the literary historian Van Wyck Brooks,

who called for the creation of a "usable past," Yankee composers
viewed tradition as the life line of culture. They posited this tradition
as an ideal world ordered by blood ties, neighborliness, and natural
status. Mason characterized this historical fiction as a "fellowship of
the past."[14]

In redemptive culture, art and tradition are responsible to one
another. Art and the prophetic future are similarly wedded. Supported by tradition, art creates perceptual frames of value, requisites
of social meaning. Musical art embodies this grammar of identity not
as a series of propositions but as immediately apprehensible form.
Living in an ideal past and an ideal future, Yankee composers conducted a jeremiad against the profane present. If they would but try,
contemporary Americans could best experience the American spirit
through musical culture. In concert, audiences could worship culture.
Through music the categories of a true civil religion could emerge.
When he felt unable to communicate satisfactorily with contemporary
audiences, a man such as Mason sought solace, influence, and immortality in a "fellowship of the future."

Racial thinking was not exactly the negation of a faith in progressive culture but an alternative and related mode of pursuing the same
ends. Mason shared with the social scientist Charles Horton Cooley a
concern with the emergence of a "natural aristocracy" of national cultural leadership. "The world of thought, and eventually the world of
action, comes gradually under the rule of a true aristocracy of intelligence and character, in place of an artificial one created by exclusive
opportunity."[15] In its most general meaning, race was the external sign
of an internal grace. Natural aristocrats were naturally the sons of
New England.[16] Even among culture critics who did not think highly
of the Yankees' compositions, many found their own feelings about
music and American culture codified in the aesthetic of identity and
religion of redemptive culture. The Yankee custodians of musical culture, preeminently Mason, set the terms of national debate concerning
the legitimacy of their modernist "sons," and the meaning of American
musical life of the 1920s and 1930s.

The centennial composers were not coopted by the cults of experience that became our century's neoromantic accommodation to the
cage of rationalization. The consumer society held little attraction for
these Yankees. They considered their works ideal counterexamples to
an unending stream of musical novelties made to be quickly popular

and quickly replaced. Mason and Ives believed that the composer who consciously seeks to "get his audience" through effects will end by making superficial, market-hungry music. They wanted nothing to do with such "mannered," "romantic" music; it lacked spiritual strength.

At every level of their beings, the centennial composers grappled with issues of will and identity. They succumbed neither to cults of the self nor to cults of the exotic other. As spiritual grandchildren of the Puritans, they might be expected to vibrate between poles of aggressive egoism and the desire to experience the solvent of pantheistic mysticism; yet they remained committed to the demands of redemptive culture. While Ives and Ruggles drank at the well of transcendentalism, their ecstatic feelings nourished a productive idealism. They did not indulge in self-centered dissolution or sink themselves into an "oceanic feeling" devoid of will or ego. The emergent therapeutic ideal, with its substitution of narcissism for morality, held little allure for these men. They would fight through the "nervous burden" afflicting them and the Yankee *conscious collective.*"

Centennial composers sought neither to dissolve nor to fortify the self through exotic experiences. Cultural otherness served them as an antithesis to their own personality and culture. Weeds grew "out there"; the grass was not greener on the other side of the fence. Although Arthur Farwell flirted for a time with a local-color Americanism that drew on Indian sources, the centennial Yankees generally considered premodern exoticism—Oriental, Negro, or medieval—extrinsic to their mission. Some, such as Mason, lost heart and came to feel that the domestic culture had been invaded by wild flowers, weeds that threatened to overgrow the American garden.[17]

1

THE NERVOUS BURDEN

Both Mason and Ives committed themselves to music as the crown of redemptive culture. But each man accommodated himself to his mission according to his own perceptions of its penalties and rewards. From childhood both men knew the scorn of peers who associated culture in general, and music in particular, with effeminate ineffectuality and undemocratic exclusivity. They struggled all their lives with permutations of these issues.

Mason and Ives grew into manhood during the early progressive era. Americans experienced the years from 1890 until World War I as a voyage into the unknown. They fit new sails to their great clipper "progress" and navigated into the shifting tides of the twentieth century. The United States had become a multiethnic urban society with an aggressively capitalist economy pressured by a broadening democratic ideology. Cities filling with immigrant Europeans and migrant Negroes seemed to breed a dangerous social disorganization. Robert Wiebe's phrase the "search for order" well characterizes the progressive mission.[1] There was some consensus among progressives that before they could master the economic and political machinery of society, the idea of "order" itself had to be expanded beyond positivist ideas about ends and means. At its heart the "search for order" was an effort to rediscover a *conscience collective*, a spiritual sextant for the new century. Moral instrumentalism served progressivism as a loose-limbed "philosophy." For all its vaunted tough present-mindedness, instrumentalism was bound together by a faith that fed on imagined pasts and imminent futures. Typically, the ideal instrument of progressivism was education. In David Noble's words, "Education revealed the natural and democratic reality toward which the American public should make progress."[2] Education was sold as a panacea. Public school would make possible a civilized mass polity. College was to be an incubus of personal and civic character for America's leaders. A strenuous collegiality bridged the years between childhood at home and the battlefield of adult responsibility.[3] At college, in the heat of the progressive era, the centennial Yankees came to grips with their mission in life. Subsequently, as college professors, some of them would try to consolidate the lessons of progress as they had come to understand them.

Young adults typically view their era as a fulcrum of historical transition, but for Mason and Ives the discontinuities of the 1890s were underlined by multiple traumas. Their fathers died unexpectedly early in the decade. Psychological loss was exacerbated by declining financial security just when they most needed help. Their personal misfortunes were framed by the severe depression of 1893, with its attendant social and spiritual dislocations. Mason and Ives had every reason to feel cut off from their roots. College was their first proving ground. At Harvard and Yale the centennial Yankees dealt with their losses and made bargains with culture.

As the first generation of American composers to study their profession in the context of a liberal arts college education, the centennial Yankees were forced to adjust to a disciplined treatment of music as culture. At Harvard and Yale they took their first steps toward defining a symbolic relationship between musical culture and democracy, between art and the vernacular. Ives and Mason tested the limits of tonal decorum and toyed with the promiscuous mixing of the classic and the vernacular. Mason submitted to the guidelines of genteel culture with minimal resistance. He fully internalized a range of humanist Victorian values to which he was predisposed in any case. The cultivated gentility of his musically renowned family prepared him to seek the company of other young men like himself, cultural idealists—poets, philosophers, and musicians. He accepted the lessons of Harvard: that dissonance must know its place, that music as art is sacred, that the vernacular is profane. Ives, on the other hand, felt himself torn apart by competing commitments. He admired his father's Whitman-like love of both classical and vernacular music; yet his father's lack of conventional social status distressed him. At Yale, Ives rebelled against genteel definitions of classical correctness. Dissonances, like free men, ought not be tied to the apron strings of genteel sensibilities. Nor would he accept the generalization, implicit in much college music training, that classicism represented sacred culture while vernacular marches or jigs were profane. Unlike Mason, Ives courted the friendship of the regular guys, of fraternity and sports-oriented upperclassmen. Yet college did not spoil Ives's love of classical music. He graduated from Yale convinced that traditional forms had yielded music of transcendent greatness. They could do so again, he decided, only if divorced from the debilitating exclusivity of weak-kneed gentility.

After college, Ives and Mason left the security of their New England homes to build careers in New York City. Each sought individual fulfillment. Mason, descended from a famous family of piano pedagogues, virtuosi, essayists, and businessmen, pursued a career as a concert pianist. Though his family connections eased his confrontation with New York, Mason failed. He withdrew to Boston to reconsider his calling, to suffer the nervous burden of his destiny. In his choice of career, Ives acted out the schizophrenic ambitions and qualms that had long troubled him. He decided to become an individual, conventional success through the insurance business. In insurance a dedicated young man could get rich quickly. And Ives conceived of insurance as a socially useful business. He relegated music to the private sphere, where it would not be dependent on the approval of nice ladies and nicer men. Thus Ives thought to avoid the toll exacted of his father's stubbornly independent musical life.

Mason emerged from his dark years in Boston dedicated to the progressive cause of great music in America. As critical essayist, teacher, and composer, he chose to missionize for musical culture. He sought to expand the audiences of his day, to introduce educated young men to the potentials of redemptive culture. From the start, his essays and books attracted widespread, favorable attention. Mason's writings led to his appointment at Columbia University. There he used the full weight of his influence to further public understanding of music in all its potential glory. By contrast, Ives refused actively to court the public, though he sincerely applauded Mason's efforts. Rather than missionize to expand the size and extend the understanding of contemporary audiences, Ives composed classical music both vernacular and tough, music that might appeal to the democratic people while scaring away some genteel ladies.

Both men succeeded in their careers; but as Yankee composers they continued to struggle under their nervous burden. Mason reached a wide American audience through his writings. At Columbia he became the first MacDowell Professor of Music. His compositions were promptly performed around the country by internationally renowned musicians. Wealthy patrons and friends enabled him to travel to Europe and compose in the New England countryside.[4] Yet Mason grew increasingly restive and unhappy with the state of music. Specifically, he felt that his own music, which he liked to think of as Yankee classicism, was not having a sufficient impact. Disconsolately, he analyzed the faults of audiences, critics, and performers. In the writings of Emerson and Thoreau, Mason sought support for his ideas about artistic leadership in a democracy. He decided that individuals emerging from the inert masses would form a saving remnant, a cultural vanguard leading the masses to appreciate the best of which they were capable. This form of progressive democracy characterized the role of the artist and educator as one who must suffer to provide ideal models for people still incapable of perceiving their greater destiny.

Ives succeeded in the insurance business. He became a respected innovator in his profession, married a bright, understanding, and beautiful woman with excellent society connections, and quickly became wealthy enough to build a country estate where he could escape from the hated pressure and noise of New York City. But fulfillment he sought through an extraprofessional affair with his true passion, music. It would be wrong to suppose, as Arnold Schoenberg did later, that Ives cared nothing about audience approval.[5] Ives desperately longed for the people to love and understand his music. He laced his works with barbed wire to keep out the sissies, and probably to assure himself that he wasn't one too. Through his music he tried to fashion a manly redemptive culture, a civil religion for all stout-hearted Americans. He conceived his music as an invitation to a mountain climb, not to a tea party. The insults of critics and musicians hurt him, as did the indifference of the public. He too turned to Emerson and Thoreau for consolation and support. But unlike Mason, who raked over the public in search of scapegoats, Ives resisted the temptation to blame Americans in general for what he took to be the failure of genteel culture itself. Instead he lashed out at "molly-coddle" critics, at "prima-donna" conductors, and at his own class, the Yankees. Convinced that Yankee gentility had succumed to the virus of "lily-livered" exclusivity, Ives bore his nervous burden by himself, until, emotionally drained at the age of forty-seven, he ceased to compose. He tinkered with his old music, adding new barriers of dissonance and writing lengthy program notes to explain his intentions. He lived just long enough to taste public adulation. When it came, he distrusted it, or himself, to the end.

Centennial Yankee composers struggled to win public recognition of their own culture as essential to American national identity. In the face of a triumphant materialist civilization, they feared that New England's idealism might fail, that in fact they represented a Yankee-hood "which stays in corners, speechless and impotent."[6] They worried lest they slip, as Emerson did, into a protective senility, safe from engagement with civilization's terrible anarchy, or, as Henry Adams did, into a paranoid, bitter defeatism.

Obsessed with the decline of Yankee will and vision, Henry Adams generalized his fears into the law of entropy in history: that until infused by barbarian invasion with new energy, every civilization winds down like the spring of a clock. Other Yankees wondered if the "stretched passion" of the Puritan errand was nearly spent. They saw barbarians, brought by the new immigration, very much in evidence. For such gentlemen as Henry Cabot Lodge and Henry and Brooks Adams, "history was indeed one goddamned thing after another," observes the historian David Hackett Fisher. Without moral order, they imagined that the anarchy of modern life would destroy the American dream itself. Perhaps history was "a steady spiral running downward toward the left, and culminating in some dark catastrophe—lava flowing through the streets of Quincy, or a tidal wave crashing upon Nahant, or a wild-eyed mob of Jews and Irishmen smashing in the doors of the Boston Atheneum and scribbling madly in the margins of books."[7]

Mason and Ives, and several of their colleagues, tried to escape these dangerous shoals of despair. They took up their errand during the progressive era; and in its spirit they voiced a determined optimism, a faith in a brighter day ahead. While they felt called to a mission, occasionally they sensed that the promise of ultimate redemption had been withdrawn. It was hard not to buckle under the strains of feeling called yet unwanted; it was difficult to bear the burdens of mission, music, and manliness. Ives tended toward Emerson's internalization of strain. A premature nervous aging forced Ives to withdraw into himself. After a near-breakdown at the outset of his career, Mason dedicated his life to a public mission on behalf of musical culture. But, like Adams, he became increasingly bitter and vengeful with age. The "nervous burden" Mason and Ives endured symptomized their sense of crushing responsibility and foreboding. Like other genteel Yankees, the centennial composers were shaken by tremors of impotence when faced by the dimensions of their task in behalf of cultural Americanism. Various forms of psychosomatic debilities, even paralysis, occasionally afflicted these otherwise healthy genteel men and women.[8]

But Yankee composers carried a double burden because of their background and profession. By the late nineteenth century, *gentility* often connoted an effete, nonproductive class of society that clung to merely traditional prerogatives of esteem. *Genteel* also designated a lifestyle, a comportment associated with education and pride in family roots. In this sense, *genteel* accurately describes the lives of most centennial composers. With their families and their maids, they moved back and forth from their city brownstones to their country homes. They bore the extra expenses of books and trips to Europe as necessities. Often they were repelled by bohemian singularity but attracted by cantankerous individuality. They participated in that broad New England-based Protestant gentility which characteristically included a few small-town professionals and farmers in its lower ranks; urban professionals, most notably university professors, in its middle ranks; and famous artists and well-to-do old families in its upper ranks. To be a genteel Yankee, it was better to be neither extremely rich nor extremely poor. But either disability could be ameliorated by humanistic education, good family history, and adequate manners. As a group, musicians seemed to epitomize the putative failings of gentility generally. Anglo-American Victorian composers were painfully aware that they were considered mere craftsmen of evanescent pleasures, artists who painted with air, architects who designed sandcastles. Individually, and collectively, they were unusually sensitive to the assumption that they didn't do a man's work.

In the United States, composers felt the sting of disrespect still more sharply. Cultural critics such as Santayana singled out Yankees as the grandmotherly carriers of a "Genteel Tradition" that isolated itself from the masculine will of entrepreneurial America. The Genteel Tradition dominated national intellectual and artistic life, asserted

Santayana. It was expressed in a "simple, sweet, humane, Protestant literature, grandmotherly in that sedate, spectacled wonder with which it gazed at this terrible world and said how beautiful and how interesting it all was."[9] The pejorative edge of such characterizations cut especially close to the Yankee composers, since they thought that American classical music was tied to the apron strings of a female, amateur patronage. In one fashion or another, they sought to divorce themselves from their female audience: by developing a broader patronage, by emphasizing the masculine character of their personal lifestyles, by toughening up their music. To be both a composer and a Yankee meant living a life doubly stressed.

The lives of Mason and Ives reveal a range of Yankee backgrounds, temperaments, and experiences. Both men shared the formative encounter of receiving advanced musical training in the context of a liberal arts education. College taught them that while music was a sacred art, musical culture must seek a picturesque ideal. From a less urbane background than Mason, Ives rebelled against genteel, academic definitions of musical culture. Yet both held an underlying conviction that music was a uniquely spiritual art. Neither man's response to the challenge of American musical culture exempted him from the calling of composing in a country that questioned the manhood of its composers.

Daniel Gregory Mason was born in 1873, a decade after the youngest of his four brothers, in Brookline, Massachusetts, a quiet, exclusive residential suburb of Boston. The Masons were the preeminent musical family in American history. Their patrilineal heritage extended back to Robert Mason, who came with John Winthrop to Salem in 1630. Daniel Gregory's grandfather Lowell Mason introduced music instruction based on Pestalozian methods into American public education. In addition, he laid the foundation for the professional training of public school music teachers. Daniel's father, Henry Mason, was a founding member of the successful piano and organ company Mason and Hamlin. His uncle William Mason succeeded as a piano virtuoso, minor composer, influential piano teacher, and author of the widely read *Touch and Technic* and *Memories of a Musical Life*. Successful as reformers, entrepreneurs, artists, and teachers, the Masons exemplified the best in the tradition of genteel Yankees.[10]

Born one year later than Mason, in 1874, Ives grew up in Danbury, Connecticut, a town on the brink of rapid economic growth and social change. Immigrant Italians were moving in, creating a large ethnic lower class. New entrepreneurs jostled old families for influence in the town's public life. Among Danbury's genteel Yankees, the Ives family stood near the head of their class. They traced their heritage to 1635, when William Ives had settled in Boston. The family was known for its enterprise and public-spirited activity.[11]

One Ives fit the family image awkwardly. George Ives, Charles's father, led the local band and church choir, not simply as a part-time enjoyable public service but as a profession. In the Civil War he had served with distinction as the youngest bandleader in the Union army. But, in the historian Frank Rossiter's words, "his commitment, as an adult in Danbury, to music as a life's work was a breach of the traditions of his family and society—a violation of what they expected of an American, a man, and an Ives."[12] Success as an educator or entrepreneur legitimated a musician's career, but leading a band was not considered a worthy, manly calling. His father's experiences cast a shadow over Charles Ives, who was tormented by issues of authority, manliness, freedom, and success.

Ives and Mason related to their fathers in very different ways. Ives worshipped his father all his life. As a boy he tagged along after George Ives, listening in, and at an early age contributing to his father's work. The shock of George Ives's unexpected death during his son's freshman year in college was a trauma from which Charles never fully recovered. In later years he spoke of his father as though he were still living. All his life Ives was haunted by his father. He agonized between loving admiration for his father's uncompromising wholeness, and shame for his father's conventional failure in the eyes of the community.[13] By contrast, Mason felt more distant from his businessman father, Henry Mason. Mason's portrait of his father also limns a way of life:

> In the little "sitting room" to the right of our front door was an arm chair where my father would receive me on his lap of a Sunday morning, to cut my finger nails. He performed this rite with a small, bright, very sharp pen-knife, as neat and exact as himself. He would press my

finger hard so as to make a clean edge. His own finger nails were super-clean, and close-textured, flat on top, and like all his person scrupu-lously cared for. He was fond of cologne-water, bay rum, and other toilet whimsies, and when I climbed into his lap those Sunday morn-ings cigar smoke would be only an overtone of sweeter scents. Week-days he paid little attention to me. James would drive him to his office at the Mason and Hamlin Company, and out again at night. Sometimes I would go along, and if it was spring James would stop the two horses at a dip in Beacon Street where willows grew, get out of the "carryall" and cut me a whistle. With my father I was always a little timid. Despite a fund of essential kindness his temperament was nervous, even irritable.[14]

Like Ives, Mason lost his father as a young man. He grew to resemble his father: personally distant, "nervous, even irritable," publicly ur-bane, a conventional success.[15]

In prep school and at college, each young man worked through his ambivalent feelings about his father's musical career in the context of heavy social peer pressures and an acquaintance with the concept of culture taught in liberal arts programs. From childhood Mason found himself attracted by the more refined and exalted aspects of life. In 1890 he attended Phillips Exeter Academy to prepare for entrance to Harvard. Always a sensitive, withdrawn boy, he discovered that at Exeter, "most of the healthy young animals despised me as a 'mother's boy' and were in turn despised by me as barbarians." On the whole, the students at Harvard represented little improvement. In the classes of Charles Eliot Norton, the great "custodian of culture," many stu-dents "would swarm down the fire-escape once their names were checked; and if they stayed it would be to . . . place [matchheads] . . . under heel, and make diverting detonations." Mason counted himself among the few who basked in Norton's "power to make you feel by the contagion of example that beauty was the supreme value of life." Teachers such as Norton, Santayana, William James, and Josiah Royce and a small group of students made Harvard worthwhile for Mason.[16]

Mason's friends were musical or poetic. He valued the poet Philip Henry Savage for his "delicate idealism." But Mason's closest college companion was another poet, William Vaughn Moody, whose "ro-mantic warmth" and Western freshness attracted Mason. After gradu-ation from Harvard in 1895, the two enjoyed a walking tour in Europe, a brief hiatus before plunging into the world of adult struggle.

Looking back a year later from a period of mutual drudgery, Mason
wrote nostalgically to his friend:

> Don't forget Pritchard, and the nut-brown sky-clear girl of the willow
> lane, and mint juleps, and rum toddy, and curacoa, and the Valde-
> Vire, and the steerage wench, and "Voulez-vous montez, Messieurs?",
> and the Charles moon, and the Caen cafe, and "Pourquoi, Pourquoi",
> and Beauvais Cathedral; and *Me*.[17]

Another of Mason's college friends, Edward Burlingame Hill, the son
of a Harvard professor, grandson of a Harvard president, followed his
lineage to become a professor of music at Harvard. Hill exuded the
cosmopolitan confidence of a Boston Brahmin in the old mold. Mason
always expressed surprise that someone with Hill's pedigree should be
so "impulsive," "brilliant," "social," and addicted to sports. Tempera-
mentally the two were opposites; Mason credited their enduring
friendship to "mutual affection and toleration."[18]

Ives went to Hopkins Grammar School in 1893–94, prior to ma-
triculating at Yale. He showed no interest in forming or joining a
cultured clique. Perhaps his proudest moment at Hopkins came when
he pitched the baseball team to a victory over the Yale freshmen. At
Yale, Ives studied desultorily, working hard instead at being a "regular
guy." He was popular enough with his peers to be elected into one of
the coveted upper-classmen's clubs. His eagerness to fit in socially
probably derived from his discomfort that George Ives had been something of an outsider in his community. And socially Yale required
more conformity than Harvard. In Ives's time, Harvard men thought
of Yale as provincial, of Yale men as "crude muckers." Yale men
typically considered Harvard men to be overly individualistic, "snobbish," effete gentlemen filled with dangerous ideas.[19]

Ives and Mason were among the first generation of Americans to
be offered a fairly complete music education at a liberal arts college.
Virtually all of the centennial composers were college men, although
many also studied music with private teachers.[20] By contrast, most
musicians were barred from full participation in the world of intellectual culture, because their traditional training through private tutorials
or professional conservatories defined them as narrow craftsmen. Even
into the twentieth century, musicians struggled to free their art from
remnants of the stigma that they were mere artisans, although vir-
tuosos were considered a breed apart. Thanks largely to the pioneering

Charles Ives (left), pitcher for Hopkins Grammar School, stands beside his catcher. Neither music nor rebellion intrudes into this energetic and tidy world of 1893. *Courtesy Yale Music Library*.

efforts of Mason's and Ives's music professors, John Knowles Paine at Harvard and Horatio Parker at Yale, music entered the American pantheon of "sweetness and light," the liberal arts college. After centuries of near-banishment, music returned to liberal education following the Aristotelian tradition that, alone among the arts, music *theory* (and, correlatively, composition) was a fit activity for a gentleman because it was an abstract and intellectual pursuit, not a lowly craft.[21] Thus Mason and Ives learned to approach music as culture.

Both Paine and Parker sought to dispel doubts as to the tough, intellectual legitimacy of their fields. In later years Ives and Mason expressed grudging admiration for their teachers as composers, but they also thought of them as pedagogically inflexible. John Knowles Paine began teaching music at Harvard in 1862, at his own initiative and without official status for several years. By 1875 he was a full professor, and music courses were accorded regular academic credit. Paine stayed at Harvard until 1905. He boasted important students, Mason among them, but was known as a particularly boring and autocratic teacher. "Probably if he had not been academic," writes the music historian John Tasker Howard, "even to the point of dryness, he would never have been tolerated in a nineteenth-century university." Paine's counterpart at Yale, Horatio Parker, was appointed in 1894, the same year that Ives enrolled as a student. Parker shaped the music department as he wished, and headed it until his death in 1919. "Parker was quite the man of the world," notes Howard. "Fastidious, immaculate, he commanded a social standing often denied musicians of his time. . . . His brusque manner frightened the timid, and he despised those who were afraid of him. In this he was something of a bully; he would often willfully confuse his pupils in class, and then scoff at their confusion."[22] Parker and Paine were major figures in American classical music at the end of the nineteenth century; and they saw to it that no one demeaned them as in any way soft. Indeed, consciously or unconsciously, they acted almost as caricatures of rigid Victorian manliness.[23]

Under the strict rules of Paine and Parker, Mason and Ives learned the prescribed limits of musical culture. Both students tested the harmonic language of classical music to discover the bounds of acceptable usage. In each case they learned that dissonance, like tough language, must know its place in culture. Mason accepted the lesson, though not the cold manner in which Paine administered it. Turning to his father for moral support, Ives refused to let Parker saddle him. Similarly, each young man flirted with vernacular music as with a girl from the other side of the tracks. For Mason, especially, such dalliance carried a spiritually risqué quality. Musical slumming cemented the implicit lesson of Harvard, that classical music was an adornment of spiritual culture. Vernacular music gave lower, coarser, less permanent pleasure. It did not elevate the soul. Ives was of two minds on the issue. Like Parker, Paine, and Mason, he believed that great music communicated a transcendental experience whose substance was essentially religious. But he had also been brought up to love the march, the spiritual, and the jig. To exclude them categorically as spiritually inferior struck Ives as snobbish. Relegating vernacular expression to illegitimacy smacked of antidemocratic elitism.

College provided the perfect environment in which to thrash out these questions. John Higham notes that "it was in a college setting about the end of the nineteenth century that the model of a youth culture came into being." At college in the 1890s a young man was expected to stretch out and try his powers. If he went too far, no one became seriously upset, because college was, among other things, a place assigned for the rituals of becoming a man. Intellectual and social experimentation helped students find the limits of their abilities and of society's flexibility. Young men like Ives and Mason found out what they could get away with—existentially and professionally.[24]

Even though Mason was a serious student, he found Paine's teaching unendurably dry. He gave up taking music courses at Harvard after his sophomore year.[25] "Professor Paine struck me from the start as arbitrary, as lacking in that first and last gift of the teacher, the ability to see things from the angle of the student." Early on Mason tangled with his eminent professor over the expressive flexibility of dissonances. "Typicaly, to give an example, was his blue-pencilling of a dissonance with which I had begun a song," complained Mason. "He said it was 'unprepared'—as undoubtedly it was; but to me it was seizing and exciting, and his prohibiting it merely cold-blanketed my enthusiasm." Ives cited a similar clash with his professor. At the start of Ives's freshman year, Parker asked him to bring in whatever compositions he had. "Among them," recalled Ives, was "a song, *At Parting*—in it, some unresolved dissonances, one ending on a [high] E_b ([in the] key [of] G major), and stops there unresolved. Parker said 'there's no excuse for that—E_b way up there and stopping, the nearest $D_\#$ way down two octaves.'—etc." Like many music students before and after them, Mason and Ives tried to stretch the prevailing "rules" of harmonic progression and resolution before they had fully mastered them. But the two students reacted rather differently to their "lessons." Ives wrote to his father and received full backing against Parker. "Tell Parker that every dissonance doesn't have to resolve, if it doesn't happen to feel like it," retorted George Ives, "any more than every horse should have its tail bobbed just because it's the prevailing fashion."[26] As eager as Ives was to be a regular guy socially, in music he was his father's son, constitutionally incapable of deference. (Ives doesn't record what he actually said to Parker's face, if anything!) Mason took Paine's blunt negativism as a sign of bad teaching; reflecting on the incident, he agreed with the justice of the theory behind Paine's admonition.

Mason and Ives also explored the boundaries segregating American vernacular music from the world of classical music culture. Mason relegated his tests of the compatibility of art and entertainment to the realm of college pranks. He excluded them from the classroom, and largely from his composing career as well. Ives went on to build a unique style around the confrontation itself, around the contentious cohabitation of classical and vernacular music. "The germ of Ives's complicated concept of polyphony seems to lie in an experience he had as a boy," noted his first biographers, Henry and Sidney Cowell, "when his father invited a neighboring band to parade with its team at a baseball game in Danbury, while at the same time the local band made its appearance in support of the Danbury team."

> The parade was arranged to pass along the main street as usual, but the two bands started at opposite ends of town and were assigned pieces in different meters and keys. As they approached each other the dissonances were acute, and each man played louder and louder so that his rivals would not put him off. A few players wavered, but both bands held together and got past each other successfully, the sounds of their cheerful discord fading in the distance.[27]

As described by the Cowells, this experiment sounds like a unique sort of happening, dreamed up by a musical Thomas Edison and later transcribed by his son the composer.

It may be true that Ives associated his interest in multiple band fireworks with his father, but Ives was not alone in his youthful enthusiasm for these rousing effects. While at Harvard, Mason and his friend Hill occasionally played two-hand or four-hand piano music in Boston society's drawing rooms and studios.

> One of our favorite battle-horses was *Between Two Bands*, a graphic representation of one march (E. B. H. in the treble) beginning very near and very loud, and gradually disappearing into space and *pianissimo*, while a different march (D. G. M. in the bass) would begin very far and soft, and equally gradually approach into deafening *fortissimo*. There was a crucial moment when both bands were about equidistant, supremely relished by us if not always by our audience.[28]

Parlor arrangements of band and dance music might be grand entertainment; and in their youth, Ives, Mason, and Hill all savored such terrific noises. But for Hill, and especially for Mason, an unbridged gulf segregated spirituality from fun. Their awareness of this chasm lent parlor band imitations a naughty quality. At college they explored the limits of experimentation and the borders separating vernacular entertainment from art.[29] But the end of college marked the end of socially sanctioned high jinks.

Ives and Mason each took seriously the requirements of manhood: that he should find his calling and succeed to the limits of his ability, and that, of course, he should marry. Each man grappled with the compromises and stresses of career choices, of art and public recognition, of money and marriage. And each man was nearly broken by the struggle. Ives chose to live a comfortable, conventionally successful life. He wanted nothing of romantic poverty. He felt that Americans had good reason to despise the poor artist as an ineffectual weakling. Poverty did not win independence from the genteel cage of female patronage. It condemned the composer to compromise his manhood, either as a responsible breadwinner or as a free artist. Ives hoped to steer between the rocks of exclusivity and the shoals of weakness. The businessman Ives would subsidize the composer Ives. Mason, too, felt that he could wrest both comfort and freedom from New York. With his family money and connections, he reasonably assumed that he could make a career as a concert pianist. He would succeed according to the rules of classical music culture. As a performer of the world's great masterpieces, he could interpret culture's spirituality to his countrymen. But neither career plan proceeded tidily. As Yankee and as musical artist, each man was forced to pay the hidden tithe of his calling.

In 1894, an earnest young Daniel Gregory Mason at the piano fits comfortably into a genteel setting. *Courtesy Performing Arts Research Center, The New York Public Library at Lincoln Center.*

After an idyllic summer in Europe, Mason moved to New York City to begin his musical career. He initially intended to use his family connections to develop a career as a concert pianist. In his memoirs, Mason recalled that "even while at college I had had occasion to realize how powerful a springboard for my untried feet was likely to prove the interest and influence of my family." At first the excitement of New York was well buffered by the presence of his uncle Dr. William Mason, who lived nearby in the vicinity of Washington Square. "The friendly environment of my family . . . could even domesticate for me a little the maelstrom of New York when in the fall of '95 I decided to plunge into it from my quiet Boston eddy." At his uncle's apartment, Mason met many notables of New York's musical world, including the pianist and conductor Ossip Gabrilowitsch, who became an ardent champion and close friend. But Mason's New York career as pianist did not take off, and he gave up after one year. "In spite of the stimulus of my study with Arthur Whiting, the inspiring contacts at my uncle's, even the praise of Paderewski . . . all my hopes of establishing myself in New York, and as a musician, soon proved vain and had to be abandoned." In the wake of his father's death in 1890, and of the depression of 1893, the family business had declined in profitability. Mason could no longer count on financial support from his family. "Almost worse still, my health, never strong . . . now gave out completely. . . . There was nothing to do but admit myself beaten for the moment . . . and crawl back to Cambridge." Mason's illness, sympathetically referred to by his friend and teacher Josiah Royce as the "nervous burden," was characterized by emotional and physical debilitation, severe depression, and inability to work. In addition, he suffered "pianist's" and "writer's" cramps. Mason called the years from 1896 to 1902 the "long dark tunnel of my life." He earned a living wage teaching English at Harvard and enjoyed intellectual companionship. But, though he had given up hopes of a pianist's career, he now pined to compose.[30]

During these years of forced introspection, Mason found his true calling as artistic and critical midwife to an American musical culture. Gradually he drifted into the mainstream of musical life by writing about music. Already he had published an article for the undergraduate paper *Harvard Monthly* on "Robert Schumann's Relation to Romanticism." A Harvard classmate of his brother Harry suggested that "there is a glorious field, absolutely unopened thus far, for the man who will tell educated people what music is, what its place and relations are, in words they can understand."[31] Through his related roles as composer, critical essayist, and teacher, Mason made a name for himself in American musical life. In 1902 he placed his first effort, "Two Tendencies in Modern Music," in the *Atlantic Monthly*, with the help of his former teacher Arthur Whiting. Whiting also obtained for Mason a commission from *Outlook* magazine for an article on Brahms, which actually made it into print a month ahead of the *Atlantic Monthly* piece.

These articles launched Mason's career. Their commitment to music as the apotheosis of culture found immediate favor among established Anglo-American musicians. Within a few months his essays on Grieg, Dvořák, Saint-Saëns, Franck, and Tchaikowsky, plus "The Meaning of Music" and "The Appreciation of Music," appeared in print. By Christmas they were available in a book, *From Grieg to Brahms*. At twenty-nine, Mason was a success. In spite of its "unfortunate" title, his book sold well and drew favorable responses from several influential men. Charles Villiers Stanford, educated gentleman, British Victorian composer, champion of Brahms, and important teacher, wrote a warm appreciation of Mason's Brahms essay. Another Englishman, Edward Carpenter, wrote of his pleasure with Mason's articles: "Music, as Schopenhauer showed . . . gives the key to the interpretation of the universe, so much more intimately and directly than the other arts; but so few musicians hitherto have been philosophers or literary folk." Whiting introduced Mason to the influential British critic W. H. Hadow. Mason and Hadow became friends. Mason sent copies of his articles to Sir Hubert Parry, a man he admired above all English musicians, not for his compositions "but as a writer, a critic, and an uncompromising upholder of fine traditions in a lax time, a character of singular transparence and nobility." Parry lauded Mason's arguments and style. Letters of praise also came from Americans: the conductor Theodore Thomas, the sculptor Abbott H. Thayer, and Mason's composition teacher Percy Goetschius. Mason's initial efforts to "mold standards of public taste" struck a consonant chord with these eminent men.[32]

Mason moved from Harvard to Princeton in 1902, his spirits and health much improved. While it is difficult to know to what extent an awkward romantic situation contributed to his depression during his stay at Harvard, Mason does tell us that "my former sister-in-law and I were married on October 8, 1904"; and a letter from Edward Arlington Robinson notes the happy resolution "of one of the worst tangles that the gods and devils ever delighted themselves with." That year Mason and his wife, Mary Taintor Mason, moved to New York City permanently. In 1905 he took on the editorship of a new magazine, *Masters in Music*, wrote articles, and gave public lectures for the New York City Board of Education.[33]

The progressive president of Columbia University, Nicholas Murray Butler, was impressed with Mason's article on "music and the educated man"; and in 1905, Mason received an appointment as a "lecturer" in music at Columbia. He moved steadily up the ranks; by 1929 he was named the first MacDowell Professor of Music at Columbia, a position he held until 1942.[34] Columbia provided Mason with a suitable pulpit from which to preach the progressive gospel of musical culture to the young middle-class men who would, no doubt, be the national leaders of the future.

After college, Ives also moved to the great city of opportunity to seek individual success. But unlike Mason, he did not pursue single-mindedly a career in music. Ives may have tested the waters in music and business simultaneously to see which would work out. The year he was graduated from Yale, 1898, Ives took a full-time job as a clerk with the Mutual Life Insurance Company and a part-time position as organist and choir director for the First Presbyterian Church in Bloomfield, New Jersey. He held two such music posts successively until 1902. Ives may have looked upon his church job as a way to pick up extra money while indulging his love of music. But he also could have been secretly committed to a musical career. With the performance in 1902 of his cantata *The Celestial Country*, Ives possibly hoped to duplicate the unusually successful premiere in 1892 of Parker's *Hora Novissima*. Ives's work was apparently inspired by his teacher's piece. The tepid critical reaction to the premiere of *The Celestial Country* may have been "one of the main reasons why Ives forsook music as a profession," argues the musicologist Victor Yellin. If so, Ives persevered little as a young man, and prevaricated much as an old man to cover his failure. In any case, he kept most of his composing to himself, as he had at Yale.[35]

Ives moved from one type of insurance job to another for several years, living a life which today would be referred to as that of the junior executive. On the Upper West Side of Manhattan, Ives and a number of similarly situated young men shared an apartment they dubbed "Poverty Flat." In 1907 Ives formed a partnership with Julian Myrick, and they built a successful insurance agency, with which Ives stayed until his retirement in 1930. He brought to the business of insurance a progressive zeal, a vision of insurance as a private, capitalist answer to the legitimate needs of ordinary people for protection in the cruel wilderness of modern individualist society.[36]

A year after entering the partnership, Ives married Harmony Twitchell, an attractive, intelligent, well-connected young woman. Trained as a registered nurse, she was the daughter of the minister Dr. Joseph Twitchell of Hartford, a close friend of Mark Twain. Ives's marriage introduced him into Harmony Twitchell's circle of artistic and society friends. He worked hard to provide the appropriate genteel requisites for his new wife and himself.

By 1912 Ives was wealthy enough to buy land in West Redding, Connecticut, and to build a country home complete with a barn. He and his wife moved out to Redding to be away from "the Hell Hole," as he called New York; and Ives settled into the life of a commuting executive. Only in the winter months did they return to their East Seventy-fourth Street brownstone. Childless, they adopted a daughter, Edith, in 1915. The art historian James Thomas Flexner became friends with Edith Ives in the 1930s. He remembers that Ives relaxed more when at his West Redding house. In New York he was "very nervous and jumpy." The pace and noise of modern life upset him. When an airplane intruded on his Redding idyll, he would shake his cane in the air and swear at the pilot. Flexner recalls Ives's "taking me out over quite a considerable estate to show me cows or pigs or something of that nature. And I got the impression that he very much enjoyed being a country squire."[37] Ives joined the army of individualists who sought in country life the symbolic roots of genuine living. New England's woods were thick with lawyers, professors, and ministers clothed in overalls, old hats jammed over their brows. Here country gentlemen practiced their crusty gentility.

"Jumpiness" and "excitability" came to be fixtures of Ives's personality from middle age on. As far back as 1906, he realized that he had a health problem. Certainly his years at Poverty Flat had placed a strain on him, physically and emotionally. The demands on this good-looking, outgoing, and ambitious fellow "were enormous, even for an athletic young man with Ives's energy. He found time to go to night school to learn something about the law, and to pitch on his agency's baseball team."[38] In 1918 he suffered a severe heart attack, from which

Charles Ives, a successful young insurance executive, poses with his adopted daughter, Edith. *Courtesy Yale Music Library.*

he never fully recovered. But Ives's "nervous burden" cannot be said to have been caused by his heart attack. He was a driven and troubled man, torn by the demands of his calling.

The strange feature of this story of an ambitious young executive is that it conceals a secret life, that of a "closet" composer. Ives's long-time country barber and friend, Anthony Lapine, never took "Charlie" for a musician: "My God, he looked like a gentleman farmer." Lapine's experience was fairly typical. In New York Ives was all business, adored by his subordinates as a generous and considerate boss. Of his music, Ives's business partner said, "I hardly ever heard anything about it." "Those who knew Ives in one role did not often catch a glimpse of him in another," writes the music historian Vivian Perlis. "Ives' daily activities until his retirement revolved around the downtown New York business world. His family and his associates thought of him as a successful insurance man, obviously capable and very intelligent, with perhaps a slightly artistic bent."[39]

Yet Ives was a composer, and had been since his teens. And he remained ambivalent about coming out of the closet throughout his musical career. As a boy he had specialized in composing funeral dirges for deceased neighborhood pets. But at thirteen he wrote his first march, *Holiday Quick Step*, for the Decoration Day parade. His father's town band performed the piece, but "Charlie was too overcome to appear in his usual place at the snare drum," relate the Cowells. "Instead, when the band came marching down Main Street past the Ives house playing Charlie's piece full tilt, the boy was discovered nervously playing handball against the barn door, with his back to the parade." At fourteen Ives became the youngest organist in Connecticut; he played for services at the First Baptist Church in Danbury, "but he dreaded being called a 'piano player' by other boys of his age." "As late as the 1920s, untutored popular sentiment regarded the playing of music as the occupation of wretched professionals and scheming young ladies," writes the scholar Jacques Barzun. "The school-boy trundling his violin was a sissy." Ives was anxiously aware of what society thought of a male who aspired to be a "serious" musician. "What do you play?" the young Ives was asked. "Shortstop!" he blurted.[40]

In his *Memos*, written in the 1930s, Ives wrote to justify "why and how a man who apparently likes music so much goes into business." He evidently addressed the argument to himself, but also to whomever he might ultimately be answerable. His first reason linked music with effeminacy:

> As a boy I was partially ashamed of it—an entirely wrong attitude, but it was strong—most boys in American towns, I think, felt the same. When other boys, Monday A.M. on vacation, were out driving grocery

carts, or doing chores, or playing ball, I felt all wrong to stay in and play piano. And there may be something in it. Hasn't music always been too much an emasculated art? Mozart etc. helped.[41]

All his life he manifested in extreme form the concern of many genteel Victorian composers that they not in any sense seem queer. Having tied his career choice to personal virility, Ives then portrayed himself as trapped between his manly responsibility as family provider and his artistic ideals as a composer of tough, dissonant music. Ives echoed Emerson's dictum: "Art is a jealous mistress, and if a man have a genius for painting, poetry, music, architecture, or philosophy, he makes a bad husband and an ill provider." In conclusion, he justified his dual life as a means of retaining his contact with "people of all conditions." Ives, the vernacular classicist, apparently feared that life as a professional composer would remove him from the masses.[42]

While Mason combined his talents and interests into a musical career that afforded him comfort, prestige, and influence, Ives divided his life into a professional, conventional business success and an intense, mostly private commitment to music. Mason's professional attitude toward music, his name, and his conservative competence won for him ready access to publishers and performers. Ives sought performances where he could find them; but he was only an amateur composer of difficult and unorthodox music. Understandably, his art found audiences slowly.

By the modest standards of success in classical music, especially in the early twentieth-century United States, Mason fared well with his available audiences. He obtained good publishers, usually within a year or two of finishing each piece, including such firms as G. Schirmer, Universal Editions, Society for the Publication of American Music, C. Fisher, Witmark, and C. C. Birchard and Company. Although his letters contain numerous complaints about the problems of securing performances, his major works were played promptly by some of the finest artists in this country.

Mason's Quartet for Piano and Strings (finished 1911, published 1912) had its premiere with the Kneisel Quartet and Ossip Gabrilowitsch. Leopold Stokowsky conducted the premiere performance of his Symphony No. 1 with the Philadelphia Orchestra in 1916. The Boston Symphony also accepted it for performance, first by Karl Muck, then by Pierre Monteux, and finally by Serge Koussevitsky, who put off his performance until 1926.⁴³ Mason's *Quartet on Negro Themes* received its first performance by the Flonzaley Quartet in 1920, a year after it was published, while his *Chanticleer Overture* was promptly played in Cincinnati under Fritz Reiner, who subsequently conducted it six times in New York. Frederick Stock also conducted the overture with the Chicago Symphony Orchestra, and Bruno Walter performed it with the New York Philharmonic. His Symphony No. 2 had its premiere with Reiner in Cincinnati in 1931, and Walter played it in New York the following season. In 1937, Mason's Symphony No. 3, *Lincoln*, was presented by Sir John Barbirolli with the New York Philharmonic.⁴⁴ But like other composers, Mason could not support himself solely by composing. Nevertheless, insofar as performance indicates relative acceptance and success, Mason, in his own lifetime, should have felt secure at the top. The list of performers of his music includes a roll call of the preeminent figures in American music.

Ives's situation contrasts starkly with Mason's relatively broad success. "In 1921," writes Frank Rossiter, "at the age of forty-seven, Ives's active life was effectively at an end. . . . Almost all his music had been written; yet his musical reputation was at its nadir. Charles Ives the composer was unknown." During the years 1903 through 1920, there were no public performances of Ives's music. What little contact he had with professional musicians did not encourage him to expose his music publicly. Friends and old classmates told him his music was "awful," filled with "horrible sounds."⁴⁵ A violinist who tried to play Ives's Violin Sonatas raged that while he could expel vile food, he could not get Ives's wretched music out of his ears. Afterwards Ives wrote:

> After he went, I had a kind of feeling which I've had off and on when other more or less celebrated (or well known) musicians have seen or played (or tried to play) some of my music. I felt (but only temporarily) that there must be something wrong with me. . . . Are my ears on wrong? . . . I began to feel more and more, after seances with nice musicians, that, if I wanted to write music that, to me, seemed worth while, I must keep away from musicians.⁴⁶

Eventually, breakthroughs came. In 1921, Ives's *Concord Sonata*, published and circulated at his own expense, struck a responsive chord with Henry Bellamann, Southern poet, lecturer, and proponent of

modern piano music. Bellamann arranged performances of the *Sonata*.
In 1924 the violinist Jerome Goldstein played Ives's Second Violin
Sonata in Town Hall, New York City. The piece received a favorable
notice by Winthrop Tryon in the *Christian Science Monitor*. E. Robert
Schmitz, a French promoter of modern music, arranged a performance
of the first two movements of Ives's Fourth Symphony, conducted by
Eugene Goosens. Reviews were mixed but attentive. The key reviews,
by Olin Downes and Lawrence Gilman, were favorable. Ives's next
important break came in 1932 with Nicolas Slonimsky's performances
in Boston and New York of *Three Pieces in New England*, and with the
airing of seven Ives songs at the Yaddo Festival in Saratoga, New
York. The performance of the entire *Concord Sonata* in 1939 by John
Kirkpatrick brought a paean from Gilman's pen and finally launched
Ives beyond his own small circle.[47]

Yet critical reviews chafed both composers. Virtually all artists
distrust the intermediaries who stand between them and their audiences. Agents, publishers, performers, producers: none are as forbid-
ding as the critic. Critics color the memory of the real, day-to-day
audiences. They lecture composers on their responsibilities to both
tradition and posterity. The "new" they attach to tradition as best they
can. They would weave culture whole. But they seldom make composers happy. Mason's works elicited much respect but little enthusiasm. He got "fed up" with "newspaper men calling me 'learned,
erudite, professorial, and academic.'"[48] Like Mason, Ives detested
professional critics as a group. An apotheosized, lily-eared critic
named "Rollo" takes quite a beating in Ives's combative marginalia.
Ives even wrote an "Ode to a Music Critic":

> In most of the concerts he goes into and out of (about 99 out of 98), he
> can sort [them] right out from his little nest of samples. Then he leans
> back quite relieved, as he doesn't have to open his ears but little if his
> satchel is open. But gracious, girls!—how fussy and bothered he does
> get when he can't find anything in the concert that's in his samples. . . .
> Sometimes he doesn't get cross when he hears something he can't find
> in his satchel, if somebody or a newspaper in some nice European city
> has O.K.'d the strange sound—for he doesn't have to bother much to
> listen, he just stamps [it] K.O. and puts it among his samples.[49]

Ives and Mason criticized their critics, and blasted the boards
controlling major musical institutions—"usually ladies," complained
Ives. They protested the antics of "prima donna conductors" who

ignored their American music.[50] But they were also forced to confront their perception of their own failure to reach a larger audience. They equated the fortune of their works with the fate of their cultural mission. Mason eventually struck out in all directions in search of scapegoats. He even blamed the mass of the American people and wavered in his optimistic assessment that progressive education could help introduce potential audiences to the value of beautiful music. Ives, too, anguished over public rejection of his music. About the nice ladies he cared little. But nice ladies could hardly account for the masses.

Ives turned his disappointment inward upon himself and his own Yankee group. His self-contained bitterness complicated the invalidism increasingly isolating him from musical society. His "nervous burden" manifested itself in every aspect of his existence. Undercurrents of helpless sadness and wrath eddied just beneath the surface calm of this pugnacious pacifist. One evening, after Ives had asked the blessing before dinner, "all of a sudden he banged his fist on the table and said, 'goddamn that Hitler!' It shocked everybody. Even Mrs. Ives said, 'Oh Charlie!' Then he became so overcome that he couldn't speak." Visitors found Ives to be "very tense and friendly and excited—shaking with excitement." Sometimes he talked "feverishly," getting so worked up he had to throw himself down on a couch, panting for breath. Like a scorned lover, he daily tasted the acid indifference of an audience toward which he scarcely dared to reach. On occasion Ives lost his temper and tongue-lashed antagonistic patrons. He stood up at a performance of his friend Carl Ruggles's music to bellow at an unappreciative concert-goer, "Stop being such a God-damned sissy!" But Ives also felt composers had no unlimited right to impose their tastes on "a public that cannot help itself. . . . In other words, a public audience, or a [church] congregation, has some rights."[51]

Speaking as a composer, not as a patron, Mason felt audiences had only the right to learn from their cultural betters what was good for them. He divided the musical public into convenient thirds. The largest group he dubbed "moronic conservatives." This type "swears by the classics, not because he perceives their beauty (a highly active process) but because he recognizes their names." Less numerous, but "far more vociferous," is the class of "moronic radical." The moronic radical "demands the latest because he lacks the taste to recognize the best. His preference is for whatever is crudely eccentric, bizarre, ugly, and cynically sophisticated." The darling of the moronic radicals is "that *enfant terrible* of sensationalism, Stravinsky." Between these extremes one could find a layer of active listeners of cultivated taste.[52]

Although Mason eschewed Matthew Arnold's specific categories of "Barbarians," "Philistines," and "Populace," he viewed his role as critic and educator in Arnoldian terms: to preserve "the best that has been said and written," and to spread "sweetness and light" among intelligent laymen. Mason insisted on reaching beyond his real audience to the untapped potential audience. "We are to play Wagner [Theodore] Thomas suggests, not merely until people tolerate or endure him, but until they like him—and that is equivalent to saying, until they understand him." Art was not merely for the few but was a participatory process, "strenuous and effortful for them as well as for us," wrote Mason, "in short, it is conceived not aristocratically as the domination of a passive herd by active masters, but democratically as the creative venture of all concerned." Mason's early writings brim with the earnest enthusiasm of progressive reform. In "Our Public School Music" (1904) Mason urged music educators on to greater efforts in their common struggle to raise the taste of the masses. Teachers must recognize that the popular love of dance and stage music indicates that "ordinary people have a susceptibility to the effects of rhythmical balance and form that needs only cultivation, expansion, and chastening to become the basis of true musical taste." Educators must work harder to transmute dross into gold.[53]

But by the end of the 1920s, Mason's missionary zeal had spent itself. Perforce, dealings with his real audience continued, but he lost faith in the educability of any potential audience. Now, wrote Mason in 1929, "we need to revise some of our ideas about popular education, and especially about the relation of the masses to the arts." The people simply should be told what is good for them; and if they won't or can't grasp the opportunity, forget them. " 'Universal education'—so used to exclaim a clear thinker with a picturesque vocabulary, 'is the trotting out of a damn' fine thing to a pack of idiots,' " snapped Mason. "Has not 'music for the masses,' in particular, proved at best a delusion, at worst a prostitution?" Just as Henry Ford tells the public what kind of cars it ought to have, cultural leaders should dictate musical taste to the public, and only to the intelligent public at that. "After all, in the nature of things, the appreciation of music can be only for the intelligent; all that the participation of the unintelligent is likely to bring about is the depreciation of music. Why not stop leading unthirsty horses to the water? They only muddy it." By this time willing to write off the masses, Mason asked the wealthy minority to increase its cultural subsidies in order to keep control of musical institutions out of the hands of Philistines.[54]

A pained ambivalence replaced the optimism of Mason's prewar writings. He tried to understand the indifference he felt among Americans for what he was attempting to accomplish as an artist. Mason felt that he offered an "attached idealism" that should appeal to a broad middle class of educated taste. His Arnoldian analysis of audiences changed as circumstances strained his optimism. In one version he abandoned the category of "moronic conservative." Adapting Van Wyck Brooks's "highbrow" versus "lowbrow" model, he assigned the moronic radicals or "snobs" to the "highbrow" bracket, reserving the "lowbrow" slot for "musical hoodlums" who liked popular music, "as nameless as it is ephemeral." He lamented that "the indifference of the plain people, the central mass of intelligent Americans," had retarded the development of a "middle body of sound taste."[55]

Mason turned to Emerson and Thoreau for solace, inspiration, and justification. "Dear Will," wrote the young Mason to his friend William Vaughn Moody in 1896, "I wish you'd read some Thoreau. Read *Walden* through to please me, and see if you haven't found another brother." In the *Harvard Monthly* (1897) Mason had published "The Idealistic Basis of Thoreau's Genius," which led to his friendship with the Thoreau biographer Henry S. Salt. Subsequently Mason wrote, but destroyed as unsatisfactory, a twenty-five-thousand-word *Life of Thoreau* for the *Beacon Biographies*. He turned to Thoreau and Emerson to buttress the individual will against the murmuring masses. "A good motto," he suggests,

> for those of us who, contemporaries of Schönberg and Stravinsky, found ourselves dreaming of something more human, was . . . from *Walden:* "If a man does not keep pace with his contemporaries, perhaps it is because he hears a different drummer. Let him step to the music which he hears, however measured or far away."[56]

Mason also emphasized the need to extract individuals from the mass who would form a free community of leadership: a "saving remnant," as Arnold called them. Characteristically, Mason turned to Emerson to sustain his belief that progressive reform was not antidemocratic. It is a "common fallacy," wrote Mason,

> that what is done for the many must be done so as to please the many—a view often supposed to be "democratic!" Emerson was more truly democratic when he told us to "cease this idle prating about the masses," and set about extracting individuals from the masses; for real democracy never forgets that the majority are always inferior, and its aim must be to give the superior minority a chance to make their influence felt. In other words, to level down to the people is to vulgarize rather than to popularize.[57]

Mason revered Emerson and Thoreau as ideal artists and critics, as heroic links connecting Yankee tradition with Matthew Arnold's vision of culture.[58]

Ives was also devoted to the spirit of the transcendentalists. He intended his *Concord Sonata* and its accompanying *Essays* to be direct portraits of Emerson, Hawthorne, the Alcotts, and Thoreau.[59] Ives felt a strong kinship with what he took to be Emerson's single-minded pursuit of truth, unmindful of whether it produced beautiful polished prose or orderly reason. He felt compelled to defend Emerson's epigrammatic rather than linear style. "A search for perfect truths throws out a beauty more spiritual than sensuous," wrote Ives of Emerson. But the *Essays* suggest that Ives cherished Thoreau's example most. "Thoreau was a great musician, not because he played the flute but because he did not have to go to Boston to hear 'the Symphony.' The rhythm of his prose, were there nothing else, would determine his value as a composer."[60] Like Mason, Ives looked to Thoreau for strength to be an individual, an artist in an age which did not understand his inner imperatives. In his sketch of Thoreau, Ives penned an eloquent and touching self-portrait:

> One hears him called . . . a crabbed, cold-hearted sour-faced Yankee—a kind of a visionary sore-head—a cross-grained, egotistic recluse—even non-hearted. But it is easier to make a statement than prove a reputation. . . . He was rude and unfriendly at times, but shyness probably had something to do with that. In spite of a certain self-possession, he was diffident in most company. But, though he may have been subject to those spells when words do not rise and the mind seems wrapped in a kind of dull cloth which everyone dumbly stares at instead of looking through, he would easily get off a rejoinder upon occasion. The personal trait that one who has affection for Thoreau may find worst is a

combative streak, in which he too often takes refuge. An obstinate elusiveness, almost a "contrary cussedness"—as if he would say (which he didn't): "If a truth about something is not as I think it ought to be, I'll make it what I think, and it *will* be the truth—but if you agree with me, then I begin to think it may not be the truth." The causes of these unpleasant colors (rather than characteristics) are too easily attributed to a lack of human sympathy, or to the assumption that they are at least symbols of that lack, instead of to a super-sensitiveness, magnified at times by ill health, and at times by a subconsciousness of the futility of actually living out his ideals in this life.[61]

Like Mason, Ives sought in Thoreau and Emerson strength to be an individualistic artist against the stupidity and insensitivity of the age. But unlike Mason, he would not systematically personify stupidity as the "masses."[62]

Ives would not judge the people, but he did question the vitality of his own class. Had the seed of 1776 gone soft? he asked. He judged his class as he judged music, measuring them by manliness and spirituality. His fear that Yankees were stricken with terminal spiritual impotence was not his alone. Henry Adams spoke for a group from whom the zest for life seemed inexorably to ebb. "He [Adams] had stood up for his eighteenth century, his Constitution of 1789, his George Washington, his Harvard College, his Quincy, and his Plymouth Pilgrims, as long as any one would stand up with him." (Adams, the Yankee, clung rather pathetically to the possessive mode: "his George Washington" indeed!) And then, with surpassing disingenuousness, Adams lamented "the whole consolidation of force, which ruthlessly stamped out the life of the class into which Adams was born." With Adams the debility is admitted, but, as with Mason, the burden of blame is shifted outward to some vague historical force. Ives simply got hopping mad at the Yankee for no longer being fittest. "Is the Anglo-Saxon going 'Pussy'?—the nice Lizzies—the do-it-proper boys of today." Ives wondered, in a passage of piquant sexual confusion, whether his America was "gradually losing her manhood."[63]

Ives intertwined his fears for the virile spirit of his class and of American music. At musicians and critics with whom he was unsympathetic, he threw the same taunting epithets—old ladies, sissies, effeminates, nice ladies, mush, soft-eared girls—that as a boy he had been afraid to hear from the guys. To be a man meant that one held to one's ideals, that one supported one's family comfortably and securely, that one maintained the freedom to express oneself frankly and roughly in words or in music. Swearing offered a man one way to assert his masculine freedom. His friend the composer Carl Ruggles was a virtuoso cusser.[64] The two men enjoyed whooping it up in front of their wives; together they'd singe the air blue. "He could even beat me swearing," averred Ruggles modestly. Perhaps dissonance, too, protected one's manliness in feminine surroundings. Once Ives walked out of a concert by the Kneisel Quartet because he could not stomach a "whole evening of mellifluous sounds, perfect cadences, perfect ladies, perfect programs, and not a dissonant cuss word to stop the anemia and beauty during the whole evening." With prickly dissonance, Ives tried to inoculate his musical culture against epicene infection. Like swearing, dissonance seemed tough; and it was better to be rejected as too tough than too soft. Elliot Carter has pointed out that Ives fortified his pieces by adding layers of dissonances through years of revisions.[65] He liked to think of composing as a manly, shirt-sleeve enterprise. Ives, the composer as inventor or tinkerer, would be a hero if he drew lightning; if not he was only fooling around. After all, men will be boys. Ives seemed ill at ease when finally audiences not only tolerated but actually applauded his music.[66] His complex psyche was sensitive to old sores still exquisitely raw.

Yankee composers tried to conform to the model of "robust gentility" typical of their era. "Like Theodore Roosevelt in politics, Thomas Davidson in education embodied the robust gentility and 'practical idealism' so central to what middle-class Americans at the turn of the century wanted to pass on to their children," notes the historian David Hollinger. "Ostentatiously vigorous, cultured and clean, Davidson . . . believed the best defense against 'violence and barbarism' was 'Culture.' "[67] Fear of the "effeminate" also coursed through late-nineteenth- and early-twentieth-century English musical literature. The British writer E. A. Baughan noted with misgivings the entrance of "gentlemen" into the ranks of British music. Baughan suggested that their "curious effeminacy of thought and outlook was most undesirable."[68] In the United States, critics associated the Victorian fear of cultural emasculation with the genteel tradition of New England.

The tone of self-pitying victimization, largely absent in Ives, runs through much genteel American literature even long after the turn of the century. Cultured Yankees sometimes looked for scapegoats in the form of abstract or personified forces of darkness. People such as

A craggy old Carl Ruggles stands before his schoolhouse home. *Courtesy Don Hunstein*.

Mason turned the double-edged blade of blame outward against those groups whose alleged materialistic energy seemed to be winning the day. *Harper's Monthly Magazine* and other publications carried laments for the "Plight of the Genteel" in the face of "Philistines" and an upwardly mobile "Populace." "They" want material goods rather than advancement toward the spiritual, humane values which "we" cherish, complains one such author. Of course this cannot be helped in a democracy, yet "what becomes of the 'genteel'? They are eliminated." Was the life of culture in the United States threatened? So thought John Jay Chapman, who decried "the Disappearance of the Educated Man." What is happening, he wondered, to the "man who knows a little something about everything that is going on in the world, and has a bowing acquaintance with what has been said and thought in the past?" This pale version of Arnold's formula came from a Harvard man who suffered devastatingly from the "nervous burden." "Chapman greatly resembled the nonconforming Henry David Thoreau, who embarrassed even his friends by his determined habit of placing himself athwart his society." Indeed, Chapman's motto could serve to characterize Ives: "What don't bite ain't right."[69]

Chapman exhibited the curious duality of the Victorian Yankee dilemma that so sharply afflicted the centennial composers. Like Mason, he thought genteel culture uplifting; like Ives, he feared and despised softness. Such men as Ives, Chapman, and Theodore Roosevelt struggled to shake off the insecurity vexing their class. Some, including Roosevelt and Mason, eventually went hunting for scapegoats. For two decades after World War I, Mason turned his frustrations outward, attacking those who seemed bent on destroying the ideal America which his own class could not yet realize. Mason dealt both negatively and positively with the problems that beset him and his class. Negatively, he attacked "highbrows," "lowbrows," modernists, primitivists, and Jews. Positively, Mason sought solace and hope for ultimate vindication in an ideal audience.

After college, both Ives and Mason laid siege to New York City to see if they could make it. Ives succeeded in business, but fled with a broken constitution from the urban purgatory. Mason faltered, retreated, regrouped, and eventually carried the day by combining his musical and literary interests. Neither man won satisfaction from his victory.

Mason's decision to pursue music as a cultural mission came after a painful adjustment to the realities of adulthood. And though his calling did not make him a happy man, it did provide a natural vehicle for his talents and convictions. Mason became the preeminent spokesman for musical culture in America. He worked to awaken in Americans a love and understanding of classical music. Increasingly, his quest to make America musical acquired a powerful subtheme: to make Americans love and understand the special virtues of Mason's kind of music, Yankee music. To this end he espoused a cultural theory of music as an art uniquely formal and uniquely moral, of audiences as the potential people. He treated Yankee musical culture as a sacred symbol system through which moral order could be extended to all Americans.

The case of Charles Ives is more complex. Mason learned and accepted the proposition that art and vernacular traditions are disjunctive. Ives could not wholly justify this view. He feared that the distinction would cut culture free from ordinary life, and hence from the responsibility that was its moral justification. Ivory-tower culture was effeminate and ineffectual. Ives was torn between belief in the mission of culture and fear that musical culture was unmanly and un-American. Fearing rejection as an emasculated musician, Ives nearly divorced himself from personal commitment to professional music. He also couched his eclectic overtures to vernacular music in a style so tough as to insure their alienation from available audiences. Ives would not put on airs to woo the prize that he, as an artist and a Yankee, desired as much as Mason. Bristling like an adolescent afraid to fail in love, Ives hesitated to court the public. In spite of their differences, both composers hoped to create what Van Wyck Brooks called a culture of "attached idealism." In the spirit of Arnold, Mason tried to believe that culture could bridge the gap between America's idealism and its material life. He did not agree with Santayana's characterization of Yankees as purveying an ineffectual "Genteel Tradition." Ives thought to take culture out of the drawing room, to grow hair on the chest of idealism.

2

REDEMPTIVE CULTURE

The Yankee composers rationalized their musical calling on the basis of redemptive culture: the doctrine that musical culture could redeem the American spirit. This loosely formulated religious ideology echoed both Matthew Arnold's theory of spiritual culture and the conventional wisdom of Victorian musical aesthetics. Mason and Ives portrayed redemptive culture primarily as a potential American civil religion. As Yankees, they considered themselves leaders of a progressive movement peculiarly American and, therefore, universal. By directly experiencing the ordering principles of redemptive culture, audiences could understand the meaning of their identity as Americans. Like romantics, the Yankee composers conceived themselves to be "unacknowledged legislators." But as Victorians they worshipped not art but culture through art.

The keystone of redemptive culture, musical art connected and completed two sides of an arching spiritual structure. Music both sustained and was supported by tradition, on the one hand, and by the prophetic future, on the other. While the composer, as artist, represents creative freedom, his freedom is contingent, responsible to an ideal past and an ideal future. However much the Yankee composer feared the power of critics, implicitly he recognized that the success of redemptive culture hinged on critical mediation. As essayist or educator, the composer himself often explained music, tradition, and the prophetic future in terms of each other. He believed an ideal criticism would help the artist court the public.[1]

A key element of redemptive culture, music was defined in terms of an eclectic aesthetic of identity. Centennial composers juggled ele-

[44]

ments of formalism, naturalism, and functionalism to shape a musical aesthetic that would justify the sometimes contradictory demands which they placed on their art. Drawing on Kant, via Schopenhauer, they praised music as the ideal art. Untrammeled by servitude to physical imitation, music alone opened a window onto the transcendental reality behind the deceiving appearances of everyday existence. Music was the "idea" behind its own sound. Excessive attention to the sensuality of sound itself diverted attention from the reality behind the music. Unlike many romantics, these Victorian composers viewed art as communication, not as expression.[2] Because music communicated, it was morally responsible. The value of a musical work reflected the integrity of its composer. Therefore a classical music for Americans should communicate essential national values as experienced by quintessential Americans: Yankees like themselves.

Tradition, "the fellowship of the past" Mason called it, served as a solace and a source of authority for the centennial composers. They anchored their mission in this "usable past." Paradoxically, by claiming the mantle of New England's errand, Victorian Yankees became dependent on "national tradition" and "genealogical boundaries," the "atavistic distinctions of race, religion, and geography" foreign to the American messianic ideal they struggled to reclaim. Strangely echoing the "genetics of salvation," as Bercovitch calls "membership by birth in the elect community," they described themselves in terms of "race." Although by *race* Yankees meant nothing very specific, the word drew considerable metaphorical power from nostalgia for a golden age of kinship when people supposedly lived as brothers. Men such as Mason and Ives believed that the true moral community of neighborliness had been born in Old New England. It comforted Yankees to think that they were of the blood of the Puritans. With genetic blocks they built the spiritual structure of their fictive history. The Yankee "race" inherited the mission of New England: to reaffirm the meaning of American community for each generation. Centennial composers would fulfill their calling if they could create through musical culture a grammar of national identity.[3]

The arch of redemptive culture curved toward a prophetic future. Rooted in tradition, art made this ideal future possible, and was in turn justified by it. By composing music addressed to a "fellowship of the future," the composer would actually facilitate the eventual emergence of the musical people. In tune with such progressive thinkers as

Charles Horton Cooley and John Dewey, Mason and Ives proposed to widen the network of human contacts in order to communicate the potential for cultural progress. By imagining the future, they would hasten its arrival. Though they worked in the troubled present, their fellowship lay in the past and future.

Proponents of redemptive culture understood musical analysis as an exercise in courting public approbation for Yankee sensibilities. For its missionaries, musical culture supplanted sectarian Protestantism; they hoped that it would redirect an American civil religion bastardized by runaway materialism. Mason and Ives believed that America needed artists to reveal its hidden spiritual harmony: intuitively grasped intervals and keys, a sense of time itself. Centennial composers believed that music metaphorically embodied categories of consciousness such as time, cause, and space. An American musical culture would promote direct communion with the archetypes of an American consciousness. Redemptive culture characterized the sacred and the profane as American and un-American, essential and superficial, masculine and feminine, white and black. Through the spiritual metaphor of musical order, composers might focus for people the ideal order behind the seemingly disconnected features of modern American life. American "society divinized" would realize itself through redemptive culture.[4]

To justify their evanescent art in an age of bourgeois ascendancy, centennial composers assembled an aesthetic of identity from among the variety of humanist Victorian assumptions about music as an art. Their homespun aesthetic cannot be dignified as a proper theory of art. Yet it served them well enough. They took what they needed from functionalism, from formalism, and from idealistic and imaginative naturalism. The coherence of their eclectic aesthetic lives largely in the eye of the beholder. Still, two individuals as different as Mason and Ives similarly defined the underlying principles of musical valuation. And at a practical level they ranked European composers with virtual unanimity.

At first glance, Mason and Ives seem to have little in common aesthetically. Mason tended toward a dogmatic formalism, Ives toward a moralist functionalism. Yet as each man reexamined the ramifications of his position, he stretched his perspective. Gradually, with their commitments to idealistic and imaginative naturalism as a common ground, they came close to sharing one another's outlook. Through musical formalism, Mason put as much distance as possible between his art and the world of dirty dealing. He maintained that the beauty of music is hermetic, and refers to no reality outside itself. Ives, however, implicitly defended music according to a kind of higher functionalism. Music *is* useful, differently useful than airplanes or newspapers. It communicates at an exalted level, directly from soul to soul. On the plane of idealistic and imaginative naturalism, Mason's and Ives's aesthetic rationales overlapped. Mason decided that through the pursuit of pure, formal beauty, the composer created a higher (i.e., spiritual) emotional that communicates itself directly to attentive listeners. In his music the composer encodes the very forms of authentic experience. Ives believed that music reveals the spiritual ideality inherent in genuine experience. Rightly heard, many natural and communal experiences symbolize transcendental truths. Ives's own music was inwardly programmatic.

Aside from the fact that the centennial composers applied the variants of their aesthetic of identity to their American errand, little distinguishes these loosely constructed "philosophies" from their English counterparts. They drew from a common pool of assumptions and faced a common materialist anarchy. Typically, Victorians admitted art to useful society as a tool of moral influence. The functionalist theory of artistic communication was used to justify art as a moral force. Art conveyed felt meaning, as everyday speech conveyed rational meaning. While romantics characteristically elided as felt meaning both emotion (including erotic emotion) and spirit, Victorians divorced the two, preferring to speak of spiritual communication.[5] Victorians cherished the belief that the power of a work of art to communicate is determined by its creator's sincerity. The work may properly be criticized according to the morality of its subject matter. Perhaps the clearest statement of this Victorian functionalist aesthetic is Leo Tolstoy's *What is Art?* (1896).[6]

Functionalism did not have the field to itself, however. A formalist aesthetic became increasingly important among those committed to the health of culture. The formalist views art as categorically distinct from other aspects of life. The artwork is treated as a self-sufficient organism. Intrinsic measures of value are sought, as compared to the extrinsic measures of the functionalist.[7] While not uninfluenced by

British empiricism, modern formalism owes its philosophical genesis to German idealism, specifically to Kant.

A third aesthetic of naturalism mediated the clash of moralist functionalism and formalism.[8] Naturalistic—or mimetic, or representational—aesthetics conceives of art as a mirror or window.[9] Naturalism may be realistic (reflecting the actual), idealistic (reflecting the ideal), or imaginative (reflecting the unreal, or unrealized). All three naturalistic aesthetics coexisted in romantic art theories, but the idealistic and imaginative achieved relatively more prominence. Idealistic naturalism locates in great artists the ability to apprehend directly the ideal reality (Kant's noumenon) behind perceptual reality (phenomenon). Imaginative realism (in practice overlapping idealistic naturalism) suggests that the artist's genius lies in his ability to create organic wholes—artworks—which are more than the mere sum of their parts. In effect, the God-like artist creates new modes of reality.

The aesthetic of identity synthesized these elements: the formal perfection of an artwork (formalist aesthetic) represents the noumena behind the distortions of everyday perceptions (idealistic naturalism) in terms which project a symbolic vision of a new reality (imaginative naturalism) communicated to a mankind in need of spiritual goals (moralistic functionalism).

By the late nineteenth century, art generally, and music particularly, was often treated as "spilt religion." In the United States the cult of art began to flourish prior to the Civil War. "Words like 'communion,' 'mission' and 'divine' set the tone of artistic discussions," notes the historian Neil Harris, "for its devotees, art developed many of the characteristics of a surrogate religion, fulfilling the needs and seeking the goals of many other sects." Romantics, and Victorians after them, gravitated toward music as best exemplifying the spiritual potentials of art. Since Plato, Western philosophy has been cognizant of music as an art uniquely abstract and uniquely affective. The paradoxes of romantic and Victorian aesthetics grew and prospered when seeded in music: the art of emotional mathematics.[10]

Schopenhauer placed idealist philosophy at the service of music. "Music is . . . by no means like the other arts, the copy of Ideas," wrote Schopenhauer, "but the copy of the will itself, whose objectivity the Ideas are. This is why the effect of music is so much more powerful and penetrating than that of the other arts, for they speak only of shadows, but it speaks of the thing itself." Some romantics viewed music as uniquely capable of directly conveying "from soul to soul" that which, in Margaret Fuller's words, was "too fine to be put into any material grosser than air." Others raised music even above art itself. "For some, indeed, it virtually became a religion," writes H. G. Schenk.[11] Critics found themselves falling into religious metaphors. A passage from the American music critic Lawrence Gilman merges Schopenhauer's idealist philosophy with the language of Christian devotion:

> It is verifiable truth that, as our philosopher [British critic W. H. Hadow] reminds us, the poet, the painter, the sculptor, are bound, to a greater or less degree, by the facts of life and nature. The musician is bound by no such laws; his work need not necessarily stand in any relation to the phenomenal world; it is privileged to pass beyond . . . [to the Platonic] 'eternal archetypes'. . . . For music, alone among the arts, can deal with those essences of which even ideas and concepts are projections. . . . this is the Holy of Holies of all loveliness.[12]

Gilman's colleague W. J. Henderson referred to the great performing musician as a "preacher of the gospel of Beethoven or Chopen."[13]

Mason and Ives believed music to be a uniquely spiritual art. As musicians they enjoyed mastering the formal challenges of their craft. But as humanist Victorians, devotees of musical culture, they looked to music as a singularly transparent art. They wished to communicate the meaning of their experiences as Yankees through this transcendental medium. "I go for something higher in this world—for music,—the highest of all the arts," wrote the twelve-year-old Mason to his brother Ned. Yet music was even more wonderful, "more than art, a sublime purpose." This youthful enthusiasm remained the guiding light of Mason's life. The boy's sentiment echoed a common aesthetic conceit of romantic and Victorian writers. The Southern poet and musician Sidney Lanier also viewed music as the model art, to which he looked for spiritual leadership against the "spider" of materialist trade. Art should reveal the ideal, the "Realities." "In 'The Symphony' (first published in 1875) this reality reemerges through the power of art, here symbolized in the various instruments of the orchestra, which, singly and in unison, speak out against trade," writes Jay Martin. Late in his life, in the 1920s, the Arnoldian literary critic William Brownell also looked to music, the art that communicated directly, to bridge the gap between aesthetic culture and the masses.

"Unconsciously but consistently, he had chosen the word 'concert' to describe his ideal organism."[14] Ives concurred. After a tip of the hat toward Mason for his musical missionary work, Ives quoted from a letter by Sidney Lanier to Bayard Taylor:

> I have so many fair dreams and hopes about music in these days. It is a gospel whereof the people are in great need. As Christ gathered up the ten commandments and re-distilled them into the clear liquid of that wondrous eleventh—Love God utterly, and thy neighbor as thyself— so I think the time will come when music, rightly developed to its now-little foreseen grandeur will be found to be a late revelation of all gospels in one.[15]

Here was, wrote Ives, "a vision higher and deeper than art itself." Ives echoed Emerson's sentiment: "There is higher work for Art than the arts." As the crown jewel of the arts, music was best fitted to serve a spiritual role in society. Impatient even with the restrictions of this most ideal art, Ives could exclaim, "My God! What has sound got to do with music!"[16] The important musical reality (ideality) lay behind the actual sound of the music itself. Ives and Mason agreed that sensual emotionalism was morally suspect. They believed that an undue interest in the surface beauty of music, for whatever reason, led to the debasement of the art from its higher possibilities. One should look not at a window but through it.

In his first articles, Mason laid the groundwork for the formalist aesthetic on which he wrote variations the rest of his life. He perceived "Two Tendencies in Modern Music" (1902), romanticism and classicism; and he saw their embodiment in the music, respectively, of Tchaikowsky and Brahms. Mason first explored the issues of romantic aesthetics while at Harvard. There he studied the philosophy of art with Santayana at the time the young professor was writing his little classic *The Sense of Beauty* (1898). Drawing upon aspects of German idealism and British empiricism, Santayana essayed to counteract the excesses of an extreme romantic idealism which deliberately blurred distinctions separating the good, the true, and the beautiful. Santayana restated Kant's theory of "disinterested satisfaction": "In the perception of beauty, our judgment is necessarily intrinsic and based on the character of the immediate experience, and never consciously on the idea of an eventual utility in the object."[17]

Mason agreed with Santayana's argument to a point. He averred that "one ideal of music is emotional expression; another is plastic beauty. . . . In all arts there is more or less conflict between beauty, the aim of the art as an art, and expression, its necessary condition as a human instrument." The instrumentalist ideal is that of romanticism. Tchaikowsky, for example, "is a poet and humanist who, finding in music an eloquent voice for the ardent and noble emotion he wishes to express, seizes upon it without further reflection and proceeds to use it for his own purposes." But the classical ideal disdains such easy fruits, seeking "inner symmetry." In modern music, suggests Mason, the work of Brahms best exemplifies classic formalism. "Our thesis is that Brahms is ever aiming at beautiful organization in his musical fabric, while Tchaikowsky strives rather for poignant emotional effectiveness." Mason's views paralleled those of the Viennese critic Eduard Hanslick, who articulated a blunt formalist musical aesthetic (*The Beautiful in Music*, 1854). Hanslick rejected the notion that music represented anything outside itself—especially feelings.[18] Mason suggested that the conscious expression of feelings was an inferior aspect of musical composition. He followed Hanslick in preferring Brahms's symphonic classicism to Wagner's operatic romanticism.

But small divergences between the positions of Mason and Hanslick carry important implications. Hanslick took his stand against music-as-feeling on the grounds that music was the least realistic art. As it did not represent trees, it could not represent feelings. But others, following Schopenhauer, advanced the idealistic argument that precisely because music did not represent trees, it could represent inner reality—spirit—including the deepest human feelings. Unlike Hanslick, Mason opposed formalism not to mimesis but to utility generally and expression specifically. Both men scorned links with exterior reality and with emotionalism. But at this point Mason emended his argument, allowing him to plant one foot in the romantic aesthetic camp without the appearance of doing so. The works of the classic masters, Bach, Beethoven, and Brahms, evoke the larger "emotion we feel when we recognize pure beauty."[19] Only the conscious pursuit of emotion, as in Tchaikowsky, destroys the possibility of attaining the higher emotion which inheres in classical art. Having opened the door to a hierarchy of emotions, Mason analogized between aesthetic and moral valuation:[20]

> Satisfaction is an effect, in art as in life, that comes only from the sense of wholeness. The artist has to renounce beauties that conflict with his central, permeating beauty, just as the man has to renounce delights

that conflict with his central ideal of happiness. And we have at least the analogy with the ethical sphere to support our belief that the integral conception of art is the higher, and that classicism is a saner artistic creed than romanticism. In the long run, the emotion that fills us when we hear a work of perfectly controlled and organized symmetry and loveliness, like [the best of Beethoven, Bach, or Brahms] . . . is a more moving emotion than all the fine heats with which we listen to Wagner, Schumann, or Tchaikowsky.[21]

Mason did not dismiss the claims of romanticism out of hand. In fact, he pictured music as progressing through history in a kind of dialectic. Romantic artists need to explore the frontiers of emotional expression. Classically oriented artists then build new structures of organic beauty with the resources discovered by romantics. "Brahms has stamped the romantic ideas of Schumann and his fellows with the organic beauty of classicism." Mason had formulated this position even as an undergraduate, and it appeared in a piece he had published in the *Harvard Monthly*.[22]

That Mason should have garnered the instantaneous praise and friendship of leading British Victorian critics is not surprising. From the beginning his writings smoothly synthesized the arguments of various late-nineteenth-century writers. Sir Henry Hadow, in his *Studies in Modern Music* (1892), wrote, in words reminiscent of Hanslick, that "in Music the distinction [between the formal and the material aspect] vanishes altogether." For this reason "the whole work of Art is either the pure presentation of abstract Beauty, as in so-called 'Classical' Music, or the suggestion of Beauty tinged with emotion as in the so-called 'Romantic' school." Mason also agreed with Hadow as to the dialectic of musical history. Each art passes through two stages of development, the classical, wherein "the rules of style are to a great extent determined by *a priori* laws and traditions," and the romantic, with a "revolt against tradition, and each artist becoming a law unto himself." The third stage is either an extension, with difference, of one or the other, or a combination. In his *Art of Music* (1895), Parry also expounded a musical law of progress modeled explicitly on Spencer's evolutionary theory, which posited an inevitable movement from homogeneity toward heterogeneity.[23]

Mason, at first gingerly but later with vehemence, played up the relationship between music and morality, a subject of ongoing discussion among English critics. In his remarkably popular book *Music and Morals* (originally published in 1871, it had gone through sixteen editions by 1892), the Reverend H. R. Haweis argued a philosophy of art essentially similar to the view expounded by Tolstoy in *What Is Art?* Art expresses feeling, and may be judged good or bad, not on the basis of beauty but on the basis of the quality of feeling expressed.[24] Art is a mirror, not of the outside world but of the artist's soul; and the moral worth of art reflects the moral worth of the artist. "Morality," wrote Haweis, "is a quality which Art may or may not possess; it does not, except in a very secondary sense, belong to its constitution. The Morality depends upon the Artist, not upon the Art."[25] Edmund Gurney, in *The Power of Sound* (1880), took issue with Haweis's claims. "It is hard to see how that which produces, according to Mr. Haweis's description, a special emotional atmosphere, uncharged (according to his own admission), either naturally or by association, with any idea applicable to life, can in any direct sense have force to mould conduct." Had Haweis argued forthrightly, as Tolstoy was to do, that a work could be aesthetically excellent, morally rotten, and hence "bad" art, Gurney might have been more appreciative of his position. "I believe as firmly as any one," wrote Gurney, "that if in life we may promote happiness through morality, in Art we may promote morality through happiness: but this belief will gain and not lose from a recognition that moral and aesthetic excellence are not Siamese twins, but 'twin-sisters differently beautiful.' "[26] Mason steered a canny course through this Victorian maze.

Throughout his first decade as American spokesman for Victorian musical ideals, Mason wrote with dogged optimism about the future of musical culture. He looked forward to a new Brahms who would synthesize the best elements in Tchaikowsky's romantic explorations. Education would pave the way, building a broad base of musical support among the people. Mason's writings of this period largely reiterated the varied aesthetic commonplaces of his time. In "Our Public School Music" (1904) he hewed to Hanslick's position. "Music is itself alone: its laws (of melody, harmony, rhythm) are its own: its message is untranslatable, its appeal is unique." Another article, "Dissonance and Evil," written the same year, essayed a hermeneutic analogy between ethical and artistic valuation. Dissonance arises necessarily because occasionally harmonic purity must be sacrificed to melodic interest. The musician uses this necessity to introduce a feeling of musical restlessness which impels the piece forward. Stubbing our spiritual toe may, like dissonance, spur us upward with our resolve further fortified. Hence dissonance in music, like evil in ethics, is a matter of perception, and is a necessary part of the pursuit of higher goals.[27]

Several years after "Dissonance and Evil," Mason espoused a full-fledged functionalism, suggesting that music was the highest medium of moral communication. In 1913 he wrote a pamphlet for the American Association for International Conciliation, *Music as an International Language*, arguing a theory of moral suasion similar to that of Reverend Haweis. "If it be true," wrote Mason, "that music is in sober fact, the only international language, the only emotional and spiritual coinage that is honored all over the world, then it must surely be an invaluable influence toward peace."[28] During these years, Mason's optimism acted as the glue holding his patchwork aesthetic together. Music was nothing but music; music was rather analogous to moral processes; music was an international language of spirit and emotion which helped ameliorate mutual human distrust.

Ives struggled with these same issues, most notably in his *Essays before a Sonata* (1920). Ives knew of Mason, both as critic and as composer. Mason's music served as a mark of excellence against which people measured Ives's work. Elizabeth Sprague Coolidge, an important patroness of American music, known by Ives through his father-in-law, lectured Ives after hearing some of his music: "Well, I must say your music makes no sense to me. It is not, to my mind music. How is it that—studying as you have with Parker—that you ever came to write like that? You ought to know the music of Daniel Gregory Mason, who is living near us in Pittsfield—he has a real message." Ives also smarted under comments made by the violinist Edgar Stowell, who compared Ives's violin sonatas with one by Mason. Stowell said that the density of ideas in Ives's music was too great and that, unlike Mason, Ives did not write real *Geigermusick*—music that fell naturally under the fingers.[29]

Yet Ives thought highly of Mason's writings. Referring to Mason's book *Contemporary Composers*, he wrote that Mason's "wholesome influence . . . is doing as much perhaps for music in America as American music is." Brewster Ives recalled that his uncle "always showed great respect for the old masters: Bach, Beethoven, and Brahms in particular. I have a book of his entitled *From Grieg to Brahms* [by Mason], and in it are many passages that he underscored."[30]

Ives and Mason shared the same pantheon of European composers. At the summit stood Bach, Beethoven, and Brahms. Sometimes

Ives seemed to feel that Bach and Beethoven existed beyond any category. He found Debussy's music to be "voluptuous," "sensuous," "luxuriant," and "slimy." "Wagner seems less and less to measure up to the substance and reality of Cesar Franck, Brahms, d'Indy, or even Elgar (with all his tiresomeness); the wholesomeness, manliness, humility, and deep spiritual, possibly religious feeling of these men seemed missing." Ives felt that Tchaikowsky was too interested in "getting his audience"; and he found his music repetitious. Ravel and Stravinsky, in Ives's opinion, were overinfluenced by the "morbidly fascinating—a kind of false beauty obtained by artistic monotony."[31] The great differences between Ives's and Mason's own musical styles simply are not reflected in their estimations of European music. Their judgments are almost totally congruent.

In the prologue to his *Essays before a Sonata*, Ives asked whether music represents only itself, as Hanslick had argued, or whether it can express values usually expressed in other terms. Ives wondered, rhetorically, "Is not all music program music? Is not pure music, so called, representative in its essence?"[32] In general Ives seemed to believe that to be the case, a position he shared with romantic figures such as Liszt, who loved to read elaborate programs into Beethoven's sonatas, for example. But no sooner had Ives put forward his belief in programmatic communication than he was seized by doubt. "A theme that the composer sets up as 'moral goodness' may sound like 'high vitality' to his friend, and but like an outburst of 'nervous weakness' or a 'stagnant pool' to those not even his enemies. Expression, to a great extent, is a matter of terms, and terms are anyone's." Ives suggested that music held the potential to become a transcendental language wholly unlike word language. But full musical communication would have to await the musical millennium, "when school children will whistle popular tunes in quarter-tones."[33]

Ives was self-consciously a composer of transcendental program music. But normal listeners could infer all different kinds of programs from a work, as Ives realized. Writing about his *Washington's Birthday*, he wryly noted:

> If this piece is played separately, without outlining the program, it may give (and it has given) a wrong idea of what it is and what it was made for. . . . [pieces like this] could be played as abstract music (giving no titles [or] program), and then they would be just like all other 'abstract' things in art—one of two things: a covering up, or ignorance of (or but a

vague feeling of) the human something at its source—or just an emasculated piece of nice embroidery! So if *Washington's Birthday* were put
on a program with no program [notes], the DAR would think it pre-
tended to have something to do with Washington, or his birthday or
'These United States'—or some speech by Senator Blowout![34]

Ives had every reason to worry. The critic Paul Rosenfeld, one of
those "not even his enemy," took the song *In Flanders Field* to be Ives's
sardonic comment on World War I. But the song was meant, in Frank
Rossiter's words, as a "heartfelt expression of Ives's sincere grief for
the fallen soldiers and of his identification of himself with their noble
purpose." Rosenfeld had taken his cue from the song's publication
date, 1919; but the piece was actually composed in 1917, when national feeling about the war was quite different. Similarly, another
critic thought he heard an "'almost Rabelaisian' musical burlesque of
religious sentiment" at the conclusion of Ives's song *Charlie Rutlage.*
But the Victorian Ives intended nothing even remotely Rabelaisian.[35]

Ives, of course, was not alone in his dilemma. Composers commonly find that people "misread" the inner program they intended
when composing their work. Stravinsky, who made his reputation as a
composer of programmatic ballet music, became so sensitive on the
issue that he insisted upon a strict formalist aesthetic: "I consider
music by its very essence powerless to express anything whatsoever."
For the public music critic, the issue of "content" constitutes a Gor-
dian knot. The critic might simply write that on formal grounds X
piece is without merit, and many of his readers would rely on his
"expertise." But other music lovers will not be told that their taste is
worthless. And they know perfectly well that three critics of equally
impressive training may have three opinions about any given work.
Faced with this conundrum, critics usually illustrate their opinions
with impressionistic descriptions. For their nonprofessional readers
they write metaphorically about musical "meaning" or "content." But
as the critic B. H. Haggin once noted, the layman is still stuck with the
opinion of the critic.[36] Rhetorical metaphors are useful illustratively; as
argument they are as worthless as the appeal to authority. Favorable or
unfavorable judgments may be illustrated with equally descriptive
metaphors.[37]

Essays before a Sonata was Ives's solution to the problem of errant
programmaticism. He intended to publish the *Essays* with his *Concord*

Sonata as a kind of transcendental program note. Titling the piece and its movements was insufficient. "That which I like to think suggests Thoreau's submission to nature may, to another, seem something like Hawthorne's conception of the restlessness of an evil conscience."[38] So for a hundred pages Ives explained himself like an inarticulate man who pleads, "Don't listen to what I say; listen to what I mean."[39] His *Essays* favorably influenced the critic Lawrence Gilman's "understanding" of the *Sonata*. But the emphatically programmatic intent behind Ives's work troubled the critic Oscar Thompson. "What, one wonders, would be the purely musical reaction of a trained and responsive listener from abroad who had never so much as heard of Concord, Emerson, Hawthorne, the Alcotts or Thoreau?"[40]

Whereas Mason took the position that music was nothing but music, only to maneuver himself into quite a different stance, Ives plumped for programmaticism. While Mason toyed with the idea that music and morals might be analogous, Ives held forthrightly to a Tolstoyan philosophy of art. Ives's moralism and programmaticism were closely related. He felt that music communication could be less vague if one kept in mind the distinction between "substance" and "manner." Ives held substance in high esteem. By substance he intended meaning or message reflecting moral character. Substance gives spiritual satisfaction and leans toward optimism. Manner is style. It gives merely artistic satisfaction and leans toward pessimism. Outer or sensuous beauty may be characteristic of manner; but only inner, spiritual beauty lives in substance. And substance represents the most valuable thing in music. Ives realized that as a practical matter one cannot yet count on people's ability to recognize real beauty, "something that Roussell-Despierres says comes nearer to what we like to think beauty is . . . 'an infinite source of good . . . the love of the beautiful . . . a constant anxiety for moral beauty.' "[41]

In her book *Charles Ives and the American Mind*, Rosalie Sandra Perry has suggested that Ives derived his categories of manner/substance from Horatio Parker's "emphasis on 'form and substance' as the 'more solid foundation for music.' " At another point she compares Ives's "exaltation of content over form" with Louis Sullivan's credo, and traces both back to Horatio Greenough. Good enough, if certain distinctions are made clear. *Form* and *substance* were commonplace terms variously used. But Hanslick made the point that in music substance was intrinsic to the medium itself: hence the "complete fusion of substance and form" in music.⁴² Parker, too, wrote of substance and form. Greenough and Sullivan did not disparage form; they simply wanted it to be determined by content. Ives did not follow Hanslick's view that music is its own substance; nor did he choose the same terminology. His categories of substance/manner carry a heavy burden of moral connotations. He did not connect them with *and*. Rather, he pitted them one against the other: "manner *or* substance." Ives intended his programmaticism to portray the inner reality which is "substance."

Ives's division manner/substance approximates Mason's dichotomy romantic/classic.⁴³ Mason referred to Tchaikowsky as romantic; Ives thought of him as a purveyor of manner. And they meant to imply the same things. They perceived Tchaikowsky's music as superficial, sensuously beautiful, artful in the sense of being self-consciously fashionable. But Brahms exemplified substance or classic virtues. Mason and Ives shared a profound admiration for Brahms, and by their praise they meant to communicate the same litany of Victorian cultural virtues. They felt that his music has a depth reflecting character, is spiritually beautiful, and is unconcerned with immediate gratification. As Ives wrote of Brahms's symphonies, "[They] seem to me to be of the finest and deepest religious import."⁴⁴

Starting from opposite sides of Victorian aesthetic discourse, Ives and Mason each moved toward the other's position. Mason began as a formalist, initially denying the legitimacy of emotional expression as a goal of music. He posited a dualism, setting formalist classicism against emotional romanticism. But then he lent legitimacy to certain kinds of emotion. Higher or spiritual emotion comes as an unsought by-product of formal beauty. To be eschewed is the lower or sensual emotion actively exploited for purposes of romantic expression. Musical progress proceeded as a dialectic between romantic musical explorers (such as Schumann or Tchaikowsky) and classical musical architects (such as Brahms). Mason made clear his preference for the latter; romantics were treated as necessary evils. Mason's hierarchy of emotion made it possible for him to analogize between artistic and moral valuation. In this way he fulfilled the goal of establishing for music a legitimate social function. Ives began as a functionalist, proposing a radical moral programmaticism. Music communicates, and can be judged on the perceived quality of its message. To aid in winnowing the wheat from the chaff, Ives devised the antithetical categories "substance or manner." Ives's substance, like Mason's classic beauty, contained spiritual emotion. Manner, like romantic beauty, expressed sensual, superficial emotion. Thus both men juxtaposed edification to cheap thrills. Faced with the fact of ambiguous programmaticism, Ives conceded the abstract nature of music by appending various explanatory paraphernalia to his music. Their common belief in idealistic naturalism brought these two very different men to share aesthetic ground.

Within the theologically labyrinthine paradoxes of musical aesthetics, Mason and Ives found sufficient maneuvering room to justify the ways of music to man. Exegesis proved the meliorative spirituality of music.

For the centennial composers, tradition embodied a fictive past revealed through culture. In Van Wyck Brooks's phrase, it was a "usable past." Brooks asked of American thought, what "ought we elect to remember?" Tradition, then, is an abstraction tensioned between history and myth. Yankees believed that America's tradition was essentialist rather than pluralist, a taproot reaching back to the origins of moral community in New England, to the beginning of the future. Increasingly, men such as Mason and Brooks spoke of tradition in terms of race. "Out of his conception of nationality (sometimes called 'race') and its interaction with great personality Brooks developed his conception of cultural nationalism," writes Claire Sprague. "Nationalism applied to literature becomes tradition, and tradition, more pragmatically defined, becomes the usable past. The usable past would provide a national literature with 'redemptive' and 'revelative' powers." "Race" borrowed the metaphorical authority of ancient blood ties for the task of fashioning a "fellowship of the past." To designate tradition as racial, as loosely Anglo-Saxon, implied that its spiritual strength was forged in the premodern fires of kinship society. The metaphorical brotherhood ordering kinship community provides the framework for racial ideology. Blood ties become racial ties. Such racial traditions long sustained Southern cultural discourse. But prior to the mid-nineteenth century, Yankees considered blood and soil metaphors un-American. New England's America defined "itself by its relation to . . . a continuing revolution based on '*a conception of the future as the present.*'"[45]

Through redemptive culture, the centennial Yankee could claim America's ongoing revolution as his own private preserve. Mason wanted to anchor his progressive vision of a continually renascent American consciousness in a central tradition. He and Ives rejected the notion that the American spirit could be expressed in terms of an outer local color. Such local color touched only appearances, not underlying realities. More important, in Mason's words, were "characteristic attitudes or temperamental tendencies." Only the deeply dyed cast of tradition truly mattered. He pointed in particular to "the reserve, the dislike of ostentation, the repressed but strong emotion masked by dry humor, that belong to our New England type." The claims of superficial, statistical Americanism did not impress him. The artist must escape this prison of contemporary existence and seek solace in the past:[46]

> This Anglo-Saxon element in our heterogeneous national character, however quantitatively in the minority nowadays, is qualitatively of crucial significance in determining what we call the American temper. The name popularly symbolizing it—the word 'Yankee'—is often extended from New England to cover the whole country; and that other and most far-reaching of all our popular symbols—Uncle Sam—is only a universalized and glorified Yankee. In our literature the type is immortally enshrined in the work of Emerson and Thoreau.[47]

And in his own music, Mason sought to encode this essential American temper.

Through their musical art, Yankee composers hoped to wed the past to the future, and thus escape the anarchic present. Redemptive culture, like religion, mediates the necessities of the real and the necessities of the ideal. As the anthropologist Clifford Geertz writes of religion, it "tunes human action to an envisioned cosmic order and projects images of cosmic order onto the plain of human experience." Mason and Ives each believed that through musical culture he could reach his ideal audience, the essential America, the People. This America dwelt in a "fellowship" of the past and the future.[48]

After World War I bled the optimism from progressivism, some centennial Yankees felt that the present no longer existed as a category of authentic experience. Ives came to believe that "a thing thought of in terms of the present is—well, that is impossible!" Nor, indeed, did Yankees find much that they wished to experience in the onrushing present of the 1920s. Increasingly, a sense of vertigo, like drifting at the edge of Poe's "Maelstrom," afflicted this generation's encounter with modern America. When, as an older man, Mason returned to his birthplace, he found his house "turned on its axis." Woods had disappeared; hills had been shoveled into ponds. "I almost preferred having things vanish completely," he lamented, "rather than remain like corpses without souls, outliving their youthful spaciousness and romance." Ives, too, discovered his boyhood home in Danbury bodily moved. His nephew remembered that Ives "actually moaned aloud when he got up there [in the City Hall Square] and saw how it had all changed from his recollection of it." Ives buried his head in his hands and "said he was sorry he had gone out at all." Ives's ideal America lived as a cinematic dream sequence of tart-tongued farmers, open-air camp meetings, brass bands, and baseball. He celebrated not so much the actual Danbury of his own youth "but rather that of his father before the Civil War, when Danbury had still been rural."[49] He neither praised the present nor courted its favor. He composed for audiences safely dead or yet unborn.

Ives and Mason believed that redemptive culture legitimated their lonely mission. Faith in their America kept them from thinking of their works as but bottled missives on an open sea. Ives looked toward an American musical millennium in which the people would experience his ideals through a transcendental language of quarter tones, tone clusters, and free-form strut. Having failed to control adequately his real audiences or to educate his potential audiences, Mason turned to the artist's last refuge: the great audience of posterity. Like nineteenth-century American artists, Mason as well as Ives "looked beyond the public, which rejected them, to an amorphous *people*."[50] This people's fellowship survived only in tradition and in the distant future. In Mason's *Artistic Ideals*, the book of which he was perhaps most proud, the chapter "Fellowship" unfolds an elaborate rationale for a utopian audience. Art involves communication, not simply expression.[51] In the absence of a real audience, the artist addresses an ideal audience. Eventually, as "fellowship" develops between them, the artist will reach a real audience which is his ideal audience made flesh and the salvation of society through culture.[52] Mason's artist creates for an ideal audience that is called into being by the artist.

Mason's theory of artistic fellowship drew upon the social thought of John Dewey and especially of Charles Horton Cooley. He admired the practical idealism of Dewey's pragmatism; and he turned to the sociologist Cooley as to a fellow spirit. Borrowing heavily from William James, Cooley posited a theory that society is mental. The self does not exist in Cartesian isolation but is built up through a process of interaction with the perceptions and expectations of others.[53] With Dewey and Cooley, Mason saw practical benefits in improving avenues of communication through education and through art. Mason agreed with Dewey that education and art are but facets of the same process of discovery. Cooley advocated widening the human perceptions which are the life of society. Artists play the key role in this process, for they, above all others, are gifted to imagine concrete new modes of reality. In the words of Julian Huxley, quoted by Mason: "The escape of thought from the imperfections of the actual into a thought-organized ideal is Art; its projection, dragging present action with it into a more perfect future, is true religion." Dewey insisted that art is a social, interactive process. It marks the point at which humanity most conspicuously breaks free from a priori bonds into brave new worlds of inspired inventiveness. Dewey and Cooley believed, as Mason had at the time he wrote "Music as an International Language," that increased communication widened fellowship throughout society and between societies. These progressive thinkers elided two separate assertions: that art creates new consciousness and that art communicates empathically. They agreed that art was the highest form of human activity. As Philip Rieff has noted, "Cooley's sociology was a variety of the religion of culture to which the cultured resort after all other religions fail them."[54]

Neither Cooley nor Dewey nor Mason viewed cultural growth as a random process of unguided interaction. As the fountainhead of new modes of consciousness, art assumes hierarchy. Not all that passes for art is equally good or equally useful to society. Art requires mediation. As the church domesticates revelation, culture harnesses inspiration. Mason believed that through redemptive culture, American musical artists could draw sustenance and fulfill their freely accepted responsibilities to their ideal audiences. The centennial composers thought that the weight and strength of American tradition passed to the prophetic future through the keystone of art, most effectively so through their uniquely spiritual art of music. They composed music designed to change the world—to re-form it. To this "fellowship of the future" they addressed their musical offerings. They looked nostalgically forward, for, as Mason wrote, "the fellowship of the future is to us even more than inspiring compansionship while we live; it is our means of immortality after we die."[55]

The fate of their redemptive culture rested on a future whose solid foundation it was the calling of centennial composers to construct. As Yankees and as Victorians, their progressive task was nothing less than to shape the future. Ives viewed "his music as an expression of theology and political thought," writes David Noble. "The rise of all to the spiritual out of the profane was how Ives defined the years of progress from 1900 to 1917." After the war, he no longer felt inspired to compose. In his writings, though, he looked ahead to a brighter age. As a leader in a nation called to lead, Ives felt that he must compose strong music, music to sing the song of America's germinal past, music to sing the universal symphony of its glorious future:

> For Ives, Americans, real Americans, the people and not the non-people, the aristocracy, were closer to God than people anywhere else in the world. . . . Americans then had the responsibility of helping the rest of the world. And Ives had the greatest responsibility of any American because it was through music alone that men could be united in a natural and not an artificial community.[56]

The centennial composers huddled at the edge of their wilderness, the terrifying and seductive twentieth century. Like their Puritan ancestors, they were called to an errand. Through their art they must invest the future with sacred meaning.

PART TWO

Ethnic Dissonance

In the 1920s, several centennial composers dominated America's academic musical establishment. Edward Burlingame Hill at Harvard, David Stanley Smith at Yale, and Daniel Gregory Mason at Columbia oversaw the musical education of the nation's bright young men. Through his many books and articles, Mason spread the gospel of redemptive culture to a genteel laity throughout the country. As preeminent spokesman for the concerns of his group, Mason articulated with increasing vehemence his call for a primary national musical culture. His writings proved popular far beyond his musical compositions. In 1924, the National Music Week Committee of New York listed five of Mason's books among the sixteen voted for inclusion in its "Two-foot shelf on musical subjects."[1] As national debate over the meaning of music swelled to an anxious, sometimes to an acrimonious, pitch, the terms of contention echoed Mason's formulation of

[65]

redemptive culture. Musicians, critics, newspaper editors, ministers, playwrights, politicians, people with differing musical backgrounds and tastes all argued the importance of ragtime and then of jazz and avant-garde music to the nation's cultural identity. Redemptive culture defined the arena of American musical controversy; but Yankee spokesmen such as Mason proved unable to control the interpretations placed on their metaphorical system. Like their New England ancestors, the centennial composers bequeathed to the nation a formulation of concern with the state of America's moral consciousness, only to see the dialectic of public debate pass them by.

Yankee composers had defined artistic and social valuation in terms of each other. They thought of redemptive culture as a progressive civil religion that advanced through a reductive dialectic: anchored in a central tradition, musical art would help create a prophetic blueprint for America's spiritual destiny. This formula could be read in any direction; each part existed for and was justified by the other parts. The skeleton of this reductive logic, stripped of its empathic optimism, soldiered the antimodernist and increasingly racialist aesthetic polemics of the 1920s. Virtually all of the centennial composers were antimodernists, though inconsistently. Most despised the avant-garde. None seems to have been a Negrophobe, but several were anti-Semitic. Most were racialists in a more general sense. Ives was neither a Negrophobe nor an anti-Semite. He held his peace as the progressivism of his early manhood passed, war-cheated, into middle age. Others, Mason most aggressively, found themselves trapped in a racialist antimodernism because they could not discipline the dialectic of American musical culture.

Jazz burst into the awareness of white Americans at the close of World War I. Both opponents and enthusiasts employed the "Jazz Age" label to describe a brash and youthful era. Jazz was believed to represent the new face of an America awakening to the reality of its involvement in the twentieth century. Musical analyses echoing the evaluative language of redemptive culture affirmed the importance of jazz to the national culture. Jazz acquired an association both with a hedonism allegedly characteristic of Negroes and, paradoxically, with a cold mechanism ostensibly true of modern urban life. Janus-faced jazz seemed to express the temper of contemporary America: its egoistic fragmentation of community, its materialism, its fascination with modernism in general and with avant-gardism in particular.

In the war over jazz, people battled to control the root metaphors of their self-definition as Americans. Increasingly racialism shaped the metalanguage of this American drama of national consciousness. Racial images constricted the symbolic interaction, the courtship of roles that would normally yield a satisfactory universe of identities. While turn-of-the-century ragtime was widely associated with a romantic racialist stereotype of Negroes as childlike, two decades later jazz was perceived by many of its detractors as the musical expression of an allegedly animalistic black temper. The journey from ragtime to jazz framed the possibilities of Negro identity in white America. On this narrow metaphorical stage, billed as "children" or "beasts," black people tried to create identities for themselves.

The metaphor of Negroes as marginal creatures defining the lower boundary of humanity extends deep into the history of the West. Color racialism derives from Biblical myths of kinship and European color symbolism.[2] The modern child/beast formula emerged after seventeenth-century English explorers discovered Negroes and large apes at roughly the same time. Europeans imagined that they had found the actual genesis of the metaphorical connection commonly drawn between animals and humans. This ontological "discovery" served as the foundation on which "scientific" racialism was built. In 1735 the Swedish taxonomist Carolus Linnaeus classified "man as an integral part of animal creation." He portrayed Europeans as "gentle, acute, inventive," Africans as "crafty, indolent, negligent."[3] Such schemas fit easily into the eighteenth century's root metaphor for hierarchical meaning: the Great Chain of Being. The Great Chain provided the intellectual shackles to bind the Negro to schizophrenic roles as child or beast. American slavery deemed the ranks of the chain permanent.[4] The Darwinian transformation of the paradigm coincided with Negro emancipation, and in turn served to justify a restricted identity for free Negroes. The Negro was treated as an instance of arrested evolutionary development, hovering between the prehuman stage of beast and the protohuman stage of child. The metaphorical web made it easy to accept the theoretical trap: in the Negro, ontogeny did not altogether recapitulate phylogeny.[5]

Modern racial thought has drawn strength from intellectual currents which are culture-bound though not explicitly racialist in conception. American racial theory leaned specifically on Herbert Spencer and later on Count Arthur de Gobineau to support notions that Anglo-Saxons were a chosen "race." From Spencer to Gobineau to Max Weber to Sigmund Freud, self-discipline has been viewed as a key to the "success" of Western civilization. "Energetic intelligence" is the hallmark of the white peoples, argued Gobineau in his *Essay on the Inequality of Human Races* (1853). Black people are "marked by animality and severely limited intellect. They possess great energy, but are characterized also by sensuality and instability of mood."[6] For Max Weber the "rationalization" of all aspects of life, most remarkably distilled in the "Protestant ethic," has distinguished advanced Western society from the rest of the world. Weber harnessed to self-discipline not the pressure of libido, as did Freud, but the engine of industriousness.[7] Diverse in their systems of thought, these intellectuals agreed that their civilization depended upon certain internalized traits. Intelligence channeled energy through attachment to distant goals. Whether comparison with the nonwhite world was explicit, as in Gobineau, or implicit, as in Weber, Western intellectuals underlined deeply held assumptions about the "genius" of the white West.

From racialism to racism, from chain to dualism, the root metaphors of Western culture narrowed the basis from which an American black identity could grow. Even when free from physical slavery, the Negro's public roles were so delimited that he existed on a mental reservation. Greed, insecurity, and the need to explain the quickening currents of modernization fed the analogic metaphors of racialism. Racialism entered the language of nationalism; and in the United States it penetrated the dialectic of American autogenesis. In the anxious twenties, the logic of redemptive culture framed a struggle over American character as embodied in the culture of several symbolic groups: Yankees, Negroes, and Jews. Writers of all backgrounds attributed a sensual culture to Negroes and a spiritual culture to Yankees. As symbols, they stood out from the multiplicity of American life as clearly as black and white.

The cultural contrast between sensual jazz and spiritual classical music was reinterpreted by several younger critics: Gilbert Seldes, Carl Van Vechten, and John Hammond. These white rebels affirmed the artistic, spiritual, and national value of sensualism. Drawing on romantic racialism, they viewed blacks' supposed hedonism as childlike. Jazz, wellspring of innocent enjoyment, would counteract Yankee coldness. As critics and entrepreneurs, Seldes and Van Vechten boosted the Negro Renaissance, a movement to advance the Negro's status by demonstrating his cultural value. These white critics often urged Negroes to exploit their alleged sensuality, in effect narrowing the inner resources of the Negro Renaissance. Yet even condescending attention by classically trained critics made jazz seem more important to whites and blacks alike.

Attention from Europe further sharpened the debates over jazz and the national identity. Since Dvořák had urged American composers to tap their varied national folk roots, including black spirituals, Yankees were divided over the propriety both of using Negro music and of following a European's advice. During the twenties these issues were exacerbated when prominent European composers, performers, and writers stated that jazz was *the* characteristically American folk music, that it *must* serve as the basis for a national musical style. Yankees preferred to define themselves, as had their forebears, in ambiguous opposition to Europe. Europe represented the parental "other" for whom and against whom they carried on their errand. While Yankees might make peace with spirituals, even rags, they were disinclined to embrace jazz at the behest of Europeans.

But European composers and critics went even beyond suggesting that jazz was grist for classical composers. Some intimated that jazz itself was the great American art. Louis Armstrong and Duke Ellington returned from European tours buoyed by the belief that their jazz was more than mere jive. Advocates of redemptive culture were stupefied. Though Europe was a decadent parent, no one expected its musical community to turn away from "sweetness and light" as an ultimate ideal. As the mold of social self-awareness, culture, they insisted, must employ qualitative distinctions lest the dark void of anarchy sweep over the West.

Reductionist criticism synthesized sensual jazz (antithesis of the deferred gratification essential to Western life) and mechanistic jazz (antithesis of organic fellowship) by suggesting that both were aspects of a modern materialism (consumption capitalism) which devalues spirit. Some critics defended redemptive musical culture by dismissing modern European music as jazz for "highbrows." Stravinsky symbolized European musical modernism for Americans, who first heard this new music during the 1920s. Critics described *The Rite of Spring* as high-powered jazz: brutal, sensuous, mechanical. Thus the jazz war spilled into a conflict over avant-gardism. Antimodernist critics asserted that, aesthetically and culturally, nothing separated the merely

new (fashionable) from the essentially modern (avant-garde). Enthusiasm for jazz by modern European composers touched off the
furor.

Europeans' reactions to jazz were conditioned by their traditional
visions of America as an outpost of precultural "natural man" and of
revolutionary "brave new worlds." Many European musicians, artists,
and intellectuals sought in jazz a Bergsonian *élan vital*, a life force with
which to revivify the Western artistic experience. European avant-
gardists also regarded America as a model for futurist expressionism.
Some avant-gardists wielded jazz as a weapon against an oppressive
cultural establishment. European fascination with the implications of
jazz culminated in Ernst Křenek's *Jonny spielt auf* (Jonny Strikes Up the
Band) and Kurt Weill's *Rise and Fall of the City of Mahagonny*. Defenders
of redemptive culture could only watch in fascinated anguish as
Křenek's Negro hero, Jonny, impudently conquered the world with
his jazz. It seemed that the mirror of Europe now reflected only a
cruelly twisted image of America's cultural identity. Although enthusiasm for jazz proved short-lived among avant-gardists, it pointed
up the malleability of the themes of redemptive culture. Neither at
home nor abroad could Yankee composers control the symbols of their
civil religion.

Meanwhile, a new generation of native-born composers vied for
attention as representative American artists. Their geographical, educational, and ethnic diversity underlined their aesthetic and spiritual
challenge to the America of the centennial composers. Whereas all of
the Yankees had married, symptomatically most of the composers
born from 1895 through 1900 stayed single. The circumspect family
lives of the Yankees contrasted with the lifestyles of some of the
younger men. By Victorian standards, these brash youngsters, hetero-
sexuals and homosexuals both, were sexually irresponsible. Their
backgrounds and their behavior could hardly be signs of election.

Two of the young bachelors, George Gershwin and Aaron Copland, became particular objects of attention in the 1920s. Everything
about them and their music seemed to demean the Yankee struggle for
redemptive culture. They were New York Jews without even college
educations. They consciously sought to shape a distinctively American musical idiom by mixing jazz with classical music. They achieved
rapid popular and critical acclaim. A broad range of observers, from
outright anti-Semites to philo-Semites, viewed Copland, Gershwin,

and the Swiss-born Ernest Bloch, also, as playing a characteristically Jewish role in the modern dilemma of American redemptive culture. Using the criterion of the aesthetic of identity, critics deemed music composed by Jews reflective of Jewish values and roles. Proponent of modernism, the stereotypical "New York Jew" became identified with a racial tradition midway between Yankees and Negroes. Specifically, discussions of American musical culture treated allegedly "Oriental" Jews as rootless middlemen trading on the base sensuality attributed to Negroes and the Anglo-Saxon, spiritual tradition associated with Yankees. While some observers of the cultural scene approved of this "spiritual miscegenation," such writers as Mason and John Tasker Howard nervously implicated the "New York Jew" with an invasion of foreign talent and with a supposed control of musical culture. Conventional ethnic "codewords" permitted some writers to suggest that which discretion forbade them to say outright. But Mason felt no such constraints. Most troublesome for friends of Yankee classicism, Jews tried to participate in the sacred ceremonies of national autogenesis through culture. It seemed that Jewish composers intended to obliterate the root distinction between high culture and merely anthropological culture. Classical and vernacular, traditional and avant-garde, white and black, hedonism and mechanism: all appeared to enter the Jewish melting pot.

But Jews plunged into advocacy of a renewed American music not because they were eclectic and rootless manipulators. Precisely because Jews possessed a durable sense of their own prophetic historicity, they could thoroughly identify with New England's mission. Acculturating Jews felt at home realizing the promise of the Yankee redemptive culture. *The Melting Pot* exemplified the temerity of this identification. The play portrays a Jewish immigrant, David Quixano, aspiring to complete the Great American Symphony. Like his fictional counterpart, the real-life immigrant composer Ernest Bloch sought to express the national spirit in a symphony called *America*. In the work's finale—The Future—chorus, audience, and orchestra are asked to join in an anthem to the spirit of unity through ethnic diversity. Mason was enraged at Bloch's presumption. Yet Gershwin, Copland, and Bloch tried to write original, rootedly American music that various audiences would appreciate. As self-consciously as any Yankee, these Jews believed in the democratic potential of music.

Proponents of an Anglo-Saxon redemptive culture preferred to pass the Yankee torch into non-Jewish hands. Shunning New York, and in the spirit of Winthrop, Emerson, and Whitman, New England's advocates sought their star of hope in the West. A broad range of critics nominated Roy Harris to be American music's "Great White Hope." Though not a Yankee, he of Lincolnesque bearing hailed from the plains. Ebulliently Harris accepted the nomination. He promoted himself as the ascendant Western star, one who could translate the land's vernal contours into lines of soaring music. But the imperatives of World War II displaced preoccupations with merely cultural nationalism, thus crippling the Yankee musical mission.

3

JAZZ AND THE ASPHALT JUNGLE

White Americans first heard jazz toward the end of World War I. Its rapidly widening popularity paralleled a crescendo of moralizing, joking, and vituperation that peaked in the mid-twenties. Never before had music seemed so important in the United States, stirring bitter public discussions. Yet neither jazz nor the reaction to it was wholly without precedent. The public reception of ragtime presaged sharper debates over the national meaning of jazz. Arbiters of cultural standards, including educators, critics, and composers, scrutinized ragtime to decide whether they should sanction its obvious popularity. Concerned to create examples of musical excellence toward which all Americans might strive, Yankee composers wondered where to place ragtime in the spectrum of the nation's musical life. Like composers elsewhere, they looked to vernacular music for inspiration, for musical roots. But in this young, heterogeneous, rapidly changing country, the centennial composers tended to seek a central tradition for American music—a taproot—in the Anglo-Saxon musical sources they knew best. At the same time they sought to draw upon the manifest variety of the American experience by taking bits of local color from what they considered the nation's "exotic" heritage, especially from music with Indian or Negro roots. But for Yankees such adventitious, democratic borrowing presupposed a deep commitment to their own sensibilities.

When at the turn of the century the Czech composer Anton Dvořák urged American composers to pay closer attention to Indian and Negro music, Yankees split in their responses to the Bohemian composer's friendly advice. Some, including Edward MacDowell, were evidently annoyed to be lectured about their errand by a foreigner, while others, most notably Arthur Farwell, actively promulgated Dvořák's formula for local-color Americanism. Few composers were untouched by the movement, even those who protested it most vehemently. In spite of their fundamentally sympathetic feelings toward Negroes, the centennial composers shied away from embracing what they considered a superficial, horizontal nationalism of local-color culture. A little of this and a little of that represented only the false surface of American life. They felt called to tap the essence of the national spirit.

Ragged Prelude

Rags flourished for roughly twenty years, from before 1897, when ragtime sheet music first appeared, through 1917. While ragtime didn't die immediately, after the World War Americans generally considered it only a distinctive progenitor of jazz, the happy-go-lucky music of a more innocent day.[1] Ragtime supposedly embodied in music the "Gay Nineties." "Ragtime was far and away the gayest, most exciting, most infectiously lilting music ever heard, and its name was a 'natural.' America's own music had come, as native as pumpkin pie and baseball, and within a year it seemed as if it had always been here."[2] The 1890s had not been so very gay, and ragtime acquired its greatest popularity after the turn of the century; memories of ragtime fed upon surreal nostalgia.

Ragtime achieved its success not without resistance; indeed, some of the criticism of rags foreshadowed the war against jazz in the 1920s. Occasionally it was attacked as banal urban music. Unlike folk music, wrote an observer for *Musical America*, a "product of the idyllic village atmosphere, mirroring the joys and sorrows, hopes and passions of the country people, [ragtime] exalts noise, rush and street vulgarity. It suggests repulsive dancehalls and restaurants." Ragtime sullied its reputation by its bad associations. What was to be done? The ragtime problem evinced several types of responses. Ignore it; it would go away, counseled some. "Ragtime's days are numbered. We are sorry to think that anyone should imagine that ragtime was of the least musical importance." Others suggested that organized benign neglect would help speed it toward oblivion. In 1901, the American Federation of Musicians declared that member musicians were to desist from playing ragtime. "The musicians know what is good, and if the people don't, we will have to teach them."[3] Organizations such as the National Music Teachers' Association and the National Association of Masters of Dancing struggled to maintain standards of taste and propriety.

Yet another approach questioned the originality of ragtime. The music critic Rupert Hughes, writing "A Eulogy of Ragtime" in 1899, ridiculed the "modern scholar who thinks he has dismissed the whole musical activity of the Negro by a single contemptuous word." Hughes condemned those who said of ragtime, " 'It is only a distorted reminiscence of Spanish and Mexican dances; behold the syncopation.' "[4] Although similar arguments reappeared in the later antijazz tirades, they were less virulent in tone and less frequently expressed in connection with ragtime.

To the extent that ragtime was perceived as black music, it corresponded to a romantic racial image of the Negro. According to this view, Negroes exemplify the soft side of humanity, unlike the enterprising, intellectual Anglo-Saxon race. "Genial, lively, docile, emotional, the affections rule," wrote the nineteeenth-century utopian thinker Robert Dale Owen, "the social instincts maintain the ascendant except under cruel repression, its cheerfulness and love of mirth overflow with the exuberance of childhood." White romantic racialism, notes the historian George M. Frederickson, "often revealed a mixture of cant, condescension, and sentimentality, not unlike the popular nineteenth-century view of womanly virtue, which it so closely resembled." Prior to the Civil War, Southern apologists sometimes used romantic racialism to justify slaveholders' paternalistic impulses. In the North, abolitionists employed its language in arguments against the inhumanity of slavery. The ideology peaked in 1864. It yielded to the other side of white racial stereotyping, which cast the Negro in the role of beast. Throughout Reconstruction, Southerners elaborated this image as they fostered the growth of segregation. But progressives and a few Southern accommodationists, reacting against the racist hysterics of local demagogues, revived elements of romantic racialism around the turn of the century.[5]

In fact, blacks had become successful entertainers of white audiences by drawing on the images of romantic racialism. Minstrel shows in numerous forms—plain and fancy, black and blackface—dominated popular music from the 1840s through the 1880s. Two kinds of Negro characters emerged: Jim Crow, "the plantation hand, a tatterdemalion of low estate but high spirits," and Zip Coon, "the urban dandy with affectedly modish ways and a fashionable 'long-tailed blue' dress coat." Black "jubilee" singing groups during the 1870s gained renown by associating their spirituals with the happy plantation skits of the minstrel shows. The historian Robert Toll argues that "minstrelsy provided a non-threatening way for vast numbers of white Americans to work out their ambivalence about race. . . . [The] minstrels created and repeatedly portrayed the contrasting caricatures of inept, ludicrous Northern blacks and contented, fulfilled Southern Negroes." Ragtime emerged out of the romantic racialism of the minstrel show, of the "coon song" and "cakewalk," first as "jig" music for banjo or band, then as the classic piano rags of Scott Joplin, James Scott, Joseph Lamb, and Tom Turpin, and finally in such Tin Pan Alley hits as "Alexander's Ragtime Band."[6]

For several interrelated reasons, a broad spectrum of white taste accepted ragtime. Classic ragtime was a composed, printed music. This fact alone lifted it to a certain threshold of respectability. Neither its popular association with minstrel music nor its regional associations threatened white sensibilities. Its hometowns were the midwestern cities of Sedalia and Kansas City, Missouri—albeit from what Rudi Blesh and Harriet Janis, historians of ragtime, call the local "sporting belts."[7] In addition, ragtime's association with marching music enhanced its status immensely.

Ragtime developed from march forms, and in turn served to reinvigorate the American march. Beginning with the Civil War, concert and marching bands grew continuously in nationwide popularity.[8] Brass bands became a focus of civic pride in towns throughout the United States. With the growing appeal of ragtime, John Philip Sousa adopted several strutting "cakewalk" numbers for his enlarged symphonic bands. Pieces such as "Smoky Mokes," "Hunky Dory," "At a Georgia Camp Meeting," and "Creole Belles" became popular band numbers. In 1901, the *New York Herald* reported that "when John Philip Sousa raised his baton to the opening measures of Composer (Abe) Holzmann's famous 'Smoky Mokes' last season the noted bandmaster's audience was nonplused. Then surprise gave way to vociferous applause. . . . and 'Smoky Mokes' re-echoed upon the pianos of a million music lovers." Furthermore, Sousa "was responsible, through his sensationally successful tours, for the spread of cakewalk syncopation to Europe."[9]

The brass band, with its masculine, nationalistic associations, served as a bridge to middle-class acceptability for diverse kinds of music. Both "highbrow" and "lowbrow" music achieved acclaim under Sousa's baton. Sousa, like Arthur Fiedler after him, eschewed the canons of Yankee redemptive culture, treating all music as entertainment. The bandleader compared his own aims against those of Theodore Thomas, founder of the Chicago Orchestra: "He gave Wagner, Liszt, and Tchaikowsky, in the belief that he was educating his public; I gave Wagner, Liszt, and Tchaikowsky with the hope that I was entertaining my public."[10]

Marches and ragtime were in vogue during the centennial composers' postcollegiate years. For Ives, whose father was a rebellious bandleader, and whose first performed composition was a march, the use of march and ragtime snatches in classical works seemed natural, if not inevitable. But other composers of his generation also freely used ragtime, minstrel music, and spirituals. Such borrowings stimulated considerable debate among American composers and critics.

While some Yankee composers toyed with the idea of developing a classical national music that might incorporate elements of popular and folk music, largely, though not exclusively, of white origin, the whole issue blossomed with the publication of Dvořák's famous *Harper's* article "Music in America" (1895), which suggested that the American composer "should listen to every whistling boy, every street singer or blind organ-grinder." Perhaps among "Negro melodies or Indian chants" American composers might find "inspiration for truly national music."[11] Dvořák argued that undoubtedly "the germs for the best in music lie hidden among all the races that are commingled in this great country. The music of the people is like a rare and lovely flower growing admist encroaching weeds. The fact that no one has as yet arisen to make the most of it does not prove that nothing is there."[12] Seconding Dvořák's advice a few years later, the London *Times* wrote, "Ragtime is absolutely characteristic of its inventors—from nowhere but the United States could such music have sprung. . . . Nor can there be any doubt about its vigour, brimming over with life. . . . Here for those who have ears to hear are the seeds from which a national art may ultimately spring."[13]

Dvořák's call for a closer regard for non-Anglo-Saxon folk music obtained institutional amplification when Arthur Farwell founded his Wa-Wan Press in 1901. An important figure among the centennial generation of American composers, Farwell was born in Minnesota in

1872, of New England stock. After his father's hardware business failed in the depression of 1893, Farwell resettled his family in Cambridge, Massachusetts, where he was studying at MIT. While at college, his musical interests were ignited by concerts of the Boston Symphony Orchestra. Subsequently Farwell studied composition with Homer Norris, then with Chadwick, unsatisfactorily. "Farwell had a great disdain for those who insisted that a knowledge of counterpoint, form and analysis were essential to the composer. It is probable that this belief clashed with Chadwick's ideas." Encouraged by Edward MacDowell, and financed by a man named Osborn, Farwell studied for a year and a half in Europe with such famous composers as Engelbert Humperdinck and Hans Pfitzner. These studies confirmed his choice of a career in composing. He taught music appreciation at Cornell (1899–1901) but decided that teaching retarded composition. No publishers in New York City would accept his scores, so he set up his own Wa-Wan Press in Newton, Massachusetts. Neither Chadwick, Loeffler, nor Foote would lend his name to the enterprise; but Henry "Hank" Gilbert, along with Edgar Stillman Kelley, and Harvey Worthington Loomis cooperated. Farwell intended to publish worthy American works of all kinds, with particular attention to those drawing inspiration from Indian and Negro roots. "All American composition needs," wrote Farwell in 1903, "is publicity."[14]

Like others of his generation, Farwell looked for inspiration from "the regenerative sunlight flooding the wide stretches of our land," while keeping an eye fixed on European standards of judgment. "Europe is watching," he warned, "to see not how well we can imitate her, but to see *what we are.*" And until the search for a national music bore fruit, "Europe will never respect America artistically."[15] Yankee composers continued New England's errand, as had their forebears, under their imagination of a watchful Europe.

Yankee composers were willing to toy with ragtime; but they would not be pushed into embracing it as the characteristic American music. When Charles Wakefield Cadman wrote, "Underneath all the asininity of most of the Broadway output . . . is found the germ of a national expression. . . . The restless energy and indomitable will of America [are] somehow symbolized in terms of an intelligent syncopation. . . . why not experiment further?" he was voicing an enthusiasm rather too strong for most of his peers, even though several of them did incorporate Indian and Negro elements into their music. Like Farwell, they peered over their shoulders at Europe; but they did not wish to nourish their artistic identity—their very selves—through Indian or Negro roots. MacDowell composed his Second Orchestral Suite, the "Indian," in the mid-1890s. But he cautioned that "nationalism, so called, is merely an extraneous thing that has no part in pure art." MacDowell seemed to have been convinced that inevitably boosterism would be the calling card of mediocre art. Likewise, Chadwick, who wanted no part of Farwell's enterprise, had spiced his "burlesque opera" *Tabasco* (1894) with "galops, marches, hymn tunes, waltzes, jigs, and a 'plantation ballad.'"[16]

For Ives's centennial generation, ragtime and minstrel music were of a piece with college pranks: outlandish, soulful, a little naughty—in short, great fun. Ives described some of his college pieces as played by the Hyperion Theater Orchestra in just this tone. "For instance, a kind of shuffle-dance-march (last century rag) was played on the piano—the violin, cornet, and clarinet taking turns in playing sometimes old songs, sometimes the popular tunes of the day, as *After the Ball*, football songs, *Ta-ra-ra-boom-de-ay*." He suggested that the "shifts and lilting" accents of ragging, once one got the feel of it, might lead "into something of value." Between 1902 and 1904, Ives wrote four *Ragtime Pieces*, which he mined for other compositions, such as "In the Inn" (*Theater Orchestra Set*, 1906–1911), the "Three Page Sonata" (1905), and the *First Piano Sonata* (1902–1909).[17]

But Ives agreed with his Yankee peers who balked at suggestions that ragtime might be *the* characteristically American music. He referred favorably to an article by Mason, reprinted in *Contemporary Composers*, attacking the critic Hiram Moderwell for his praise of ragtime as "the one original and indigenous type of music of the American people." Of ragtime Mason wrote, "It is a rule of thumb for putting a 'kink' into a tune that without such specious rehabilitation would be unbearable. It is not a new flavor, but a kind of curry or catsup strong enough to make the stale old dishes palatable to unfastidious appetites." As for its national characteristics, Mason readily admitted that ragtime may catch the "restlessness" that lies at the surface of American life. "The question is whether it is really representative of the American temper as a whole." Neither Ives nor Mason considered ragtime the seed of an essentialist redemptive culture; but Ives did not dismiss the new music categorically. Ragtime, wrote Ives, "is something like wearing a derby hat on the back of the head, a shuffling lilt of a happy soul just let out of a Baptist church in old Alabama." He liked ragtime and admitted that it had "possibilities. But it does not 'represent the American nation' any more than some fine old senators represent it. Perhaps we know it now as an ore before it has been refined into a product."[18]

The young centennial composers characteristically thought of ragtime as frivolous, and perhaps a little wicked. To toy with rags was to engage in spiritual slumming. Edward Burlingame Hill, in a post-college letter, teased his friend Mason with word of Hill's use of Negro music. The thrill of genteel naughtiness coursed through Hill's letter:

> I've gone and done one silly sin. I got hold of a little tune which seemed to me to be rather 'nigger' and I have worked it into a little *Scherzino*. I can imagine your groans and other exhibitions of disgust when you receive it, but just the same I must confess it. Strangely enough this little piece has for me a programmastic [*sic*] flavor about it. I can see the niggers, men and women, dancing under the sway of the fascination of the rhythm until the sweat fairly rolls off them, and the little singsong goes on and on with monotonous persistency.[19]

This minstrel characterization of black life also permeates various works by Henry Gilbert and Charles Wakefield Cadman. Gilbert composed several of these pieces, including *Negro Episode Americanesque* (later changed to *Humoresque*) on *Negro-Minstrel Tunes* (1903), a *Comedy Overture on Negro Themes* (1905), and *Dance in Place Congo* (1906).

Gilbert used Negro themes for local-color interest; but he, too, dissociated himself from the movement to portray Negro music as characteristically American. His *Dance in Place Congo*, a symphonic poem, was rejected by Karl Muck, director of the Boston Symphony Orchestra, as "Niggah music," unfit for the concert hall. Returning to his original inspiration (an article in *Century* magazine by George Washington Cable, "The Dance in Place Congo"), Gilbert reshaped his work into a ballet score, in which guise it had its premiere at the Metropolitan Opera House in 1918.[20] Hiram Moderwell's review detailed the sort of plantation life caricature that passed for innocuous local color among cultivated Northern whites:

> The "Place Congo" . . . is a flat space beside the bayou, overhung with trees, surrounded by the huts of the lazy slaves, and backed with a great orange sun setting across the dark waters. Here one sees the beautiful slave Aurore lolling by her hut, awaiting the hour of the dance. In one corner an old negress is sitting over a caldron, interminably smoking her clay pipe. One after another an overseer or two strolls

in, equipped with the traditional lash, then a dandy of the town comes
to see the sights and then two negroes, lovers of the girl, one apparently
a quadroon and the other a half-blood. The pickaninnies dance across
the stage, or stride about, eating their watermelon.[21]

A few reviewers claimed that themes of black local color were the
only originally American element in the nation's musical culture. A
review of Gilbert's *Comedy Overture on Negro Themes* praises its nationalistic use of ragtime, "the only distinctive thing in our music. . . .
[H]ow the elect do rage about it still as a noxious weed in their carefully tended garden of art! Yet being a plant indigenous to the soil, and
consequently of hardy growth, it thrives despite them." Eventually,
perhaps, the review concluded, "it will come to be recognized as no
weed but of worth as an outflowering from our land." Gilbert himself
felt as uncomfortable with such effusions as did Ives and Mason,
which probably explains why he substituted *Humoresque* for *Americanesque* in the title of his *Negro Episode*. His own view was that "the
future edifice of American art-music will rest upon the substratum of
European folk-music." In later years he said that his "Negro phase was
left behind years ago as I considered it only one element in our coming
American music."[22]

Most centennial composers rejected Dvořák's suggestion that local
color provided the materials for a distinctive and distinguished American musical culture. They thought local color painted but a shallow
national portrait. Mason and Ives distrusted superficial nationalism as
they distrusted superficial emotionalism. A true and deep national
expression, like spiritual emotion, must emerge spontaneously. They
espoused an inner programmaticism: local color could not substitute
for portrayal of the American soul. Mason decried the musical
nationalism that "mistakes the conception of the average for that of the
ideal type, and supposes that the man in the street represents the best
taste in America." Although he espoused spiritual nationalism, Mason
attacked local-color nationalism because "it condemns any attempt at
universalizing artistic utterance as 'featureless cosmopolitanism' or
'flabby eclecticism,' and suggests that the musician who speaks, not a
dialect but a language understood over the civilized world . . . has 'lost
contact,' as the phrase goes, 'with the soil.'"[23]

Mason echoed MacDowell, who rejected nationalistic music as
mere "tailoring." MacDowell aimed his remarks directly at Dvořák
and his followers:

No: before a people can find a musical writer to echo its genius it must first possess men who truly represent it . . . and in the case of America it needs . . . absolute freedom from the restraint that almost unlimited deference to European thought and prejudice has imposed upon us. Masquerading in the so-called nationalism of Negro clothes cut in Bohemia will not help us.

MacDowell did not oppose all nationalism in music, but the vehemence of his protests against Dvořák's meddling sometimes gave that incorrect impression. Ives, too, decried the straining for effect that marred the obvious pursuit of nationalism. Using his antithetical categories of manner/substance, he argued that such unnatural straining reflected an insistence upon the artificiality and narrowness of manner. "The same tendency may be noticed if there is overinsistence upon the national in art," wrote Ives. "Substance tends to create affection; manner prejudice." A true nationalism, like a true and natural relation to local roots, was universal in the reach of its love.[24]

By itself, ragtime did not seriously threaten the pursuit of an ideal American musical language. Yankee classicism could exploit this snappy, good-time music, redolent of the march. The racial overtones of ragtime were romantic, not frightening. Through minstrel stereotypes, centennial composers viewed the Negro as an interesting character from a separate section of the country, comfortably far away. Yankees were happy to use ragtime, spirituals, and shouts to lend a democratic vitality to their music. But some of them objected when Dvořák butted in, suggesting that here grew the local roots of a national musical identity. Black was not their local color. In fact, the local-color approach to cultural nationalism made many centennial composers nervous. Implicitly it challenged their assumption that a truly national music must grow from an essentialist taproot. American redemptive culture should represent the "universal color."[25] The Yankees' America could not be reduced to an ethnic patchwork.

Bête Noire

Jazz challenged the Yankee musical mission because it achieved an instant popularity that illuminated white nervousness over the rapid ethnic transformation of Northern cities and because trained musicians and critics, both abroad and at home, paid serious attention to it. Jazz served as a scavenger symbol for the cultural traumas of the

1920s. Responses to jazz revealed a process in which racial and aesthetic issues were metaphorically defined in terms of each other. Redemptive culture denoted a measure of value for opponents of jazz; but enthusiasts analyzed jazz in ways that twisted the symbols of redemptive culture, effectively subverting the errand of the centennial composers.

Jazz went public in 1917. A white group, the Original Dixieland Jazz Band, moved into Reisenweber's Cafe in New York on January 15. After a few shaky weeks they "hit it solid." Within a month they cut a record for Victor. In November of the same year, the U.S. Navy closed down the "Storyville" brothel section of New Orleans, sending jazzmen on their way.[26] A number of important black jazzmen traveled northward, joining the Negro migration to urban centers. In New York, the way for the ODJB (as the band was nicknamed) had been prepared by black bandleader James Reese Europe's "syncopated" Society Orchestra, which played orchestrated ragtime. In fact, Freddie Keppard's Creole Band had brought New Orleans jazz to New York in 1915 in a vaudeville act, but Keppard failed to strike fire. The ODJB's debut spawned hasty imitators. For two years "novelty" or "nut" jazz predominated, with gags and animal imitations as their mainstays. By 1919 novelty bands had waned, and the blues influence was more strongly felt.[27]

No clear lines demarcated the varieties of protojazz and society syncopation. The popular imagination associated ragtime with the Tin Pan Alley songs which had taken up elements of the rag. Spirituals, in concert versions by F. Rosamond Johnson and Harry T. Burleigh, remained a category apart, approved of by genteel whites and self-conscious blacks. A notice in the *New York Times* in 1919 praised "the old negro melodies and songs of religious fervor" at a concert by Will Marion Cook's Orchestra. Cook espoused a genteel syncopation. But the *Times* review reveals that Cook did not resist altogether the popularity of "novelty" music. In the "many humorous selections . . . the antics of the trap drummer in the back row cannot be overlooked in this kind of entertainment." The same article notes a concert by the Clef Club, of "many old and new songs, all the way from before-the-war plantation melodies to the latest discords of 'jazz.'" At the end of the concert "W. C. Handy led his 'Memphis Blues.'"[28]

As a fad, jazz was a label pasted over all popular syncopated band music that was not obviously ragtime. Composer and noted jazz histo-

This group portrait of the Original Dixieland Jazz Band underlines the whacky side of early jazz. *Courtesy Frank Driggs.*

rian Gunther Schuller argues that "Handy was primarily a minstrel musician, cornet soloist, and band director," not a jazz musician. In spite of Handy's title as "Father of the Blues," Memphis Blues, notes Schuller, "was not a blues at all: it was closer to a cakewalk than to anything else." Schuller makes his point to counter the weight of popular association, because Handy did acquire a reputation as a jazz/ blues composer. Men such as Handy, Cook, George Morrison, and Fletcher Henderson were drawn into the orbit of jazz. Jazz was "the coming thing," and black musicians of classical and minstrel training became "jazz" musicians, sometimes against their own preferences. By 1919 Americans clearly were experiencing a "jazz invasion," as Mason called it in retrospect.[29]

Yet the "jazz invasion" was but the cultural sign of a larger constellation of problems. Newspapers reeked of bad news. The Palmer Raids reflected widespread fears of immigration, socialist agitation, even the potential for Bolshevik revolution. A prolonged steel strike

intensified fears of revolution. Since the turn of the century, the nation's racial problems had followed migrating Negroes out of the
South and into Northern metropolises. In the decade 1910–1920, the
black population of Chicago jumped 148 percent compared to an overall city population increase of 24 percent. During the same period,
New York City's Negro population rose by 66 percent. By 1930, more
Negroes lived in New York than in Birmingham, Memphis, and St.
Louis combined. Racial tensions swelled like a boil. In Chicago, "occasional skirmishes of the pre-war period gave way to organized guerrilla
warfare." The *Chicago Tribune* said bluntly, "Black Man, Stay South!"
In July 1919 the boil burst, over the segregation-related death of a
black youth. "For six days, white and Negro mobs terrorized the city
[of Chicago], clashing on street corners, murdering passers-by, and
destroying property. Thirty-eight died, 537 were injured, and over
one thousand were rendered homeless."[30]

A new Ku Klux Klan, founded in 1915, rapidly gained popularity
after 1920. Membership grew from a few hundred to four and a half
million by 1924. The Klan Constitution pledged "to unite white male
persons, native-born Gentile citizens of the United States of
America." The Klan promised "to maintain forever white supremacy,
to teach and faithfully inculcate a high spiritual philosophy through
exalted ritualism, and by a practical devotion to conserve, protect, and
maintain the distinctive institutions, rights, privileges, principles, traditions and ideals of pure Americanism." The Klan enunciated a
widely held ideology of "100% Americanism." Its popularity peaked
in 1924, just as criticism of jazz crested. A twin racial explosion, in the
streets and in the culture, haunted the minds of many Northern
whites.[31]

As the brassy symbol of Negro migration, jazz particularly enraged family-oriented white spokesmen. H. E. Krehbiel, music critic
of the *New York Herald Tribune*, worried that more jazz would "soon
emanate from the Negro brothels of the South."[32] The closing of New
Orleans's Storyville underlined sexual and underworld associations
with the word *jazz*.[33] It was known as "nigger music" and "whorehouse
music." The decade's newspapers ran fantastic tales of jazz as an agent
of moral degradation. A certain Dr. Beets warned that if American
Indians heard jazz, they would go wild again. The Cincinnati Salvation Army opposed the building of a theater next to a home for girls,
on the grounds that the music would implant jazz emotions in babies

born at the home. From England came word that, upon hearing American jazz, a cornetist to Queen Victoria had dropped dead. In 1931 the National Association of Teachers of Speech listed *jazz* as one of the ten most offensive words in the English language.[34]

In the bitterly ironic title of J. Hartley Manners's 1922 play, jazz was becoming *The National Anthem*. Immorality among the young—cigarettes, alcohol, immodest dress, loose language, and still-looser sex—was at least characterized and perhaps created by jazz.[35] Left unchecked, it would hasten the decline and fall of American civilization. Act 1 of *The National Anthem*, set in a country club in "Northchester," details the dissolute doings of spoiled rich youths. John Carleton, a hard but moral self-made man, expresses disgust to an unconcerned friend that his own son, Arthur, lacks a sense of his social role. The working people see brats like Arthur fooling around, and "they go back to their wretched little homes and spread it. It's eating in like a cancer. . . . And a pretty sullen lot the workmen of today are becoming because of the Arthurs."[36] Carleton, suddenly hearing a burst of jazz, exclaims:

> Listen to that damned senseless, barbaric discord. The kind of sound you'd expect Indians or negroes to beat out when they're frenzied with rum. . . . Listen! You can hear their brains rattling in their skulls. God! It's become like a national anthem! Whenever a band strikes up a jazz I feel like standing up and taking my hat off. It is our national anthem![37]

At the end of the play John Carleton jeers, "Why it's ridiculous. London is jigging to it. . . . Paris is deafened by it. It has become the National Anthem of Civilization." Manners's character echoed the sentiment expressed in the *Ladies' Home Journal*: "Jazz is a signboard on the road that was travelled by Greece and Rome. Orgies of lewd dancing preceded the downfall of those nations." Manners's wife, Laurette Taylor, the actress who played in the lead role of *The National Anthem*, underlined its main point: "Jazz, the impulse for wildness that has undoubtedly come over many things besides the music of this country, is traceable to the negro influence."[38]

The licentiousness imputed to jazz was associated with the Negro. Here was a racial role significantly different from the happy-go-lucky minstrel black of the ragtime stereotype. The romantic racialism of the North turned rancid with the rapid migration and urbanization of Negroes. Many Northern whites painted a new portrait of the jazz-age Negro derived from the Southern image of "the black brute" as popularized by novelist Thomas Dixon. Dixon warned, in *The Leopard's Spots* (1902), "It may shock the prejudices of those who have idealised or worshipped the negro as canonized in 'Uncle Tom.' Is it not time they heard the whole truth? They have heard only one side for forty years." In *The Clansman: An Historical Romance of the Ku Klux Klan* (1905), Dixon characterized the Negro as "half child, half animal, the sport of impulse, whim, and conceit . . . a being who, left to his will, roams at night and sleeps in the day, whose speech knows no word of love, whose passions, once aroused, are as the fury of the tiger." *The Clansman* reached even wider audiences in D. W. Griffith's extraordinarily powerful film *Birth of a Nation*, which itself was midwife to the new Ku Klux Klan in 1915. The race riots of 1917 and 1919 sparked a wildfire of "black beast" racism throughout the North.[39] The jazzman seemed to personify the hedonism and violence that underlined the anomie of modern life.

A web of racial metaphors closed around the American Negro and his culture. The beast image shared with "romantic racialism" the notion that Negroes were inherently undisciplined and lazy. Racist thinking believed violence to be an inherent characteristic of the Negro, carried within him from the jungle, and fundamentally unaltered by the patina of civilization. Typically, a black man's sexuality was circularly defined in terms of his other alleged characteristics. Thus the lazy, undisciplined Negro was viewed as a sensualist, like a cat stretching in the sun. But catlike, the Negro could spring with sudden violence. Racists believed that sex, for the black man, tends to be rapacious. "A single tiger spring, and the black claws of the beast sank into the soft white throat."[40] According to the dominant racial stereotypes, Negroes were inherently undisciplined, lazy, violent, and oversexed. Furthermore, lower-class urban life seemed to exacerbate these traits, making the black "problem" into America's urban problem. In the most graphic manner possible, emerging Negro slums demonstrated that cities concentrated class extremes. The blackness of the lowest classes at once sharpened awareness of their existence while allowing white people to perceive the Negroes' lower-class status as merely a reflection of racial deficiencies. The tightening spiral of such analogic reasoning left Negroes with no metaphorical leverage for an appeal to reason. Racialism had become an absolutely hermetic, self-fulfilling ideology.

Observers applied racial stereotypes of Negroes to their analysis of jazz. Through redemptive culture, they made social and aesthetic norms serve together in the interest of an ideal grammar of national identity. To the extent that it was perceived as a kind of black anticulture, jazz was criticized as though it were the basest form of musical romanticism. Thus redemptive culture provided the model for a jeremiad of antitheses against the so-called jazz ethos. Black was sensual; white was spiritual. Jazz was an assemblage of superficial mannerisms; classical music communicated an organic sense of substantive logic. Black jazz exuded violence; white classical music inspired love. The emphasis of jazz on improvisation was untempered by the hard-won inner discipline of classical music, the formal apotheosis of Western culture.

Conditioned by their Victorian upbringing, centennial composers rejected sexuality as an integrally expressive and liberating element in art. They felt that emotionalism consciously pursued was tainted by sexuality. Ives rejected "manner" as the superficial, sensual appeal of such artists as Tchaikowsky, Debussy, and Stravinsky. Mason also downgraded the sensual appeal of "Romantic" art which tried to express emotion directly. On "aesthetic" grounds such as these, jazz was condemned as dangerously sexual music.[41] The extent of such an identification is indicated by the fact that H. L. Mencken, who disliked jazz but loved to pummel "puritanism," claimed that jazz was *not* sensual:

> The delusion seems to persist that jazz is highly aphrodisiacal. I never encounter a sermon on the subject without finding it full of dark warnings to parents, urging them to keep their nubile daughters out of the jazz palaces on the ground that the voluptuous music will inflame their passions and so make them easy prey to bond salesmen, musicians and other such carnal fellows. All this seems to me to be nonsense. Jazz, in point of fact, is not voluptuous at all. . . . Compare [*Der Rosenkavalier's*] first act to the most libidinous jazz ever heard of on Broadway. It is like comparing vodka to gingerpop.[42]

But many did fear the dark sexuality they perceived in jazz. In the words of black clarinetist Buster Bailey, whites worried that "we'd go after their women."[43]

As rape was thought to be the black man's preferred sexual act, jazz was believed by guardians of America's values to be a cultural agent of violence and lust. "Jazz," warned the music chairman of the General Federation of Women's Clubs, "originally was the accompaniment of the voodoo dancer, stimulating the half-crazed barbarian to the vilest deeds. . . . [It] has also been employed by other barbaric people to stimulate brutality and sensuality."[44] The association of jazz with the jungle linked it with images of carnality and violence.

Moreover, jazz appeared to flout the discipline of responsibility, the ostensible mortar strengthening the arch of redemptive culture. Redemptive culture imagined art not merely as instinctive expression; those who chose the calling of art must also accept the burdens of self-control. An ideal American music required the duty of discipline. The Negro, portrayed as wholly without self-discipline, was believed to be the living antithesis of the Protestant ethic. As the Negro's music, jazz supposedly appealed to sensuousness through undisciplined primitive forms followed only by people without musical training. The moral standards of a work ethic were applied, derogatorily, to jazz musicians. Real music, wrote Mrs. Elise F. White, "demands much time and thought; the music of artistic cultivation, of humble ambitions, prayerfully and earnestly followed; of obedience to teachers; of self-denial, renunciation and sacrifice; of the worship of beauty, and the passionate desire to express it."[45] In the aesthetics of identity, the communication of art reflected the worth of the artist. On such grounds art could be judged by association. If anarchic jazz was to be judged by its irresponsible creators, then it was scarcely music at all.

While jazz was believed by cultural critics to reflect the Negro, its hedonistic creator, its success mirrored the deluded taste of the masses, the bastardization of the democratic ideal. Jazz mocked the spirit of discipline and effort which both artists and audience must expend if a culture is to evolve. The music critic Fritz Laubenstein viewed black jazz as a misshapen child of World War I's destructiveness. "In war . . . as in jazz, 'all the artificial restraints are gone,' and we become intoxicated, emotional and natural." A professor of romance languages wrote: "Most of the jazz music, like jazz literature and jazz thinking is the product of an untrained mind." In the same vein, critic John Gould Fletcher attacked Louis Untermeyer for not being "content with the vocabulary of Shakespeare and the structure of Addison. . . . But after all, this new art is fairly familiar to our ears. We can hear its counterpart already in the performances of any Jazz band."[46] Its critics castigated jazz as the symbol of anarchy throughout society.

Community leaders opposed jazz as they had opposed ragtime, but with a heightened sense of crisis. Ignore it; ban it; segregate it. As early as 1919, Robert Cole announced a "Conspiracy of Silence against Jazz." In an imaginary interview with a representative of the Masters of Dancing, he discovers that the person does not hear him each time he asks a question about jazz. The National Music Teachers' Association forecast the imminent death of jazz at a meeting in 1920. Six years later, the *New York Times* again reported predictions of the death of jazz.[47] But it was a hardy infestation.

If it would not expire peacefully, jazz should be killed, argued some. In 1919 the National Association of Dancing Masters organized to forbid "vulgar dancing and cheap jazz music to be played." The United States Public Health Service distributed an antijazz booklet by the Dancing Masters to welfare agencies. In 1923, the General Federation of Women's Clubs pledged its two million members to "annihilate" jazz. The Kansas City, Missouri superintendent of schools called for prohibition laws against jazz as well as liquor. Many localities did legislate against jazz, so that by the end of the decade over fifty cities, including Cleveland, Detroit, Kansas City, Omaha, and Philadelphia, had banned jazz in public dance halls. In New York State, the 1922 Cotillo Bill allowed the city's commissioner of licenses to regulate both jazz and dancing.[48] But jazz, like liquor, would not go away.

A third line of attack sought to segregate jazz. Let it stay on its side of the tracks. This "moderate" stance found support among Yankee composers. Mason, in his article "The Jazz Invasion," inveighed against jazz in a tone of lofty, sweet reasonableness. He granted that perhaps jazz tried "to express universal thoughts and feelings." But it failed because it "did not stop to distinguish the ideal, which has in it something divine, from the average, which works out uncomfortably near the sub-human." Mason was annoyed by the practice of "jazzing the classics"—jazzy interpretations of classical pieces. He quoted with approval Ernest Newman's "pertinent advice" to "keep their dirty paws off their betters."[49]

Another of the Yankee composers, David Stanley Smith, seconded Mason's segregationist sentiments toward jazz. Smith was born in Ohio in 1877, of Scotch parentage. His father was a businessman, church organist, and composer of religious music. His mother, of old Connecticut stock, was a singer. He and Ives became friends while studying with Horatio Parker at Yale. A Parker protege, Smith succeeded his teacher as head of music studies at Yale in 1920. He sought to carry on the work of Yankee composers who "had the task of converting an indifferent America to a due regard for the art of something worthy of a real man's life work." Music was a noble calling, not "a joke." In an article, "Putting Jazz in Its Place," Smith objected to those who professed "to find in jazz a veritable treasure of art which is to represent America before the world." Jazz should not be compared with "big, deeply felt compositions where joking may be an affront." Jazz is narrow, and reflects "no knowledge of the romance of the New England hills or the vast spaces of the Western plains. Jazz is not the folk-lore of the nation."[50]

Most of the Yankee composers turned their backs on jazz. In the 1920s, Arthur Farwell moved away from his Indian-inspired works. He taught on the West coast, composed music with titles about mountains, and became a zealous exponent of Oswald Spengler's doctrines. In "The Zero Hour in Musical Evolution," Farwell wrote that "jazz is the heritage of all. But these things have nothing to do with a full and normal flowering of the music in the life of the people."[51] Ives's composing career ended before the jazz boom; he wrote nothing on the subject. Ruggles's surviving works, beginning with *Men and Angels* (1920), make no bow toward jazz. He had opinions on everything but apparently committed none of them to paper. Carpenter showed some interest in jazz as an exotic, humorous folk resource with which to spice his works. On the whole, Yankee composers appear to have been uninterested in jazz. The fact that most Yankee composers ignored or rejected jazz does not mean that they condoned the rabidly Negrophobic tirades conducted against jazz by many of their fellow guardians of "sweetness and light." No longer young, men such as Ives and Mason were less susceptible to the attractions of popular music than when ragtime was current. There is no reason to suppose that they should have embraced jazz, the music of the young set. Nevertheless, many advocates of redemptive culture identified classical music with a spiritual Anglo-Saxon tradition, and contrasted the deferred gratification which they believed characterized responsible masculinity with the unfettered sensuality attributed to Negroes. Some custodians of culture even convinced themselves that jazz insinuated an irresponsible black expressionism into the unformed minds of middle-class white youths.

White Rebels and the New Negro

Claims that jazz represented America offended composers and critics committed to the creation of a native classical musical culture. These claims emanated primarily from two sources: domestic white critics with impeccable old-line Protestant credentials, and foreign observers caught up in the romance of America as a symbol of cultural freedom. In their breathless and often short-winded espousal of black culture, including jazz, the former tried to invert every canon of Victorian aesthetics. And they tried, in Spengler's popular terms, to substitute a Copernican for a Ptolemaic view of cultural values, a world view for a European perspective. In this effort they were inconsistent. While eager to flaunt their taste for exotic lore, generally they retained an ultimate preference for what they understood to be the disciplined spirit of Western culture. Nevertheless, their interest in fashionable passion threatened to derail the Yankee musical mission. Critics such as Gilbert Seldes, Carl Van Vechten, and John Hammond committed a kind of class treason against the old-stock families from which they sprang. Their serious treatment of jazz threatened claims that Yankee musical culture should become the "ideal" model of American imaginative life. In addition, they meddled in Negro efforts at cultural self-definition, a movement which paralleled attempts to realize a Yankee redemptive culture.

Born in Alliance, New Jersey in 1893, Gilbert Seldes, like his older brother George, became a popular journalist and author during the 1920s. He was educated at Harvard, graduating in 1914. After college he worked as music critic for the *Philadelphia Evening Ledger* until the United States entered World War I, at which time he and his brother became foreign war correspondents. Following the war he served briefly as Washington political correspondent for *L'echo de Paris*. Then, after a short stint as an associate editor of *Colliers*, he moved over to the *Dial*, where he became managing editor before his departure in 1923.[52]

Seldes became known as an expert on both "highbrow" and "lowbrow" culture. At the *Dial*, and subsequently as a movie reviewer for the *New Republic*, he boosted popular culture, becoming the foremost advocate and aesthetician of the Lively Arts. In his sprightly, punchy style, mixing colloquial Americanisms with French and Latin phrases, he argued that critics should treat seriously, but not solemnly, those cultural creations which fall outside the formal categories traditionally defined as high art. Movies, for example, are not simply cheap imitations of staged dramatics; they are valuable on their own terms. Each genre must be judged individually. Seldes inverted the Victorian emphasis on artistic content, arguing that a creation's worth is determined by its handling of the medium. Of course art must be invested with passion; but it is not the critic's task, said Seldes, to judge the sources of the inspiring passion, even if they are politically or morally unacceptable.[53]

Seldes paid attention to black culture as well as to white. Impressed by James Europe's ragtime band arrangements, he considered the 1921 Broadway show *Shuffle Along* to be a happy continuation of Europe's black inspirations. *Shuffle Along* revived the tradition of black Broadway music, which had gone into eclipse with the deaths of Ernest Hogan, Bob Cole, and George Walker, key figures in black entertainment. Written by Noble Sissle and Eubie Blake, and featuring an extraordinary array of talent, including William Grant Still on oboe, Hall Johnson on viola, Josephine Baker, Florence Mills, and Paul Robeson, the show served as a springboard for talented Negroes in the 1920s. Seldes believed that productions like *Shuffle Along* might save Broadway from sterility. Watching "the responsive animals who sing and dance," wrote Seldes, "one feels that the show is a continuous wild cry and an uninterrupted joyous rage, that the *elan vital* is inexhaustible and unbridled and enormously good."[54]

In "Toujours Jazz," published in the *Dial* in 1923, Seldes took as his point of departure Clive Bell's *New Republic* article "Plus de Jazz." Jazz, Seldes wrote, "is the symbol, or the byword, for a great many elements in the spirit of our time—as far as America is concerned it is actually our characteristic expression." Bell attacked jazz as symptomatic of the "impudence" of the modern view that formally untrained Negroes could produce art worthy of attention. Seldes counted that

> if jazz weren't itself good the subject would be more suitable for a sociologist than for an admirer of the gay arts. Fortunately . . . [jazz

has] qualities which cannot be despised; and the cry that jazz is the enthusiastic disorganization of music is as extravagant as the prophesy that if we do not stop "jazzing" we will go down, as a nation, into ruin.

Seldes believed that the Negro roots of jazz express, in a more intense way, "something which underlies a great deal of America—our independence, our carelessness, our frankness, and gaiety." But in spite of his praise of the natural energy which he perceived in Negroes and their jazz, in effect Seldes agreed with Bell's call for intelligence and craftsmanship, qualities he too associated with whites. Lacking intelligence, the Negro has been unable to develop his inheritance, he argued. "Nowhere is the failure of the negro to exploit his gifts more obvious than in the use he has made of the jazz orchestra." While the average black jazz band surpasses its white counterpart, "no negro band has yet come up to the level of the best white ones, and the leader of the best of all, by a little joke, is called Whiteman." Paul Whiteman, in his smooth, "sweetly" running band, has yet kept all "the free, the instinctive, the wild in negro jazz which could be integrated into his music." Other notable "jazzmen," for Seldes, included Zes "Kitten on the Keys" Confry and Irving Berlin. Seldes saw a bright future for jazz, with such promising talents as George Gershwin and Cole Porter.[55]

While Seldes and other young writers expressed reservations over the Negro's artistic potential, they did so in the language of "high-brow" criticism. This fact alone boosted the reputation of jazz among whites and blacks alike. Articles like Virgil Thomson's "Jazz," billed as explanations of jazz for the educated public, sprinkled musical terms throughout their texts. Thomson's expert credentials included a sport's acquaintance with cabaret life, a composer's ability to analyze music, and a writer's facility with words. "Jazz, in brief," began Thomson, "is a compound of a) the fox-trot rhythm, a four-four measure *(alla breve)* with a double accent, and b) a syncopated melody over this rhythm. . . . The combination is jazz. Try it on your piano. Apply the recipe to any tune you know." Thomson implies that he is unimpressed with jazz. It is nothing but "the fox-trot with a monotonous rhythm underneath. That rhythm shakes but it won't flow. There is no climax. It never gets anywhere emotionally. In the symphony, it would either lose its character or wreck the structure. It is exactly analogous to the hoochie-coochie."[56] Thomson affects a witty Menckenesque boredom with jazz. Yet his use of technical terms to describe jazz actually lent strength to Seldes's argument that it was something more than mere entertainment. A mock lament in the *Nation*'s commentary column made exactly this point. Having read Seldes's and Thomson's analyses, the writer "has lost all illusions about the happy spontaneity and careless freedom of his once-loved jazz."[57] Philip Curtiss developed the same theme in "Amos 'N' Andy 'N' Art" in *Harper's Magazine*. Curtiss worried that momentarily some expert would end his own innocent delight with Amos 'n' Andy by calling it "great art."[58]

The issues of primitivism and sophistication in jazz loomed yet larger in the context of the emerging Harlem Renaissance and the New Negro movement. Van Vechten in the mid-1920s and Hammond in the 1930s served as talent scouts, interpreters, and boosters of black musical culture. Van Vechten, thirteen years older than Seldes and thirty years Hammond's senior, became the undisputed impresario of the Harlem Renaissance. His biographer finds it necessary to point out that Van Vechten did not invent the Harlem Renaissance by himself. In fact, he did have a large hand in selling the idea of the New Negro, and he was not at all shy about his own importance as an "excavator" of talent.

Carl Van Vechten was born and raised in Cedar Rapids, Iowa. His father's family traced their American heritage to 1638, when his Dutch forebears settled near Albany, New York. His mother studied at Kalamazoo College, his father at Columbia Law School. The family ambiance was that of Midwest gentility, just one generation from frontier roughness. It incensed his father that Carl's pipe-smoking maternal grandmother "insisted on spreading her voluminous skirts to urinate on the front lawn." Carl read, studied music, and played the role of big-city bohemian. "He grew one long, talon-like nail on the little finger of his right hand. . . . He sported a derby and pointed, patent-leather boots; he affected Ascots; and he had the highest collars and the tightest trousers in town." As Van Vechten described his own youth, "There was no one quite like me in Cedar Rapids. . . . I couldn't wait to get out." He escaped to the University of Chicago, and then to New York, where, to him, life "was all gay, irresponsible and meaningless, perhaps, but gay."[59] On West Thirty-ninth Street he lived down the hall from Sinclair Lewis. He talked Theodore Dreiser into an article for *Broadway Magazine*, "Salome: Most Sensational Opera of an Age." Hanging out at the *New York Times*, he picked up occasional assignments. By November 1907, less than two years after he first landed in New York, he was appointed assistant music critic to Richard Aldrich of the *Times*. In 1913 he met the wealthy, radical Mabel Evans Dodge, and entered her orbit. From that moment Carl Van Vechten made a profession of scooping all other watchers of fashionably offbeat culture. In the words of the historian Nathan Huggins, "He thrived in that thin, dangerous, and exhilarating atmosphere where one makes *approving* critical judgments about the very new and the very off-beat. It is remarkable how often his judgments—usually daring, seldom cautious—were right."[60]

With a series of articles in 1925–1926 for *Vanity Fair*, Van Vechten transformed himself into the foremost white promoter and interpreter of the Harlem Renaissance. The articles culminated in the publication of his novel *Nigger Heaven* in 1926. Well-heeled visitors to New York who wanted to go slumming in Harlem sought out Van Vechten as their guide. He delighted in being provocative, and he succeeded. *Time* wrote that "sullen-mouthed, silky-haired author Van Vechten has been playing with Negroes lately, writing prefaces for their poems, having them around the house, going to Harlem."[61] Actually, Negroes and their culture had long fascinated him; but as a matter of publicity he decided to raise public consciousness of black art and entertainment in 1925.

If *The National Anthem* had been a warning of a "jazz tendency" in American life, no better exemplar of Manners's prediction could be imagined than the real Carl Van Vechten. In his life and in his fiction, Van Vechten flaunted the jazzy decadence of a Fitzgerald story. "Van Vechten produced a kind of mock decadence unique in American literature. His novels are hyperaesthetic, perverse, and often devoted to esoteric or archaic lore. His characters are restless sophisticates forever seeking sensation and running from boredom."[62] In his consuming interest in the high and low life of Harlem, Van Vechten showed no shyness in interpreting black culture for whites. He did so through a sensibility attuned to the exotic and offbeat aspects of life. Nor did he shrink from giving public advice to black artists and intellectuals on how best to "exploit" their own experiences.

Van Vechten brought his interest in black music to the public early in 1925, in a series of articles stimulated by the Aeolian Hall premier of Gershwin's *Rhapsody in Blue*. The opening article hailed popular jazz in general and Gershwin in particular. Van Vechten wove himself throughout the history of jazz, noting his every presence

A theatrically lighted prop lends modernistic drama to Carl Van Vechten's Babbitt-like features. *Courtesy New York Public Library, Manuscript Division.*

and rationalizing every absence. Once again he staked his claim as a cultural Columbus. His next article surveyed "The Folksongs of the American Negro" and arrived at Dvořák's conclusion that spirituals were "the most important contribution America has yet made to the literature of music." He noted with approval that "intelligent" Negroes were taking the lead in the perpetuation of the spiritual. He asserted that whites had no business singing spirituals, and advised blacks to avoid a cultivated, inauthentic manner of performance. In "Black Blues" he continued the education of his readers. Blues and jazz-backed blues were unpopular with blacks, just as spirituals once had been, because of the "humbleness of their origin and occasionally the frank obscenity of their sentiment." But Van Vechten perceived their worth. "They are not only an essential part of Negro folklore but also they contain a wealth of eerie melody, borne along by a savage recalcitrant rhythm."[63]

Van Vechten had built up his case to the point where he was ready to offer his "Prescription for the Negro Theatre." He argued that black performers were stuck in a minstrel show pattern of limited audience appeal in 1924. Instead of light-skinned dancers, he suggested a rainbow extravaganza of "six black girls, six 'seal-browns,' six 'high yellas,' and six pale creams." He suggested that Broadway recreate on stage a Harlem night spot, and possibly "a wild pantomimic drama set in an African forest with the men and women as nearly nude as the law allows."[64]

Returning to Gershwin, the stimulus for his first jazz-related article, Van Vechten proceeded to "A Discussion of the Negro's Reluctance to Develop and Exploit His Racial Gift." Although people recognized the black roots of jazz, "soon Irving Berlin, and later George Gershwin—to name the two most conspicuous figures in a long list—were writing better jazz than the Negro composers." Van Vechten sympathized with black irritation over white exploitation of their "picturesque life." Yet he contended that Negroes such as W. E. B. DuBois misled their race by emphasizing the development of intellectualism. Intellectual life is colorless, without characteristic content; but the "low-life of Negroes offers a wealth of exotic and novel material." Van Vechten was happy to note, however, that "a new school of coloured writers . . . have perceived the advantages of writing about squalid Negro life from the inside." In general, though, he found that the Negro left his special potentials to "exploitation" by the white man.[65]

Not to be outdone, Van Vechten himself had prepared a modest example of how such exploitation might best be accomplished. "*Nigger Heaven*," complained DuBois, "is a blow in the face. It is an affront to the hospitality of black folk and to the intelligence of white." DuBois's central criticism was that, to Van Vechten, "the black cabaret is Harlem." The writers Claude McKay, James Weldon Johnson, and Langston Hughes defended Van Vechten. But even Hughes later suggested, "Perhaps, like my *Fine Clothes to the Jew*, Mr. Van Vechten's title was an unfortunate choice."[66] Van Vechten, the outsider, made two unpardonable ethnic slips: he arrogated to himself the right to be crudely familiar and to air dirty laundry in public.

Van Vechten's exploitation of Harlem cabaret life points up a central paradox of the Negro Renaissance. It was, in Nathan Huggins's words, "as much a white creation as it was black." Black intellectuals believed that through art the Negro would rise phoenixlike to create culture that could not be denied. By demonstrating his "civility" through high art, the Negro would undercut the roots of bigotry.[67] Alain Locke wrote that "Negro life is not only establishing new contacts and founding new centers, it is finding a new soul. There is a fresh spiritual and cultural focusing." James Weldon Johnson believed that "through artistic achievement the Negro has found a means of getting at the very core of the prejudice against him, by challenging the Nordic superiority complex." W. E. B. DuBois insisted that "until the art of the black folk compels recognition they will not be rated as human." Black intellectuals, like other progressives in the twenties, sought through culture the identity and stature withheld by politics. But writers such as Van Vechten portrayed Harlem as an "erotic utopia."[68] *Nigger Heaven* was followed by black novels which also mined sordid aspects of black urban life. Claude McKay's *Home to Harlem* contained "lurid and sensational" characteristics which "doubtless contributed to its commercial success."[69]

Thus the New Negro, who was to prove himself—indeed, to create himself—through his art, found that the only inner resources that would sell were those stereotypes that had burdened the Old Negro. Blacks could not get their bearings without reference to a cultural compass that pointed north to intellect and discipline or south to sensuality and license. Negro artists, wrote Johnson, "are bringing something fresh and vital into American art, something from the store of their own racial genius: warmth, color, movement, rhythm, and abandon; depth and swiftness of emotion and the beauty of sensuousness." Exploiters of the Harlem Renaissance took the stereotypes of savages and made of them culture heroes, or at least antiheroes. Jazz represented a savage abandon which would cure the spiritual anemia of the Protestant ethic. Not discipline, not work, but sensual emotion was the elixir to save American society. Van Vechten had Mary Love, a cultured, light-skinned Negro, lament: "Savages! Savages at heart! And she had lost or forfeited her birthright, this primitive birthright which was so valuable and important an asset, a birthright that all the civilized races were struggling to get back to." Similarly, the writer of the article on jazz in Locke's volume *The New Negro* argued that "it has been . . . a balm for modern machine-ridden and convention-bound society. It is the revolt of the emotions against repression." The author quoted Leopold Stokowski as saying of jazz: "America's contribution to the music of the past will have the same revivifying effect as the injection of new, and in the larger sense, vulgar blood into dying aristocracy."[70]

In effect, the Harlem Renaissance developed schizophrenically, as attitudes toward jazz revealed. Writers such as DuBois wished to project a dignified intellectual, high-culture image of the New Negro who would earn entrance to the hallowed halls of Yankee culture. Jazz did not fit into DuBois's Negro Renaissance. Only Langston Hughes among black writers loved jazz and accepted it into his vision of an emerging black culture. And Hughes, as in his poem "Nude Young Dancer," drew on the image of the Negro as sensual creature of the jungle:

> What jungle tree have you slept under
>   Midnight dancer of the jazzy hour?
> What great forest has hung its perfume
>   Like a sweet veil about your bower?
>
> What jungle tree have you slept under,
>   Dark brown girl of the swaying hips?
> What star-white moon has been your lover?
> To what mad fawn have you offered your lips?[71]

Creators of the primitivist New Negro turned redemptive culture inside out and set racialism on its head.[72] But racialism it remained.

However, the savage-beast imagery had to be altered if boosters were to sell an exotic, erotic Harlem. So the black stereotype underwent a sex change: cabaret life in Harlem was feminine, not masculine. Violent rape did not stalk the cabarets. Rather, they were warmed by the sexuality of tantalizingly bare, black female dancers. The "Cotton Club Girls" were advertised as "Tall, Tan and Terrific."[73] In Harlem's cabarets, fear was a familar affair among blacks; the white clientele was to be thrilled but not threatened. The Depression effectively killed the Harlem Renaissance, but not the confusion of stereotypes generated by the search for the New Negro.

John Hammond, who made a career of discovering and recording popular musicians, especially jazz musicians, inherited the remains of Van Vechten's mantle. Hammond was born in New York in 1910. His mother was a Vanderbilt:

> The Hammond life style while I was growing up consisted of summers at Dellwood, chauffeured trips to Lenox to visit my Vanderbilt relatives, and, for longer journeys, a private railroad car which was hitched to the back of trains heading toward our destinations. The Vanderbilt children had no reason to play with toy trains. We had real ones.[74]

While in grade school, Hammond persuaded a governess to escort him to a Negro review. "We sat in the balcony, watched scantily clad show girls and shocking skits, and I loved it all. Of course, my governess thought that I was only interested in the music." As a boy he studied piano, then violin. He became an avid collector of jazz records from age twelve. At thirteen he went to Europe, and heard jazz bands in England. As a teenager he attended all the jazz reviews he could get into, spurred on if the production was disapproved of by the Parents' League, of which his mother was president. After graduating from the Hotchkiss School, he enrolled at Yale. Partly as a result of pursuing his jazz studies on weekends, he dropped out of Yale. His knowledge of black jazz secured for him jobs writing for the English publications *Gramophone* and *Melody Maker*. Each year Hammond bought a new Hudson convertible, in which he traveled about the country. "My visits to American towns and cities included stops at variety and burlesque houses, as well as jazz clubs. I was still the voyeur, the theater buff, curious to know everything that was going on, being printed, played, or flaunted."[75]

Born too late to have heard firsthand the early "hot" jazz bands, Hammond made up for this loss by his attachment to small, black improvising groups as models of good jazz. His contacts in the jazz world were cemented when Benny Goodman became his brother-in-law. His social position, his earnest enthusiasm, and his knowledge of classical music made it possible for him to introduce several classical

John Hammond (2d from left), in Chicago, 1940, with friends: Earl Hines (4th left), Helen Humes (upper right), Dave Dexter, jazz writer (4th right), Count Basie (2d right), and Benny Goodman (bottom right). *Courtesy Frank Driggs.*

music critics to an appreciation of jazz, among them B. H. Haggin, Irving Kolodin, Gama Gilbert, and Winthrop Sargeant. Both Kolodin and Haggin credit him with enormous influence in jazz circles. Haggin, who had been Hammond's boss for a time at the *Brooklyn Eagle*, did not let friendship interfere with professional relations. He called Hammond to task for an apparent conflict of interest when Hammond, a reviewer, took a position with Columbia records. The conflict was important, argued Haggin, because of Hammond's bias in favor of his brother-in-law Goodman, and his general preference for black musicians. Years later Hammond graciously conceded the correctness of Haggin's call to conscience on the point of the conflicting jobs. But at the time, Hammond shot back a defensive letter to the editor. He would no longer be acting as a critic, Hammond wrote; and he "bitterly" denied "that I am more partial to a musician because his color is black." But Haggin's point was rather more general. Hammond

listened . . . with ears, sensitiveness, judgment deflected by his sense of
importance and power, his loyalties and animosities. . . . [H]e had been
aware of presenting to the world the remarkable phenomenon of a rich
young man with intelligence, one also with a heart and conscience that
ranged him on the side of the oppressed against his own class of oppres-
sors.[76]

People perceived a combination of reverse racial and class snob-
bery in Hammond. He generally preferred rougher, blues-influenced
jazz that retained the small-group improvisation characteristic of early
New Orleans and Kansas City jazz. In line with these views, he
criticized Duke Ellington's more extended, symphonic works. Jazz
critic Barry Ulanov notes that Hammond and his friend Spike Hughes
(alias "Mike" in the *Melody Maker*) didn't like the smooth, virtuosic
sound of trombonist Lawrence Brown, whom Ellington had found in
California. "These well-bred youngsters, very proper in look, manner
and dress, wanted jazz to flagellate their sense of propriety," comments Ulanov. "When Duke achieved any considerable mel-
lifluousness in his music . . . they panned him." Increasingly they
found his work "arty" and "pretentious." Hammond always retained a
real, but cool, regard for Ellington's genius as a bandleader. He continued to feel that Ellington had "lost contact with his origins." He
notes that Ellington played to exclusively white audiences, even in
Harlem, and refused to press for integration of either his audiences or
his band.[77]

Certainly Ellington considered himself an entertainer, one who
could not afford the luxury of ignoring the expectations of his paying
customers. Thus when he moved into Harlem's Cotton Club, he
changed his band's name from the Washingtonians (reflecting his origins) to Duke Ellington's Jungle Band (in keeping with the Cotton
Club's ambiance). Orchestrations and titles reflected his "jungle-istic"
theme.[78] The jazz writer Marshall Stearns evoked the Cotton Club
during Ellington's stay:

I recalled one [floorshow] where a light-skinned and magnificently
muscled Negro burst through a papier-mache jungle onto the dance
floor, clad in an aviator's helmet, goggles, and shorts. He had obviously
been "forced down in darkest Africa," and in the center of the floor he
came upon a "white" goddess clad in long golden tresses and being
worshipped by a circle of cringing "blacks." Producing a bull whip
from heaven knows where, the aviator rescued the blonde and they did

an erotic dance. In the background, Bubber Miley, Tricky Sam Nan-
ten, and other members of the Ellington band growled, wheezed, and
snorted obscenely.[79]

Jazz was Harlem, and Harlem was, in the title of a book, one of the
Sinful Cities of the Western World. The sensual, undisciplined call of the
jungle lured white civilization to its doom. Here one could see "white
women trot along, prancing and strutting with negroes." There were
"swarms of people with banjoes and ukes strumming, gurgling sensual
music."[80]

The moralist's observations were essentially correct, averred
Seldes, Van Vechten, and Hammond. Jazz was, or should be, elemental and seductive. But the moralist drew the wrong conclusion. Here
was the protest against a mechanized, achievement-oriented, Victorian
culture, a protest which could save white culture from atrophy and
death. A bit of fun might heal the hell-haunted white psyche.[81] This
inversion of Victorian moral and aesthetic values sharpened the struggle over the emerging identity of American musical culture. Hammond, Seldes, and Van Vechten gravitated to jazz at least in part
because of the black sexuality they associated with it. Hammond
yearned for an "Ur-jazz," elemental and earthy as Bessie Smith's
blues. Yet Hammond was a moving force in the racial integration of
jazz bands. He wanted to integrate people, but not music. Van Vechten and Seldes admired the "low-down" blues, too; but their ideal was
for jazz to be musically integrated into classical music. Van Vechten
could not decide if whites should play with black music. While he
advised whites not to sing the blues, he saw jazz as a black music
which whites should exploit if Negroes wouldn't. Seldes, Van Vechten, and Hammond inverted Victorian aesthetic canons and racial
stereotypes without fundamentally rethinking them.[82] Emotional re-
lease was good; and Negroes were naturally endowed with the free
emotional life based on unfettered sexuality which was expressed in
jazz.

Devotees of jazz appeared to urge a kind of spiritual miscegenation, an infusion of vital blood to revivify the American imagination of
itself—the national identity. The transcendental "mystery" of the
New England errand seemed to have lost its hold on Americans if
some of its foremost representatives could imagine that the culture of
Negroes, the lowest "deviant" rung on the social ladder, could represent the American spirit.

As this publicity shot of Ken Johnson and Bessie Dudley illustrates, the Cotton Club projected a cheerful and seductive spirit. *Courtesy Billy Rose Theatre Collection, The New York Public Library at Lincoln Center.*

Motor Music

Symbol of the surface of American life, jazz was perceived primarily as carrier of dangerous romantic blackness, of undisciplined sensuousness. But for many critics it also represented a second constellation of features associated specifically with modern civilization: materialism, mechanism, and urbanism. Jazz was "exactly adapted to a pampered and mindless capitalistic public," asserted Mason. Unlike the artistic values of classical music, those of jazz could be reduced to the economic denominators of modern life. "Jazz is turned out for immediate consumption, by rubber-stamp. Its relentless monotonous rhythm shows that. (Its supposed rhythmic subtleties are all superficial—the basis is machine-made thump-thump.)"[83]

Writing in *Behold America*, a symposium on American life in 1931, modeled on Harold Stearns's influential 1922 collection *Civilization in the United States*, Mason devoted his entire entry on American music to "The Jazz Invasion." By contrast, in the 1922 symposium, Deems Taylor had failed even to mention jazz as he assessed the state of music in the United States. Yet, on the eve of the Depression, and at the peak of his own success as a composer, Mason could speak of nothing but jazz. He found himself wholly distracted. He identified jazz as a symbol of materialistic capitalism, of mechanism, of urban ills. "Jazz is so perfectly adapted to robots that the one could be deduced from the other. Jazz is thus the exact musical reflection of modern capitalistic industrialism."[84] Materialistic jazz reeked of the marketplace. True music smelled sweetly of the spirit.

The purpose of culture, as Arnold had defined it, and as Mason reaffirmed, was to lead materialistic civilization. Humanist Victorians assumed the importance of the self-discipline upon which civilization rests, but opposed the overweening materialism that was the hallmark of economic success. Culture helped one either to rise obliviously above or to reform civilization.[85] Civilization could not lead itself; near-sighted, it pursued only the carrot of gold. The humanist Victorian saw civilization, capitalism, and materialism as roughly synonymous. Because religion could no longer offer sufficient solace and guidance, artistic culture must create healing beauty, must imagine the future.

Mason adjusted Arnold's imperatives to the mode of national self-creation. Civilization measures itself quantitatively, culture qualitatively, in Arnold's view. How, asks Mason, is America to measure itself? Jazz deserves credit for aiming at "a kind of democratic inclusiveness and Whitmanesque cordiality." But the proponents of jazz mistake the "average" for the "ideal." One must make distinctions. "It was of distinction that Matthew Arnold wrote: 'Of this quality the world is impatient . . . [yet] it ends by receiving its influence, and by undergoing its law. . . .' But in the meantime how disheartening is the insistence on quantity of those blind to quality, and especially of the enthusiasts of jazz." Head counts do not determine the quality of music—either artistic or national. "It is not the number of asses that nibble at a branch that determines its value, but its own inherent greenness and fragrance."[86]

Mason saw that fate had chosen jazz to test America. This trial of the national purpose required leadership at the most profound levels of consciousness. As music critic, composer, and American, Mason was called to prophesy for "the land of Lincoln and of Emerson."

> If jazz is thus right in its desire for democratic breadth of appeal, but wrong in seeking it through the prostitution of music rather than through the cultivation of the people, it is also right in its sense that twentieth-century American music should be a product of twentieth-century America (rather than an importation, say, from nineteenth-century Germany) but seems to be wrong in the qualities it has picked out as permanently characteristic of that America.[87]

Mason here confronted jazz as the personification of the materialism of modern mass society. The jazz impulse did not represent America; certainly not the ideal America. America was Daniel Gregory Mason's prophetic imagination of it. Mason adopted the myth of national self-renewal in the manner of Emerson. "We have listened too long to the courtly muses of Europe," proclaimed Emerson. If Emerson "castigates his countrymen for their base 'materialism,' observed Sacvan Bercovitch, "he does so in order to sever the apparent from the ideal."[88] In the spirit of Arnold, Mason fought the good fight of culture against civilization, of quality against quantity; and, in the spirit of Emerson, he did so in the name of America.

Those who touted jazz as art failed to perceive its fundamentally mechanistic nature, argued Mason. Artistic wholes were beautiful in their cohesive organicism. But jazz represented the antithesis of organic cohesion. It was mechanism. Mason's attack on "mechanistic jazz" combined traditional romantic anti-Lockean arguments with what H. Stuart Hughes calls the modern revolt against positivism. Everyday experience confirmed Herbert Spencer's sociological generalization: modern civilization advanced through an ever-mounting heterogeneity and specialization in all aspects of life. Not only must culture counter the cash-nexus of materialism, it must, as well, provide holistic replacements for the ad hoc eclecticism of mechanism. With Coleridge, Mason opposed the deadening scientific outlook of mere "understanding." Only the "imagination" of artistic creativity can combat this scientific anarchy. In Mason's eyes, jazz lacked the larger vision of artistic imagination. Like the banal scientific empiricism of most modern life, jazz contents itself with merely superficial originality. "It is a foolish literalness, a pathetic lack of vision, that leads people in a mechanical age to try to make art mechanical too," wrote Mason of jazz.[89]

For Mason, jazz represented the whole complex challenge of modern civilization. Mechanistic, materialistic jazz exacerbated rather than counterbalanced the unpleasant aspects of urban life. In jazz Mason heard transience, noise, and inauthenticity, elements which soured his enjoyment of cosmopolitan urban life. Was jazz, as Hiram Moderwell enthused, the "perfect expression of the American city, with its restless bustle and motion, its multitude of unrelated details, and its underlying rhythmic progress toward a vague nowhere?" Mason readily conceded that Moderwell described exactly "the present life of our unhappy land." Indeed, American cities were notable for "congestion, confusion, lack of privacy, physical luxury masking mental poverty, over-stimulation of nerves and consequent nervous exhaustion. And no one would deny that of these objective qualities jazz was a singularly accurate subjective reflection."[90] Jazz, in H. L. Mencken's memorable damnation, was like the "sound of riveting." It painted a clear but grim portrait of exactly those features of American civilization which it was the calling of musical culture to transcend.[91]

Thus the war over jazz raged on two intellectual fronts. On the one hand, jazz was made to stand for the devolutionary forces of sensual blackness against which culture has always struggled. In America this evil now took the concretely national form of Negro jazz. On the other hand, paradoxically, some critics perceived jazz as the antimusic of robots and riveting machines, the technology of urban civilization. Here loomed Matthew Arnold's old nemesis, mechanism. Through Arnold, the Yankee aesthetic of identity was rooted in romantic distinctions between mechanistic and organic art. Critics applied these standards derogatorily to jazz: a truly American music must not reflect the superficial banalities of national life; it must found its prophetic mission on an ideal America of organic, village fellowship.

4

The Distorted Mirror

Forced to take notice of jazz when young, white, counterculture critics hailed jazz as a sensual art, advocates of redemptive culture were stunned when Europeans took to jazz. Apparently, it became widely popular abroad, even among musicians, artists, and intellectuals. Concerned critics recognized that if Americans were successfully to create a musical culture based on European forms, albeit purified and democratized, then Europe must pay attention to American efforts. Ultimately Europe was the mirror in which they verified their own progress. As the scholar Perry Miller wrote of New England's second- and third-generation Puritans:

> If an actor, playing the leading role in the greatest dramatic spectacle of the century, were to attire himself and put on his make-up, rehearse his lines, take a deep breath, and stride onto the stage, only to find the theater dark and empty, no spotlight working, and himself entirely alone, he would feel as did New England around 1650 or 1660.[1]

If Europe turned away from the principles of redemptive culture, then perhaps the centennial composers, too, might be on a "fool's errand."

For this reason, the European infatuation with jazz galled people such as Mason. Actually, European opinion covered a broad spectrum. But Europeans tended to view jazz as both black and prototypically American. Therefore custodians of American musical culture were discomfited even by those Europeans who detested jazz and blamed America for exporting such degeneracy.[2] Most foreign jazz buffs appraised it in much the same terms as Seldes, Van Vechten, and Hammond: the exotic *élan vital* of jazz stimulated artists working

[109]

in traditional forms. Some Europeans, committing the ultimate cultural heresy, thought of jazz *itself* as a new musical art form. Indeed, Europe's affair with jazz was enough to chill a Yankee's heart. But Negro jazzmen returning from European tours basked in a new sense of their own artistic worth.

Europeans' opinions of jazz were colored by their common stereotype of America as an ever-new, exotic, aboriginal land. In Locke's words, "In the Beginning all the world was *America*."[3] Transatlantic misunderstandings over jazz underscored the discontinuity between modern European and Yankee interpretations of the Adamic American myth. Looking for "natural man," some Europeans hunted for him in Harlem's asphalt jungle, while Yankees insisted that in America, nature and cultured civilization interacted synergistically to produce a "new man." Promoters of the Yankee musical mission were chagrined to see Europe reflecting a perversely distorted image of the American identity.

When Europe crowned jazz, defenders of Yankee classicism reacted, typically, by collapsing several issues into a single symbol. Those who subscribed to redemptive culture believed that jazz was the musical expression of the evils of modern civilization. Mason depicted America reeling before a "Jazz Invasion" that was un-American or foreign. Classical critics considered Negroes functionally "deviant" to the Yankee ethos, foreign to normative American culture. Simultaneously Europe exported avant-garde music, alien in every respect. "Modernism" was the linguistic wastebasket into which writers like Mason disposed of the modern jazz spirit and its foreign fellow travelers. For Americans, Igor Stravinsky, and specifically his *Rite of Spring*, symptomized musical modernists who dressed up the jazz spirit to titillate the jaded tastes of pseudosophisticates. As a catchall symbol, "modernism" encompassed a variety of new art movements, ranging from European avant-gardism through fashionable culture, and material civilization itself.

But Yankees built their reductive damnation of modernism on a partial truth. Sometimes European modernists like Darius Milhaud did equate jazz with their "myth of the new." Worse yet for Yankees, the avant-garde often equated its expressionism and futurism with "Americanism." The European avant-garde drew on myths of the New Golden Land: America as exotic wilderness and America as seedbed of revolution.[4] Thus while "jazzers" and "modernists" were bastardizing the very symbolic language of redemptive aesthetics, Europeans pursued their own aesthetics of identity and assiduously ignored the Yankee composer.

Europe Crowns Jazz

Jazz struck Europe "almost like a start of terror, like a sudden awakening, this shattering storm of rhythm, these tone elements never previously combined and now let loose upon us all at once." So proclaimed French composer Darius Milhaud in 1924. Bemused by attention from Europeans, American observers reported back every jazz conquest, every official opposition. "Jazz 'er Up!" headlined the *New York Times* in 1921 of "Broadway's Conquest of Europe." "American composers of 'jazz' tunes . . . have accomplished in their field something which American 'highbrow' musicians, in theirs, have never even come within hailing distance of accomplishing. They have utterly vanquished their European rivals." Enthusiasm for jazz reportedly swept Tokyo. The British queen opposed jazz, as did the pope. In 1926 jazz dancing was banned in Italy; a year later dance "speakeasies" circumvented the prohibition. In Germany, imported recordings ignited a vocal jazz craze. The Montparnasse police banned jazz, as did the Soviet government. Turkey claimed its own king of jazz. Jazz classes at the conservatory in Frankfurt caused a furor. By April 1928, Americans received the shocking news that jazz had actually "invaded" Vienna, the inner sanctum of musical culture.[5]

But Europeans had already been enchanted by the varieties of ragtime, minstrel entertainments, and cakewalk dancing. Bert Williams and George W. Walker had introduced quality black variety shows to England. The French were astonished by the virtuoso strutting ragtime of James Europe's Hell Fighters Band during World War I. Debussy, Satie, and Stravinsky evidenced interest in the charm of ragtime.

In soil prepared by ragtime, jazz spread luxuriantly. As soon as Victor began recording jazz bands in 1917, Europeans imported the discs. Parisians were the first Europeans to hear live jazz, in November 1918. Black clarinetist Sidney Bechet and the Southern Syncopated Orchestra introduced New Orleans jazz to England in 1919.[6] Bechet's tour overlapped a yearlong stay by the Original Dixieland Jazz Band. Seventeen English recordings of the ODJB signaled their success. In

1920–1921, Billy Arnold's Negro Band visited England. A stream of jazzmen followed, some to join native English and Continental jazz bands, others as part of touring aggregations.

Interest in jazz peaked with trips to England by Louis Armstrong in 1932 and by Duke Ellington the following year. Previously, jazz aficionados had feasted on Armstrong's feats via his recordings of 1928–1931. Years of performing fulfillment led to fundamental changes in Armstrong's relationships. He formed his own touring band, and broke with Lil Hardin, wife, pianist, and promoter. Like so many black jazz musicians of his era, Armstrong considered himself an entertainer, nothing more. He and his band listened religiously to Guy Lombardo's radio broadcasts, in appreciation of the white bandleader's style. Armstrong had, as yet, no strong sense of himself as an Afro-American artist. His four-month English tour didn't achieve unqualified success. The English considered Armstrong's group a "good 'nigger' band," an appellation used patronizingly but without rancor, notes jazz critic Barry Ulanov. Nevertheless, Armstrong was buoyed by a new sense of his value as a performer.[7] His reception planted the notion that his entertainment was also art.

Ellington's English tour also produced mixed reviews, but it likewise served to boost his sense of his music's importance. Ellington's supporters emphasized his cultural aspirations in a substantial promotional campaign that preceded him. His press agent assured Cedric Belfrage of the London *Sunday Express* that the bandleader was "well-educated and gentlemanly in his bearing." The composer Percy Grainger compared Ellington with J. S. Bach and Frederick Delius. The British were intrigued. Nonetheless, it was difficult to find hotel space for the Negro band. How black was Ellington? Did he have a flat nose and crinkly hair? Was he, indeed, well behaved? The English were astonished to find Ellington "quiet, friendly and deferential."[8] He wasn't known as "Duke" for nothing.

Ellington's musicians were genuinely surprised by the greetings of numerous people who already knew the history and repertory of the band. Harry Carney, a baritone sax player, later said, "We couldn't understand how people in Europe, who heard us only through the medium of records, could know so much about us." Spike Hughes, a leading English jazz critic, tutored audiences on how to react to Ellington's music. "When Trick Sam [Nanton] plays you mustn't laugh . . . it's art; and no applause in the middle of numbers." Ellington, attuned

Louis Armstrong and his Chicago band star in this delicious fantasy of jazz heaven for a 1931 movie. *Courtesy Performing Arts Research Center, The New York Public Library at Lincoln Center.*

to audience response, tailored his musical persona to their expectations. Sensing that his slow numbers were not a hit, he changed styles: "I went back and gave a vaudeville show." As just an entertainer, Ellington always felt it his job to accommodate the expectations of his audiences. Like Armstrong, Ellington and his men were genuine, if ambivalent, admirers of white jazz musicians. Ellington also came to feel that Europeans valued him as a black artist. The tour raised his self-esteem. "The main thing I got in Europe was *spirit*. . . . If they think I'm *that* important . . . then maybe I have kinda said something, maybe our music does mean something."[9]

Critics came from all over Europe to report on the Ellington band. On the whole they heard what they expected to hear. Ernest Newman decided that Ellington was "a Harlem Dionysus drunk on bad bootleg liquor." The *Era*'s "Stanley Nelson kept up a peppery discussion of the aphrodisiac qualities of Ellington's music." But John Cheatle of the *New Britain* perceived "over-sophisticated jazz players, whose music is almost entirely European in character." And Constant Lambert, a

Sartorially elegant, Duke Ellington stands at ease, as usual. *Courtesy Performing Arts Research Center, The New York Public Library at Lincoln Center.*

champion of jazz, wrote, "Ellington is no mere bandleader and arranger, but a composer of uncommon merit, probably the first composer of real character to come out of America."[10]

By 1932, jazz criticism was already an established form in
Europe. From the Continent came leading jazz commentators, writers
for *De jazzwereld* (Holland), *Music* (Belgium), *Jazz* (Switzerland), *Jazz
Tango Dancing* (France), and *Music Echo* (Germany). Jazz criticism developed faster in Europe than in the United States. When *La revue
musicale* began reviewing records in 1926, it included jazz and classical
music from the start. Henry Prunieres launched the reviews with the
proclamation "Decidedly, jazz reigns on the earth." The American
musicologist and critic Carl Engel noted with surprise that Robert
Goffin's *Aux frontieres du jazz*, published in 1932, was the first good
book on the subject. The Belgian's study was followed two years later
by *Le jazz hot*, by the French writer Hughes Panassie. The French
contingent, Prunieres, Panassie, and Charles Delaunay, wrote enthu-
siastically of the Ellington band.[11]

The voracious interest of established European intellectuals, composers, critics, conductors, and performers carried weight with
American commentators. The composer Marion Bauer observed that,
like hungry dogs, French composers leaped at the bone of jazz; and not
only composers devoured jazz. The writer Jean Cocteau wrote,
"American Negro orchestras . . . fertilize an artist's imagination as
much as does life."[12] Like Seldes, Van Vechten, and Hammond, many
European enthusiasts associated jazz with a Bergsonian life force, a
kind of cultural fountain of youth which could nurture the withering
roots of Western artistic creativity. Conductors Serge Koussevitsky
and Ernest Ansermet found admirable qualities in jazz. Ansermet's
praise turned for comparison to the greatness of J. S. Bach:

> [These blues improvisations had] richness of invention, force of accent,
> and daring in novelty and the unexpected. Already, they gave the idea
> of a style, and their form was gripping, abrupt, harsh, with a brusque
> and pitiless ending like that of Bach's second Brandenburg Concerto. I
> wish to set down the name of this artist of genius; as for myself, I shall
> never forget it: Sidney Bechet.[13]

The violinist Jacques Thibaut praised American jazz, as did the composers Albert Roussel, P.-O. Ferroud, Maurice Brillant, and Maurice
Ravel. Interviewed for *Musical America*, Ravel said, "Jazz is a very rich

and vital source of inspiration for modern composers and I am astonished that so few Americans are influenced by it."[14] An interest in jazz
helped to unite the French composers dubbed "the Six": Auric,
Honegger, Tailleferre, Durey, Poulenc, and Milhaud.

Milhaud, who increasingly divided his time between France and
the United States, sought out jazz bands on both sides of the Atlantic.
After hearing jazz in a London taxi-dance hall in 1920, Milhaud composed his low-life ballet score *Carmel mou* in 1921. In 1922 his jazz
horizons expanded when he heard the Leo Reisman orchestra at the
Brunswick in Boston. Reisman's white band played a smooth style of
jazz. Milhaud noted as salient jazz characteristics: constant syncopation, intricate soloistic percussion playing, and new orchestral tech-
niques.[15] To appreciate fully the coloristic palette of a jazz orchestra,
contended Milhaud, one had to hear a band like Paul Whiteman's or
Billy Arnold's.

Milhaud credited Negroes with giving jazz its life force. "There
can be no doubt that the origin of jazz music is to be sought among the
Negroes." The American Negro retains "primitive African qualities,"
and these are the source of the "tremendous rhythmic force" and
"expressive melodies" of jazz. "Here we are at the first sources of this
music, with its deep human content which is about to create as complete a revolution as any of the masterpieces now universally recognized." From the union of black jazz, with its seminal energy, and
traditional classicism, with its refined intelligence, Milhaud believed a
new art would be born:

> In jazz the North Americans have really found expression in an art
> form that suits them thoroughly, and their great jazz bands achieve a
> perfection that places them next to our most famous symphony orches-
> tras like that of the Conservatoire or our modern orchestras of wind
> instruments and our quartettes.

Milhaud was entranced. The ballet *La Creation du Monde*, which was
launched with a suitably scandalous Paris premiere in 1923, was
Milhuad's own contribution to the "concert repertoire" which "these
magnificent orchestras need." He looked forward especially to the
continued harmonic development of jazz. "There can be no doubt that
in a few years polytonal and atonal harmonies will prevail in the
dances that will follow the shimmies of the 1920's."[16]

Like most of his peers who sought inspiration in the alleged primitiveness of black jazz, Milhaud was committed to the ideal of craftsmanship he associated with high art, with intelligence, with whiteness. As yet another exoticism to be used up by traditional artists, jazz retained for Europeans the charms of distance, a quality it sorely lacked for genteel white Americans. Jazz, in the early 1920s, stood for gay, irresponsible freedom. "What I love about jazz," wrote the protodadaist composer Erik Satie, "is that it's 'blue' and you don't care."[17]

By 1926, Milhaud was done with it. Like a hungry dog, he had feasted on jazz; but the bone he had so eagerly gnawed in 1924 had lost its succulence. Now he haughtily distanced himself from the popularity of jazz. "Even in Harlem, the charm had been broken for me. White men, snobs in search of exotic color, sightseers curious to hear Negro music, had penetrated to even the most secluded corners. That is why I gave up going." A year later Pierne wrote, "The jazz influence has passed already, like a beneficent storm after which one rediscovers a clearer sky, more settled weather."[18]

Yet European fascination with jazz survived. France continued to be an especially receptive host for American jazz, even after French composers had had their fill. English love of American jazz was balanced, politically, by attentiveness to the employment needs of native musicians. Two years after Ellington's tour, the Ministry of Labor imposed on non-English musicians a ban lasting twenty years.[19] In Germany, jazz interest among classical composers peaked later than in France. As German society came unglued, the identification of jazz with freedom increasingly acquired a political edge.

Looking to see themselves mirrored in the eyes of Europeans, American critics asked who was the fairest of them all. The persona they perceived looked not at all like Uncle Sam. The eminent critic W. J. Henderson, writing for *Scribner's Magazine* in 1924, described the quandary which jazz caused for would-be creators of a national music consciousness:

> This jazz orchestra is American. It has impressed itself upon the artistic European mind just as the ragtime and jazz music [in its rhythmic life] has captured the popular fancy of Europe. Can any such thing be said of any other American musical creation? In the admirable compositions of the learned Athenians who walk in the groves of the Boston Common one finds all the urbanity and all the lofty contemplation that characterize the works of the fathers. But has Europe hearkened to

them? Has a European musician stretched out the arms of his flagging inspiration toward them and clasped to his throbbing breast their needed support? Alas, no! But ragtime and jazz rule the feet of France and Britain.[20]

Europe, implied Henderson, would tell Americans who they were. Jazz reflected the American soul. "It expresses our ebulliency, our care-free optimism, our nervous energy, and our extravagant humor—characteristics which our foreign critics tell us demark us from the rest of the world." But earlier attempts by cultivated Yankee composers to incorporate Negro elements invariably failed, "because the public declined to embrace the slave music when dressed in the unbecoming robes of Teutonic tone poems."[21] And, Henderson might have added, genteel Yankees generally refused to embrace jazz in any guise.

Antijazz partisans could draw no solace, even from European opponents of jazz, who typically confounded jazz as black and as American. It was a diseased exhalation of the New World wilderness, in their opinions. Even Carl Engel, who was himself guardedly optimistic about the prospects for incorporating jazz into American classical music, expressed outrage that Europeans should blame their own degenerate handling of jazz on America:

> If America can make musical capital out of its first true folk-music, all the better. If Europe sees in it only an escape into musical idiocy and filth, we do not wish to interfere. But we may be pardoned for protesting against a possible inclination on the part of learned musicologists, to call this latest chapter in the history of European music: "The American Infection."[22]

How could America, the New Jerusalem, be a source of moral disease? As Mason argued in the Emersonian mode, America was not the surface aspects of mass society, of politics, or the marketplace. America was the new dawn as imagined by New England. That Europeans, against whom and for whom New England charted the progress of its errand, should view jazz as the spirit of American music, indicated the seriousness of the Yankee dilemma. If, as the sociologist Charles Horton Cooley said, "each to each a looking-glass / Reflects the other that doth pass," then social reality had degenerated into mocking fun-house mirrors in a tawdry spiritual circus.[23] Who was the fairest one indeed!

Modernism: Errant Symbols

Jazz represented the manifold paradoxes of modern life: hedonism and urban mechanism, the components of consumption capitalism. Jazz "bears all the marks of a nerve-strung, strident, mechanized civilization," wrote a contemporary analyst. "It is a thing of the jungles—modern, man-made jungles." "The Jazz Age" was a conceptual portmanteau, a way of containing the confusions of modern life by giving them a single handle. As they unpacked the metaphor of jazz, critics "discovered" the secret of modernism. Lacking the concreteness of a good metaphor, "modernism" itself could not resolve the paradoxes to which it referred. But like a guide to the perplexed, "jazz" lent perceptual coherence to phenomena as discrete as European musical avant-gardism, bureaucratic and scientific rationalization, even contemporary faddism. F. Scott Fitzgerald suggested that the age was corrupted "less through lack of morals than through lack of taste." Redemptive culture implied that the two were inseparable. As a metaphor for modernism, jazz confirmed their identity. "In a broad sense," wrote the popular critic and author Sigmund Spaeth, "modernism and jazz amount to the same thing. Both may be most simply defined as the distortion of the conventional in music." Jazzy modernism encompassed the fashionably contemporary, the avant-garde, and the structural modernism of capitalist civilization.[24]

But the categorical confusion over "modernism" and its referents was also shared by sectors of the avant-garde. Jazz proponents and avant-gardists alike disputed the various meanings of "modernism." Elements of the French and then the Italian and German avant-garde grasped at jazz, and for a moment brandished it aloft. In this spirit, some rebellious young American composers also touted jazz as modern music, providing an excuse for men such as Mason to tar both avant-garde music and jazz with the same broad brush. The avant-garde could be equated with faddishness—extreme "romanticism" or "manner"—essentially jazz-for-highbrows. Avant-garde music was only perverse, jazzy entertainment decked out in intellectual garb. Lacking spirit, it could not really be art. Modern composers such as Stravinsky intoxicated the "moronic radicals," as Mason called them, who pushed their way into concert halls in increasing numbers. Under an intellectual costume, Stravinsky secreted the essence of jazz, sneaking the whole, like a Trojan horse, into the hallowed precinct of the concert hall.

Musical conservatives bristled when contemporary critics and composers advocated the modernism of primitive music. As early as 1915, the Australian composer Percy Grainger called his colleagues' attention to the complexity of primitive folk music, noted its inaccessibility for most musicians, and touted its utility for contemporary composers. It was widely assumed that, like Picasso, Stravinsky had drawn inspiration (e.g., for *The Rite of Spring*) from African sources. As Leo Ornstein symbolized for Americans (in his performances of Scriabin and in his own piano compositions) the preshocks of modern music, Stravinsky dominated the popular and professional notion of avant-garde music through the 1920s. When he finally toured the United States in 1925, people clamored to know about this terrible Slav. In Boston, *The Rite of Spring* was performed six times that year. The *Boston Evening Transcript* reported, "To the schism over jazz succeeds the schism over Stravinsky."[25]

Audiences were primed by criticism that described Stravinsky's modernism as primitive sensualism or as mechanism. At its 1922 American premiere, *The Rite of Spring* was denounced as jungle music:

> The Paleozoic Crawl, turned into tone with all the resources of modern orchestra, clamored for attention at the Philadelphia Orchestra concert when Igor Stravinsky's *Rite of Spring* was given its first airing on this side of the vast Atlantic. It was the primitive run riot, almost formless and without definite tonality, save for insistently beating rhythms that made tom-tom melodies of the gentle Congo tribes seem even super-sophisticated in comparison. . . . Without description or program, the work might have suggested a New Year's Eve rally of moonshine addicts and the simple pastimes of early youth and maidens, circumspectly attired in a fig leaf apiece.[26]

Philip Hale, in the *Boston Herald*, produced just such a program, an "outline of Stravinsky's *Rite of Spring*, a tone picture of spring-fever in a zoo . . . suggested as a means for helping the uninitiated to understand and enjoy this epoch-making work." "It is an orgy," wrote Olin Downes, "and an explosion of force, but very brutal and perhaps perverse." Annoyed by such reviews, Stravinsky replied to a reporter's query on quarter tones, "No, I do not write in quarter tones. I am richer than an African or Papuan. I was born under the . . . [well-tempered] Clavier and I seek my new effects with our familiar tempered scale."[27]

In *The Dilemma of American Music*, Mason announced that

"Prokofieff, Stravinsky, and Casella in part of his work, complete the downward curve of decadence [begun by the atonalists and impressionists] and arrive back at the starting point of rhythmic development—the crude childishness of 'jazz.'" To his own satisfaction, Mason proved that "Stravinsky as a Symptom" threatened the continuity of Western music:

> Now, if we were to take this formula of jazz—short rhythmic or metrical figures, formally inane but physically pungent, mechanically repeated—and put at its disposal all the resources of modern musical technic, particularly in the matter of complex harmony and tone-color, what would we get? We should get, should we not, the so-called ultramodernist composers, headed by Stravinsky? . . . The reason we do not usually recognise this curious aesthetic kinship, this atavism by which the traits of savage ancestors reappear in neurotic descendants, is that the modernist composers have drawn the red herring of harmony and tone-color across their trail.

Mason quoted with approval critic George Dyson's assessment of *The New Music:* "Asia and Africa are imported into the concert room, and the drum is beaten harder than ever before."[28]

Stravinsky also symptomized the avant-garde celebration of antihumanist technology, of urban consumption capitalism. In 1920, before Americans had even heard *The Rite of Spring*, Deems Taylor wrote, "Assuming . . . that Stravinsky is mechanism become music . . . I don't want it." Taylor's fellow critic Paul Rosenfeld expressed his distaste for Stravinsky's *Concertino* in similar metaphors. "It is like a locomotive which has fallen off the track, making its wheels revolve in air. Rhythms prolong themselves out of sheer inertia; pound on wearily." How like modern civilization, a derailed locomotive, machine without reason. "It is this piecemeal, mechanical, inorganic structure that seems, despite other differences, to be characteristic of the whole contemporary movement of which Stravinsky is the outstanding figure," wrote Mason. "Modern music avoids the long living curves of rhythm, and becomes ever more choppy and mechanical."[29]

According to Yankee redemptive aesthetics, Stravinsky represented an unholy union of the jungle and the metropolis. Jazz symbolized the incivility of the modern industrial cityscape, whose alien nature was epitomized by the anomic presence of a new class of strangers. Identifying the avant-garde with jazz, and both with the superficial features of contemporary civilization, Mason denied that they were truly art, and on these grounds refused them entrance into the holy pantheon of Western culture.

Even John Alden Carpenter, more liberal toward jazz than his centennial Yankee peers, sometimes equated jazz with a crude capitalist urbanism. Ultimately he agreed with the underlying sentiment of Mason's arguments. When commissioned by Diaghilev to compose a "ballet on modern American life,"[30] Carpenter produced "Skyscrapers," which ambiguously associated jazz with a desperate alternation between mechanistic work and distracted entertainment:

> With the parting of the curtains, blinking red lights are revealed on either side of the stage—"symbols of restlessness." Then dancers wearing the semblance of overalls go through motions of violent labor, while shadows in human shape move listlessly by. The whistles blow, the workers come out, and each steps into the arms of a short-skirted, barelegged partner for a fun-mad, dance-addled scene of scenic railways, ferris wheels, etc.[31]

Carpenter, a wealthy, worldly man, friend of Stravinsky, was not as censorious as Manners or Mason, but he shared their concern for the future of the American musical spirit. The work of the arts is to provide national spiritual leadership. "Their task is to nourish and sustain people. The day of American leadership has dawned," he wrote. "It is not enough to deal with things. In addition, we must express our ideas and ideals. It is the role of music and the arts to be the medium for this expression." Given the chaotic condition of modern American life, Carpenter recommended "prayer and a return to religion and art as solutions to today's problems. They speak to the best that is in us. These troubled times," he concluded, "are not a healthy period for the creator. Artists cannot be afraid of today and afraid for tomorrow and express themselves freely."[32] Only the spirit of art could reflect the true soul of America, its eternally new becoming.

All parties to the debates over jazz and modernism pursued reductive arguments, polemics simultaneously social and aesthetic. Critics played a linguistic shell game in which the referents of "modernism" constantly shifted. Opponents of jazz and avant-garde music defined "modernism" most broadly as the whole of contemporary material civilization. The jazzy musical culture of this urban civilization they explained either as an atavism to precultural savage life or as the degradation of production capitalism into consumption capitalism. Some critics defined jazzy "modernism" more narrowly as the merely fashionable. In terms of redemptive culture, such music lacked spiritual content and was characterized by "manner" or "romanticism." It represented the perverse fashion of "highbrow" fascination with "lowbrow" trash. Critics such as Mason reduced the protean confusion of the 1920s into a single Janus-like evil, a jazzy "modernism" which combined a "brutal," "crude childishness" and a "piecemeal, mechanical, inorganic structure."

Redemptive culture clashed with an avant-garde aesthetic that defined itself as the spirit of eternal birth. The fault lines of the disagreement clarify the curious connections between the European avant-gardist's "America" and the genteel Yankee's "America." The New World long held a paradoxical place in the European imagination as an exotic precivilization and as a source of revolutionary trends. In America, land of prehistoric forests and of the first modern revolution, land of frontier plains and of steel skyscrapers, and in jazz, music of Negro naturalness and of mechanistic newness, the European avant-garde found ready symbols for its attacks on the bourgeois estate of culture. From the romantic search for folk roots sprang avant-gardists' insatiable appetites for primitive art. To the South Seas, Africa, and South America they went in search of vitalism. The German expressionist Emil Nolde wrote, "There are enough overrefined, pallid, decadent works of art and perhaps that is why artists who are vital and developing seek guidance from vigorous primitives."[33] The subjectivist avant-garde's love of primitivism resonated with Gauguin's desire to be "far from that European struggle for money."[34] Society in the United States was ostentatiously capitalist; yet the search for an American fountain of youth ended here with Negro jazz. Black jazz seemed to thumb its nose at bourgeois culture. It boasted unimpeachable primitivist credentials.

Like the Yankees, European avant-gardists adopted an aesthetic burdened with a mission. But the mission of the avant-garde resembled the centennial composers' errand turned inside out. Irving Howe suggests that avant-garde modernism is "an unyielding rage against the official order. But modernism does not establish a prevalent style of its own; or if it does, it denies itself, thereby ceasing to be modern." Avant-garde manifestos hacked away at the carefully tended hedges delimiting the garden of culture. The avant-garde, on the military model, would destroy the hegemony of culture. In this respect it resembled political and social revolution. Though its manifestos sometimes attacked art, the dead hand of the museum was its real target.

Without revolution, new art would be stillborn, suffocated by the custodians of culture.[35]

The Italian philosopher of art Renato Poggioli argues that the avant-garde—what he terms "modernity," or the "myth of the new"—is always threatened with cooptation by the fashionably contemporary—or "modernism." This faddish "modernism" is "nothing but a blind adoration of the idols and fetishes of our time." This "snobbist variant of romantic 'local color' sometimes takes the form of 'Americanism.'"[36]

In the 1920s, the confounding of avant-gardism and fashionable modernism was common. Poggioli's true avant-garde seeks, in the romantic tradition, a birth of the wholly new, "a birth rather than a rebirth, not a restoration but . . . a construction of the present and future not on the foundations of the past but on the ruins of time." Some European avant-garde partisans did in fact pursue the "myth of the new" as a form of "Americanism"—with or without jazz. They proceeded in the spirit of Goethe and Hegel, who idealized America as a land without memory, a land of the future.[37]

The futurist avant-garde looked to a new art of revolutionary "dynamism," of vital Bergsonian becoming, rather than being. F. T. Martinetti, in his manifesto of 1908, called on futurists to "free Italy from her numberless museums which cover her with countless cemeteries." Like a Whitman unmoored from democratic faith, he proclaimed their intentions:

> We will sing the great masses agitated by work, pleasure, or revolt; we will sing the multicolored and polyphonic surf of revolutions in modern capitals; the noctural vibration of arsenals and docks beneath their glaring electric moons; greedy stations devouring smoking serpents; factories hanging from the clouds by the threads of their smoke; bridges like giant gymnasts stepping over sunny rivers sparkling like diabolical cutlery; adventurous steamers scenting the horizon; large-breasted locomotives bridled with long tubes, and the slippery flight of airplanes.[38]

Although their urban, mechanized dynamism was modeled on the land of the skyscraper, America, the Italian futurists were chary of openly associating their movement with the European cult of Americanism.[39]

Avant-garde manifestos proclaimed both a radical expressionism, devoted to expression even at the cost of organic unity, and a radical materialism, celebrating the sensual flux of industrialization. Actually two ideal-typical poles of avant-garde aesthetics are represented here: radical materialism's (futurist-dynamist) celebration of the external world sensually experienced, and radical expressionism's preoccupation with the display of the inner self. Both oppose the teleological ramifications of art-as-the-servant-of-culture. Internally both tendencies are tensioned between an aesthetic nihilism (dada) and a gestalt formalism of medium (e.g., cubism). By treating industrial, technological civilization as though it were nature, futurism assaults the cultured sensibility. In its glorification of will, expressionism emphatically denies the mediative prerogatives of culture. This avant-garde art is antiteleological because it detests the presumption that culture is the end-all. Romanticism had maintained a tense, unstable allegiance: both to expressionism and organicism and to sensual materialism and spiritual idealism. But these ideals tended to break apart as the nineteenth century progressed, although the lines of definition remained somewhat ambiguous.[40] Typically, the streams of avant-gardism mingled inextricably, and both were associated with "Americanism."[41]

Americanism found its way into many avant-garde works, such as a sculptural "New York Manager" that Picasso created for Satie's balletic happening *Parade*. Picasso bedecked his "manager" with "cowboy boots, red pleated shirt-front, stove-pipe hat, and a huge superstructure like a skyscraper."[42] Yet the flood of futurist musical manifestos, such as Luigi Russolo's "The Art of Noises" in 1913, produced little music.[43] Edgard Varèse most obviously fulfilled the programmatic American fantasies of Italian futurists. Varèse and his chroniclers have insisted that the French composer developed his musical aesthetic wholly apart from futurists like his friend Russolo; but the important distinction between them was that while futurists composed manifestos, Varèse composed music.[44]

Medically unfit to fight in the First World War and unable to pursue a conducting career during hostilities, Varèse moved to New York late in 1915. Five years later he composed *Amèriques* for large orchestra with augmented percussion. Varèse explained his "purely sentimental title":

> I was still under the spell of my first impressions of New York—not only New York seen, but more especially heard. For the first time with my physical ears I heard a sound that had kept recurring in my dreams as a boy—a high whistling C sharp. It came to me as I worked in my Westside apartment where I could hear all the river sounds—the lonely

foghorns, the shrill peremptory whistles—the whole wonderful river symphony which moved me more than anything ever had before. Besides, as a boy, the mere word "America" meant all discoveries, all adventures. It meant the unknown. And in this symbolic sense—new worlds on this planet, in outer space, and in the minds of man—I gave the title signifying "Americas" to the first work I wrote in America.[45]

Like the futurists, Varèse was inspired by the industrial dynamism of the American cityscape. *Ameriques* was among the most important compositions of avant-garde "Americanism" which did not refer to jazz.[46]

European avant-garde fascination with the implications of jazz culminated in Ernest Křenek's *Jonny spielt auf* ("Johnny Strikes Up the Band") and Kurt Weill's *Rise and Fall of the City of Mahagonny*. A year after *Ameriques* premiered, Křenek's "jazz opera" was performed in Leipzig. It quickly became an international sensation and was translated into eighteen languages. In the opera, the black bandleader Jonny makes eyes at Anita, the opera singer and girlfriend of Max, unstable composer and contemplator of glaciers. Even more desirable than Anita, for Jonny, is the violin of one Daniello, also attracted to Anita. At the end of many misadventures, Daniello is pushed under a train by Yvonne, chambermaid bedmate of Jonny. Jonny is bound toward America possessing his three desires: Yvonne, violin, and Anita. In the opera's apotheosis, the train station clock becomes a "giant globe, bestrided by Jonny. The Statue of Liberty is behind him, and he is triumphantly playing the violin, finally outstretching his arm in imitation of the statue. The chorus below him dances in hypnotic rapture as the world falls under the spell of the compelling music."[47]

Europeans were "intrigued" with the novelty of having a Negro sing Jonny's role. When Křenek's work premiered at the Metropolitan Opera in 1929, there was no such novelty: a white singer performed Jonny in blackface, "his performance at times reminiscent of Al Jolson, who was also in attendance." The "score utilized not only jazz, but radio loudspeakers, the sound of a train and other appurtenances of the era."[48] The critic Lawrence Adler described the work as having "infested Europe with its popularity":

[It is] a good replica of a thoroughly impudent American Negro, and seems more plausibly grotesque in foreign setting. . . . [If Křenek] is fond of jazz, he likewise does not distrust the processes of the atonalists. And from the modern point of view, what could be more entirely apropos? Jonny, the pivotal figure of the play, is a highly unmoral personification of many latter-day ideas and impulses. Live vociferously, be sure of yourself, and obey the voice of the moment. . . . Could anything be more in keeping with such a gesture than the principles of atonality?[49]

Three years after *Jonny*'s premiere, Kurt Weill's *Mahagonny* opened in the same Leipzig theater, threatened by packs of Nazi thugs. Weill's jazz-tinged opera portrays the rotting self-destruction of this "city of nets," this frontier America of capitalist anarchy. Members of the audience were simultaneously repelled and thrilled by the opera. At the work's conclusion, amid the tumult, one middle-aged man stood applauding and booing. Politicizing clouded the once-clear lines of the European avant-garde's "Americanism." Avant-gardists assailed bourgeois culture, only to be attacked themselves from the extreme political left and right. Of *Jonny* a Soviet critic wrote, "Here love is perverted into an animal, cattle-like cupiscence; there is nothing in it but filth, dirt, cold cruelty and sticky frog-like sexuality, combined with the dry rationalism of a biped calculating machine."[50]

No Yankee could have said it better. And in fact, centennial composers and Soviet critics shared a Victorian anti-avant-gardist aesthetic, one in the service of national redemption, the other in the service of bourgeois-Marxist apologetics.[51] Yet with such "friends," how could New England cope with its enemies?

Having drawn their symbols from the common fund of Victorian cultural discourse, Yankees were condemned to see others dip into the same reservoir. Yankee composers could not hope to provide cultural leadership for America if they could not control the meaning of the metaphors central to such a task. They had invested heavily in symbols which, manipulated by adversary critics, took on lives of their own. New England and Europe were no longer speaking the same language, as it were. What was culture? What was modernism? What was jazz? What, in the light of all that was America? And whose?

5

PASSING THE TORCH

The great trial of Yankee redemptive culture came in the 1920s, just at
the time when the centennial composers were grooming America's
future musical leaders. Mason at Columbia, Smith at Yale, and Hill at
Harvard presided over university departments through which the responsible musical leadership of the future could be expected to pass.
Although they had not written the Great American Symphony, these
men could feel that their efforts constituted an overture to such a
monumental symbolic event. As composers, educators, and critical
essayists, they were fulfilling their calling, heavy though their cross
might sometimes be in these trying times. The coming generation
would surely reap the harvest nurtured by their labors.

If New England were to be the morning star heralding the sun in
the West, if indeed Mason's critical efforts reinforced the effect of his
art, he could feel pride as a prophet of the Great American Symphony.
Like Thoreau, he would have overcome the self-doubts that ate at him
as a young man. In an early draft of *Walden*, Thoreau had written, "I
could tell a pitiful story respecting myself, with a sufficient list of
failures, and flow as humbly as the very gutters." Thoreau's revision of
this passage "became the motto" of *Walden* itself: "I do not propose to
write an ode to dejection, but to brag as lustily as Chanticleer in the
morning, standing on his roost, if only to wake my neighbors up."[1]
This latter version supplied the inspiration and title for Mason's most
popular composition, *Chanticleer Overture*. It was the keynote of his
life's work.

Had the cultural dislocations of the 1920s not overwhelmed Yankee musical ideals, Mason could have employed his analogy between

evil and dissonance to explain away the blues. Like Thoreau or Emerson, the centennial Yankee could have drawn a kind of prophetic strength from the bleakness of his present situation to project yet brighter days for the Republic. Dissonant jazz brought Americans face to face with the banal aspects of their civilization. Like evil stumbled upon in the dark hour of the soul, jazz could serve to remind Americans that their true self, embodied in a transcedent national culture, was yet to be fully realized. But the jazz spirit was no mere stumbling block; it was more like an alien plague that had infected the next generation of American composers, a generation apparently intent on selling out the Yankee mission.

Mason had articulated better than any member of his generation the desire to create a Yankee musical identity, to compose an overture to tomorrow, to pass the torch of culture to forthcoming generations. Of course, passing the torch to younger artists necessarily involves certain tensions. The members of the old guard must expect to be affronted by antiestablishment gestures. Some of their own dreams would be incompletely fulfilled by the youth they tutored. But the centennial Yankees never got the chance to play indulgent parents to their rambunctious progeny. The young turks of the 1920s were no spiritual kin of New England.

The native-born composers of emerging prominence in the twenties, born during the years 1895–1900, were diverse in every respect. Too many of them failed to pass through Columbia, Harvard, or Yale to become disciples of the centennial Yankees; some missed the beneficent touch of college altogether. They were ethnically, geographically, and aesthetically a motley crew: William Grant Still (1895), a black man from the deep South, studied at Oberlin and New England conservatories and eventually settled in California; the New England representative was Roger Sessions (1896), an eclectic-modernist, both serial and neoclassic, via Harvard and Yale; Howard Hanson (1896), of Swedish parents, educated in his native Nebraska, in New York (with Percy Goetschius), and at Northwestern University, a modern-romanticist, made the Eastman School of Music a vehicle for mainstream American composition; Virgil Thomson (1896), Missouri rebel via Harvard and Paris, composed elegantly daft Americana and wrote wickedly brilliant criticism, both of enduring quality; Henry Cowell (1897), born in Menlo, California, was allowed by his parents to do as he pleased, and what pleased him early were experiments in musical sonority; Roy Harris (1898), of self-celebrated Oklahoma birth in a log cabin, studied with Arthur Farwell; George Gershwin (1898), Lower East Side Jewish, studied piano and harmony classically but went straight to Tin Pan Alley; George Antheil (1900), from Trenton, of Polish parents, created a futurist-dadaist career as "Bad Boy of American Music" until he tired of it; Aaron Copland (1900), like Gershwin a Brooklyn-born Jew and student of Goldmark, like Thomson and Harris a Paris student of Nadia Boulanger, composed in modern idioms both popular and severe. This heterodox, heterogeneous assemblage represented in microcosm much that the centennial Yankees feared.

Most of the younger men seemed indifferent to marriage, that Victorian bulwark of personal responsibility and social continuity. Several led bohemian lifestyles; some were evidently homosexuals. Their lack of adherence to Victorian standards in life and art marked most of them as unfit to inherit the mantle of the Yankee musical mission. George Gershwin made no secret of his bachelor philanderings.[2] Nor could Virgil Thomson's lifestyle have been calculated to calm worries about the respectability of the American musical community in "gay Paree." From among the younger group, Ives had made friends with Henry Cowell, an explorer in sound after Ives's own heart, and a man not attracted to the objectionably bohemian lifestyle of Varèse. Cowell's efforts in behalf of Ives's music were prodigious. But in 1936 Cowell was arrested for having homosexual relations with a minor.[3] Ives, the genteel Victorian, was crushed. He not only refused to help Cowell, he swore never to see him again. Eventually Ives softened his adamant stand, but only after Cowell redeemed himself through marriage. This younger generation seemed a sorry lot to take up the torch for an emergent American musical culture.

The Jewish Nexus

Nationalistic use of jazz by several prominent Jews among the younger composers transformed a generational spat into an ethnic free-for-all. George Gershwin and Aaron Copland elided elements of popular jazz and classical music. Gershwin approached this synthesis from a popular, Copland from a classical, background. Gershwin, Copland, and Ernest Bloch, an older, Swiss-born Jew, seemed to challenge the Yankees for control of America's musical destiny. These Jewish composers sought to write characteristically American music. Their critical and popular success attracted attention to their Jewishness, much of it adverse, almost all of it stereotypical.

Writers of every stamp associated Jews with the success of jazz, with the fusion of jazz and classical music, with the domestic avant-garde movement, and with an overall challenge to Yankee leadership of musical culture. A few were pleased with their perceptions; some were horrified; most were bemused and irritated. Overall, Jews were viewed as the linchpin of a nominally American modernism. Yankee composers saw redemptive culture threatened by a radical romantic expressionism rooted in the undisciplined hedonism of the black jungle, and by mechanistic civilization, based on the worship of things. The Jewish nexus linked hedonism and mechanism in con-sumer capitalism through a concern with superficial creature comforts. Whether approved or disapproved, whether articulated by Jew or gen-tile, by anti-Semite or philo-Semite, the Jewish nexus seemed to ex-plain the popularity of jazzy modernism. Critics interpreted music such as Ernest Bloch's *America* and Gershwin's *Rhapsody in Blue* as emblematic of a Jewish interest in redemptive culture.

For those already mesmerized by the logic of race, a dialectical turn sufficed to explain why Jews seemed to be conducting a black mass in the church of national consciousness. Western history was ripe to rotting with racial metaphors for Jewishness. In Europe prior to the French Revolution, religion, not color, nourished the images and asso-ciations that defined Jewishness. As religious aliens, living representa-tives of a past that Christianity was supposed to have replaced, Jews had long been forced into legally and economically marginal roles. They were defined as social deviants: rootless, manipulative middle-men. Since the early nineteenth century, when Jews were admitted to citizenship status in several Western countries, the religious metaphor of Jew-as-horned-Devil was replaced gradually by the racial metaphor of Jew-as-Oriental. Orientalism, expressing the Jews' spiritual exclu-sion from the nation, sucked like an undertow at the advancing wave of emancipation. Legally Jews might be citizens of the state; but cultur-ally they could be portrayed as a rootless race, alien to the ideal of a unitary people.[4]

The metaphor of Jews as middlemen was given a specifically racial formulation by the Count de Gobineau in 1853. His *Essay on the Inequality of the Races* exhibits one of the major preoccupations of post-revolutionary "sociologies": "the definition and creation of an 'elite' to replace the aristocracy." Instead of Jefferson's "natural aristocracy," Coleridge's "Clerisy," or Arnold's "Saving Remnant," Gobineau "proposed a 'race of princes,' the Aryans." Though Aryans were the most "noble, intelligent and vital" white stock, they were particularly susceptible to miscegenation. Gobineau termed "semitization" the miscegenation whereby black blood pollutes white blood. A gradual simplification of Gobineau's racial categories by others fixed Jews as Oriental agents of "semitization." By the end of the nineteenth century, Jews were characterized as Oriental middlemen between whites and blacks. Jewish stereotypes, like Negro stereotypes, tended to be dualistic. Jews were projected as the personification of coarse sensuality and of manipulative cleverness.[5]

This ambivalence toward Jews and their role in Western culture had been true of Gobineau, a man with anti-Semitic tendencies; it was true of Lazare Saminsky, a Jewish composer and cantor in the 1920s; and it remains true of John Murray Cuddihy and John Higham, contemporary sociologist and historian respectively. Gobineau felt that though "semitization" sapped the social strength of Nordic civilization, it fed the efflorescence of the arts, music especially. On balance, Gobineau denounced "semitization."[6] Saminsky, a Russian-born New York Jew, distinguished two roots of Jewish musical culture: Hebrew and Judaic. "The Judaic type is grounded in the sharply rhythmic and ultra-expressive, orientalized idiom showing an abundance of borrowed and neutralized traits." Saminsky despised "Judaic" music, created, he believed, by Diaspora ghetto existence. He acidly attacked much of Copland's music as the product of a scheming, ghetto Jew. By contrast, the "Hebraic order is rooted in the traditional religious melos with its rich and calm ornamental recitative, with its fine major turns so characteristic of the old synagogal song."[7] John Murray Cuddihy, a gentile sociologist, writes in a time when *race* has lost virtually all positive resonances. *Ethnicity* is today's euphemistic substitute for *race* as it was understood in the 1920s. And in some quarters the "Protestant ethic" serves as a laundered equivalent for what used to be called Anglo-Saxon spirit. Cuddihy accepts sociologist Talcott Parsons's Weberian interpretation of modernization "as a secularization of Protestant Christianity" demanding "differentiation" in all sectors of life. Cuddihy portrays a characteristically plucky, culturally obtuse Jew who blunders through contemporary Protestant civilization because he cannot suppress his id; he lacks "civility." Whatever Cuddihy's terms, he still pigeonholes Jews between WASPs and, by implication, the hopelessly hedonistic Negroes.[8]

John Higham, a sympathetic scholar of American immigration history, portrays Jews as the vanguard for a modern culture that "has undermined puritanical attitudes toward worldly enjoyment."

> A consumption ethic, in short, has superseded a production ethic. As this transition went forward swiftly in the 1940's and 1950's, the cultural distance closed between Jews, who had always appreciated pleasure and other Americans. Jewish entertainers . . . novelists . . . and . . . literary critics . . . became leading disseminators of an urban morality which gave a new emphasis to hedonism, intellectuality, and anxiety.[9]

While Cuddihy emphasizes the role of Jews as strangers from the past who have stayed to haunt even a secularized Christian culture,[10] Higham portrays Jews as harbingers of a modern American consciousness "saturated with the emerging hedonistic ethos of mass consumption, mass culture society."[11] Consumption capitalism is the common ground where Higham's modernist Jew and Cuddihy's atavistic Jew meet.

And so it was for writers such as Mason, who supposed that Jews reconciled in the marketplace the two faces of jazzy modernism: urban mechanism and jungle hedonism. Mason was among those who wondered aloud whether Jews supplied the artists, controlled the channels of distribution, and filled the concert halls with a new kind of audience. Not only were Jews increasingly prominent among American composers and performers; they alone among the new immigrants dared to meddle in things sacred—the national culture itself. Mason felt that composers such as Copland and Bloch were despoiling redemptive culture and creating in its place a musical asphalt jungle.

The attitudes of Mason and Ives must also be seen against the particular history of Yankee attitudes toward Jews. Yankees had a long, intimate, and ambiguous relationship with Judaism and Jewishness. Sacvan Bercovitch notes that "total identification—literal, spiritual, and figural—of Old Israel and New is a distinguishing trait of the jeremiads in the last decades of the seventeenth century."[12] With that in mind, Yankees distinguished the "noble ancient Hebrew" from the "repugnant modern Jew." In the mid-nineteenth century, a complex mixture of philo-Hebraism and anti-Semitism could be found among Brahmins such as James Russell Lowell and Charles Eliot Norton. The emergence of Jews "from ghettos into polite society became a recurring topic of conversation . . . among the Cambridge circle of the 1870s." Social gains for Jews underscored a sense of loss among Yankees.

Barbara Solomon distinguishes the ambivalence of Norton's and Lowell's generation from the unbalanced anti-Semitism of Henry Adams, common among his Yankee generation. Adams no longer felt the call of New England's mission. He sank into a savage despondency. Mason's response to Jews varied from the ambivalence of Norton to the viciousness of the older Henry Adams. Charles Ives, on the other hand, was rather more like Charles W. Eliot, who wrote, "I should like to be saved from loss of faith in democracy as I grow old and foolish. I should be very sorry to wind up as the three Adamses did. I shall not, unless I lose my mind." Like Eliot, Ives refused to blame immigration for what he took to be the loss of will among the Yankees themselves.[13]

Centennial composers such as Mason had scripted themselves as America's democratic elite, the cultural vanguard of progressivism. Through tradition, redemptive culture justified their calling to create the symbols of a prophetic future. Race was but a minor rhetorical sign of their inner grace. But during the 1920s, the scavenger metaphors of racialism ravaged the ideal of tradition from the inside. Racialism grew at the expense of the idealism that had allowed Yankee composers to tout redemptive culture as a civil religion. Critics identified the alleged hedonism of jazz with the music's genesis among Negroes; similarly, the popularity of jazz and its challenge to classicism came to be associated with Jews. If black jazzmen personified the primitivist atavism of modernism, Jewish composers personified the "semitization" of American culture. Jews allegedly mistook the centripetal energy of civilization for the cohesive power of culture. Thus the centennial generation felt that when Jews such as Gershwin composed classical music, they communicated not the spiritual harmony of the country's oldest lineage but the anarchic rattle of urban America.

While anti-Semites made Jews scapegoats for the anomic features of modern life, others saw Jews as heroes for trying to bridge the widening chasms of sensibility in American society. But most observers were simply puzzled, unable to resolve into a common focus their images of Jews, jazz, modernism, and America. Attitudes were seldom unmixed.

The American concert public associated the superhuman presence of great virtuosi with a Slavic pedigree. Liszt's magnetism was the model of a nineteenth-century concert idol. Paderewski's visits to the United States in the 1890s were greeted by a clamor that had as much to do with his romantic aura as with his pianism. Because the Slavic element of the new immigration was mostly Jewish, popular usage increasingly blurred the distinction between Jews-as-Slavs and Jews-as-Orientals. The myth of Slavic charisma was a heavy burden for aspiring American musicians with homely names. To acquire a Slavic pedigree, a darkly romantic one, even a Jewish one, would not hurt a classical musician's American career. Thus when concert manager Henry Wolfsohn learned that the talented and beautiful pianist in his office was named Lucy Hickenlooper, he knew they had a problem. "No Mayflower business should be suggested by your name," admonished Wolfsohn:

> If anything connects you with New England, everybody will find you cold. You could smash a piano at every concert and they would still say you had no artistic temperament. . . . *You* will be alone on a bare stage playing abstract music on a black and white piano. God help you if anybody finds you cold in the bargain. No, you can't take any of these Anglo-Saxon names. Haven't you anything Slavic anywhere?[14]

Lucy Hickenlooper became Olga Samaroff and later, by marriage, Olga Samaroff Stokowski. While it is impossible to know whether Wolfsohn was sensitive more to his own or his audiences' preconceptions, Olga Samaroff succeeded as a concert pianist, teacher, and critic.

Unlike Lucy Hickenlooper, Jacob Gershvin was born with a Russian Jewish name. Before he became involved in a musical career, Jacob Gershvin became George Gershwin.[15] Though he never gave up his anglicized name, Gershwin retained a humorous awareness of its import. In 1921, just before he catapulted from Broadway to the classical concert stage, he wrote, with his brother Ira (born Israel), a song about "Mischa, Jascha, Toscha, Sascha," who "all began to play the fiddle / in Darkest Russia." The refrain explains the moral:

Temp'ramental Oriental Gentlemen are we:
Mischa, Jascha, Toscha, Sascha—
Fiddle-lee, diddle-lee, dee.
Shakespeare says, "What's in a name?"
With him we disagree.
Names like Sammy, Max or Moe
Never bring the heavy dough
Like Mischa, Jascha, Toscha, Sascha—
Fiddle-lee, diddle-lee, dee.[16]

Born in the Brownsville section of Brooklyn in 1898, Gershwin grew up in the streets of Manhattan's Lower East Side. From 1900 to 1917, the family changed addresses twenty-eight times, following the many enterprises of Morris Gershwin. At ten, the rough-and-tumble George came under the spell of music in the person of Maxie Rosenweig, a neighborhood violin prodigy. Two local piano teachers failed to crush Gershwin's nascent musical enthusiasm before Charles Hambitzer took the fourteen-year-old under his wing. Gershwin supplemented Hambitzer's piano lessons by two years of harmony, theory, and orchestration studies with an excellent musician named Edward Kilenyi. Gershwin found work as a song plugger with the successful Tin Pan Alley publisher Jerome H. Remick. He made his way up through the popular-music business until, in 1919, he wrote the music for the successful Broadway show *La, La, Lucille*. That same year his song "Swanee" caught the ear of Al Jolson. Gershwin's career was launched.[17]

By 1923, Gershwin was attracting the attention of critics and musicians of all types. Gilbert Seldes hailed Gershwin for expanding the expressive range and subtlety of jazz. Eva Gauthier, in an Aeolian Hall song recital, mixed Bellini, Purcell, Schoenberg, and Milhaud with Berlin, Kern, and Gershwin. Gershwin accompanied the popular songs, to the delight of the audience and of critics Deems Taylor and Carl Van Vechten. Gershwin's interest in classical music continued as a quiet, private stream paralleling his popular songs. In 1919 he composed a "Lullaby" for string quartet. His chamber opera *Blue Monday* (or *135th Street*), composed hastily in 1922, impressed scarcely anyone but Paul Whiteman. Brief harmony studies with the composer Rubin Goldmark in 1923 aborted because, unlike Kilenyi, Goldmark was cool toward experimentation.[18]

Gershwin's *Rhapsody in Blue*, commissioned by Paul Whiteman for a jazz concert at Aeolian Hall, galvanized opinions about the proper relationship between jazz and classical music. Gershwin, who had ruminated on the piece during idle moments, actually composed the *Rhapsody* only after a newspaper announced the concert and its date, February 12, 1924. He thought to call it *American Rhapsody*, but his brother Ira dubbed it *Rhapsody in Blue*. Gershwin decided "to kill" the "misconception" that jazz "had to be in strict time," that it "had to cling to dance rhythms." He completed the first duo-piano version in two weeks; then Ferde Grofe orchestrated it a page at a time for the specific musical talents available in Whiteman's dance orchestra. Billed as an "Experiment in Modern Music," the concert included "a handsome twelve-page program, its covers in decorative purple and gold . . . [with] annotations by Gilbert Seldes." A gaggle of musical luminaries attended: John Philip Sousa, Walter Damrosch, Leopold Godowsky, Sr., Jascha Heifetz, Fritz Kreisler, John McCormack, Sergei Rachmaninoff, Leopold Stokowski, Moritz Rosenthal, Mischa Elman, Igor Stravinsky, Victor Herbert, Ernest Bloch, and Willem Mengelberg.[19]

The concert started with the "True Form of Jazz," as in "Livery Stable Blues" and continued at length with illustrations of "Comedy Selections," "Contrast—Legitimate Scoring vs Jazzing," "Recent Compositions with Modern Score," a "Zez Confrey" collection, "Flavoring a Selection with Borrowed Themes," "Semi 'Symphonic Arrangements of Popular Melodies" by Irving Berlin, "A Suite of Serenades" by Victor Herbert (including Spanish, Chinese, Cuban, and Oriental pieces), "Adaptation of Standard Selections to Dance Rhythm," "Rhapsody in Blue," and Elgar's "Pomp and Circumstance." The audience had grown cool to the sameness of the material by the time Gershwin stepped out to play his piece. Several minutes into the *Rhapsody*, Whiteman sensed the magnitude of the occasion. "Somewhere in the middle of the score I began crying. When I came to myself I was eleven pages along." The piece achieved instantaneous popular success. Victor made a recording that sold a million copies. In its first decade, the *Rhapsody* earned Gershwin a quarter of a million dollars. As a collaborative effort, it boosted the reputations of all concerned: Gershwin, Whiteman, and Grofe.[20]

Critical reaction varied widely but was generally serious. Deems Taylor chose to emphasize the "latent talent" which the piece exposed. H. O. Osgood compared it favorably to *The Rite of Spring*. Henry T.

The smartly attired George Gershwin also wears an expression of mixed emotions. *Courtesy Mrs. Grancel Fitz.*

Finck liked it better than "Schoenberg, Milhaud, and the rest of the futurist fellows." Lawrence Gilman, at the other extreme, wrote, "Weep over the lifelessness of its melody and harmony, so derivative, so static, so inexpressive. And then recall, for contrast, the rich inventiveness of the rhythm, the saliency and vividness of the orchestra color."[21]

Reviewers for periodicals mused over the extramusical significance of Gershwin's foray into classical music. Whether Gershwin's Tin Pan Alley and Broadway music were jazz or not, critics took it as given that his "classical" pieces of the twenties, including the *Rhapsody in Blue*, *Concerto in F*, and *An American in Paris*, melded jazz and classical music. In the *Nation*, Henrietta Straus asked if this was the music of the melting pot:

> With it all one cannot but wonder whether this now Slavic, now Oriental element in jazz is not due to the fact that many of those who write, orchestrate, and play it are of Russian-Jewish extraction; whether, in fact, jazz, with its elements of the Russian, the Negro, and the native American is not that first distinctive musical phase of the melting-pot for which we have been waiting so long and which seems to have such endless possibilities.[22]

Carl Engel defended the *Concerto in F* on historical grounds, citing Haydn's use of popular "dance-hall" music. He chided those who have always "clamored against cross-breeding in art as a foredoomed *mesalliance*." Engel praised Gershwin "especially because his jazz-concerto does not contain a trace of the vulgar." Perhaps that was just what American music needed: "An addition of a little red blood has often saved the weakened blue." Mindful of the black origins of jazz, H. O. Osgood called Gershwin, "in sporting parlance," the "White Hope" of jazz.[23]

In the symbolic arena of musical culture, who would confront this rude Jack Johnson, this jazz, and take its measure? Like true sports, critics bet on their favorites. Gershwin held an early edge. But soon he was challenged by Aaron Copland, another Brooklyn-born Jew, two years Gershwin's junior.

On sociological grounds, Copland himself is rather astonished that he should have become a composer. "I was born on a street in Brooklyn that can only be described as drab. It had none of the garish color of the ghetto, none of the charm of an old New England thoroughfare, or even the rawness of a pioneer street." There was nothing in Brooklyn to attract a musician's muse. "It was simply drab." By himself, at the age of thirteen, he found a piano teacher. Two years later he tried to study harmony by correspondence course, having decided to become a composer. Inharmonious results led him, with help from his piano teacher, to Rubin Goldmark. Copland laconically identifies his teacher as "a nephew of Karl Goldmark, the famous composer of the *Queen of Sheba*." On his own Copland found the "moderns," like Scriabin. Goldmark "actively discouraged this commerce. . . . That was enough to whet any young man's appetite."[24] From his teacher he learned musical fundamentals. Increasingly he kept his composing experiments to himself.

Copland made no move to attend college; but when he first heard of plans for the Fontainebleau music school for Americans, he applied, buoyed by the dream of flight from drab Brooklyn. In 1921 he made his way to France. He found the teaching pedantic until he stumbled upon the harmony class of Nadia Boulanger. Copland mentions his pride in being the first of many young Americans to study with Boulanger. The excitement of his studies was heightened by the experience of listening to premiers of avant-garde works at the Concerts Koussevitzky. He returned to the United States in 1924 with a commission from Boulanger for a symphony for organ and orchestra. Within the year Walter Damrosch conducted his *Symphony*, with Boulanger as soloist. By extraordinary luck, Koussevitzky, who was just beginning his tenure with the Boston Symphony Orchestra, liked Copland's *Symphony*, and chose to champion the young composer. Paul Rosenfeld, critic for the *Dial*, also approved of Copland's music, and arranged for him to receive the first of the fellowships from the Guggenheim Memorial Foundation. It was a most auspicious beginning.[25]

With the acceptance of two of his piano pieces by the League of Composers, an organization formed in 1923 to promote American modern music, Copland began his long association with the league. Its founders were primarily schismatics from the International Composers' Guild (1921), which was dominated by Varèse. The guild dissolved in 1927 and reemerged in 1928 as the Pan American Association of Composers. The league was less international, less premiere-oriented than its rivals. Whereas "several of the leading Pan Americans—Cowell, Ruggles, Adolf Weiss, but *not* Ives—had tendencies toward anti-Semitism," the league was often privately dubbed "the League of Jewish Composers."[26]

When, in 1925, Koussevitzky asked Copland to compose a piece for a League of Composers concert, the young composer "was anxious to write a work that would immediately be recognized as American in character." Copland recalled, "I wanted frankly to adopt the jazz idiom and see what I could do with it in a symphonic way." He had listened to jazz at Harlem nightspots like the Cotton Club in 1920–21, but it didn't catch his imagination until he heard it in a Viennese bar in 1923. Copland noted that the "impression of jazz one receives in a foreign country is totally unlike the impression of such music heard in one's own country. . . . When I heard jazz played in Vienna, it was like hearing it for the first time." Arnold Dobrin writes that "during his first years in Paris, Aaron was astonished to discover the high respect with which so many cultured people regarded jazz."[27] After Koussevitzky played Copland's *Music for the Theatre* at the League of Composers concert in October 1925, Copland began his second, and last, major piece to use jazz elements. His *Concerto* for piano and orchestra was premiered in January 1927, with Koussevitzky conducting the Boston Symphony Orchestra and Copland himself at the piano.

Paul Rosenfeld praised Copland, while denigrating Gershwin. He described Gershwin's *Concerto in F* as "a *ragout* of many flavours, multi-colored little pieces of not too fine a quality." Rosenfeld seemed offended by the eclecticism of Gershwin's concerto: "Jazz beats and shuffles. Blues add the Yiddish to the darky wail." Gershwin, he thought, tried to rise above jazz to use classical material, but Copland drew upon jazz from within the walls of musical culture. "Art," emphasized Rosenfeld, "is Copland's distinction." In three of the movements of *Music for the Theatre*, "the composer has found the first, early state of his personal idiom, while in the two jazz episodes he is still moving toward an ironic, barbaric scherzo-style equally true to his clear balanced sensibility."[28]

The popular critic and author Isaac Goldberg bet on both composers, underlining the benefits of a black and Jewish symbiosis. "Perhaps the ready amalgamation of the American Negro and the American Jew goes back to something Oriental in the blood of both." Carried away by his enthusiasm for the new jazz classics, Goldberg made over Copland's youth, suggesting that he was weaned on ragtime and jazz. He praised Copland for introducing "into jazz a spiritual content."[29]

Others perceived the matter differently. John Tasker Howard

In 1928, Brooklyn-born Aaron Copland gazes placidly through the camera. *Courtesy Performing Arts Research Center, The New York Public Library at Lincoln Center.*

expressed an ambivalent estimation of Copland's *Concerto:* "Copland has taken jazz formulae and developed them so that they are formulae no longer. Some complained that the work had no spiritual value, only animal excitement; but what else has jazz." In New York and Boston, Copland was reviled for desecrating sacred concert halls. The *Boston Evening Transcript* was moved to editorialize against this "most anti-human" outrage. Critic Philip Hale deplored Copland's "shocking lack of taste, of proportion." In New York, Samuel Chotzinoff (himself a champion of Gershwin's music) described the work as "barnyard and stable noises . . . Scriabinish fanfare." Goldberg related that in "New York a critic who wrote in Copland's favor was accused of bribery; Boston, for weeks after the concerto, echoed with remonstrance and rage."[30]

Some critics viewed Jews as Oriental agents of cultural infection. Jews brought the animality of jazz and modernism to a peak of apparent success. "As for jazz, the Negro may if he wishes claim the questionable distinction of being its originator," wrote the critic Fritz Laubenstein; but had Negro jazz "not suffered the Jewish (Semitic!) direption, it would probably have developed its own independent melody, rather than have become a parasitic mannerism preying upon the classics." Paul Rosenfeld, championing the music of Ernest Bloch (born Swiss, in 1880, Bloch settled in the United States in 1916), felt it necessary to dispute those who associated the Jewish Bloch with jungle animality. "Figuration of Bloch as the *hetman* of a tribe of unusually ferocious chimpanzees is so inevitable that it is easy to forget that the tenderest, most reverend spirit in contemporary music issues from him." In the twenties, every arbiter of public opinion concerned himself with the character of American music. Henry Ford's organ, the *Dearborn Independent*, took note "of the organized eagerness of the Jew to make an alliance with the Negro." In the United States, "picturesque, romantic, clean" popular songs had been replaced by "the African period, being the entrance of the jungle motif . . . which swiftly degenerated into a rather more bestial type than the beasts themselves arrive at." Jews took over and directed the spread of this "monkey talk, jungle squeals, grunts and squeaks and gasps suggestive of cave love" to the general public. The Jews provided just the right "touch of cleverness to camouflage the moral filth."[31] The *Dearborn Independent* serves as a touchstone of extreme anti-Semitic opinion during the 1920s. Its analysis of the Jewish relationship to jazz differs in viciousness, but not in character, from the spectrum of opinions expressed elsewhere.

"The Jew" was held responsible for spreading the sexual characteristics of Negro jazz and blamed for insinuating a jazz element into classical music, thus creating avant-garde gibberish. He was also called to account for the fusion of the jungle with the inhumanity of mechanistic, urban civilization. "The Jew" functioned always as a middleman, it seemed, making possible the devolution of native Anglo-Saxon music. As the Jewish neighborhood preceded the black neighborhood—the "asphalt jungle"—Jews paved the way for an urban anticulture of mechanism and primitivism.

While there was fairly wide agreement that Jews were popularizing jazz at the expense of Yankee classicism, the desirability of the process was debated. Gilbert Seldes found himself with more questions than answers as he probed these issues:

> Can the Negro and the Jew stand in the relation of a folk to a nation? And if not, can the music they create be the national music?
>
> There is this possibility: that as the American winds around himself layer after layer of civilization, he diminishes a little the vigour of his specific characteristics. . . . The Negro, certainly, holds to a pace and a rhythm different from these of our large cities; he still loafs, is carefree, avoids business a little, remains a trace more primitive in the expression of emotions not altogether foreign to the white man. Possibly, then, the outcast and the foreigner can apprehend certain spiritual truths about America.
>
> That hypothesis . . . would hardly explain the snap and surprise of current jazz. It is a rough generalization that the rhythm of jazz corresponds to the rhythm of our machinery. . . . we cannot say that a simple civilization (the African) by accident hit upon the complex one (our own). (Perhaps the African civilization was of a high order, like ours.) We could then account for the dominance of the Russian-Jewish composer, in the use of this material, as the advantage of one who remains above the battle and holds fast, as those in the *melee* cannot, to his artistic impulses.[32]

Seldes was convinced that he had found the pieces to a coherent puzzle, but he didn't know how they should be arranged. Mason, too, found himself uncertain how to characterize modern music, how to relate his musical perceptions to his social beliefs. The trouble with the modernists, he wrote, is their "concentration on the sensuous moment rather than on the mental span." But earlier in the same book he attacked this modern music "whose interest is less aesthetic than intel-lectual or social."³³ Is modern music characterized by "the sensuous moment" or by "intellectual and social" factors? Mason thought both; but he could not easily combine such apparent opposites.

By contrasting "the Yankee" and "the Jew," Mason found a satis-fying answer to the apparent schizophrenia of modern music. Pre-cisely that: "the Jew" and his so-called avant-garde aesthetic represent a moral sickness, a schizophrenia of the spirit. Having no rootedness, no focus in his artistic vision, "the Jew" gropes about and patches together inorganic works by means of eclecticism:

> Why [the Yankee] . . . attitude thus based on moderation should have received so far such slight and sporadic expression in our music, instead of infusing it with a pervasive and dominating individuality, is not hard to understand when we reflect that the particular type of foreign pres-tige to which we have most completely capitulated is precisely that Jewish type which, if not exactly based on the "falsehood of extremes," at least tolerates, perhaps even enjoys, extremes, as a soberer music cannot. The Jew and the Yankee stand in human temperament, at polar points; where one thrives, the other is bound to languish.
>
> And our whole contemporary aesthetic attitude toward instrumen-tal music, especially in New York, is dominated by Jewish tastes and standards, with their Oriental extravagance, their sensuous brilliancy and intellectual facility and superficiality, their general tendency to exaggeration and disproportion.³⁴

Cosmopolitan urban commercialism, recently aggravated by the Jew-ish invasion, threatened Yankee culture, thought Mason.

While he believed that "the Yankee" represents the vital center of American character, Mason recognized the existence of other superficially "more widespread" traits, known as "American hustle." "Its natural musical expression is found, of course, in jazz." But jazz "is a commercial product, like so many others 'put over' upon the people." In any event, "it reflects, not our health, vitality and hope, but our restlessness, our fatigue, and our despair." How could that be? How could the American people be sold such a bill of goods? " 'But how do the Jews do it?' is a question often asked," noted the *Dearborn Independent*. "The answer is, not public demand, nor artistic merit, nor musical ingenuity, nor poetic worth—no; the answer is simple sales-manship." In his pursuit of the dollar, "the Jew" concentrates all his crafty intelligence on the sale.³⁵

Jews were accused of picking at the cheap tinsel of American life, arranging it with eye-catching, superficial originality, then selling it to one and all. Variants of this argument were directed against Jewish composers (collectively and individually) by writers of every stamp. "In this business of making the people's songs, the Jews have shown, as usual, no originality but very much adaptability," wrote the *Dearborn Independent*, "which is a charitable term used to cover plagiarism, which in its turn politely covers the crime of mental pocket-picking. The Jews do not create; they take what others have done, give it a clever twist, and exploit it."[36] Here was the surface glitter of American life, argued Mason, not the national heartbeat. Mason used Copland to illustrate the cosmopolitan Jewish type of composer overrepresented in Boston, at the expense of "more American" composers like himself.[37] Eclectic Jews "put over" on people their tricked-out jazzy modernism.

Although the Holocaust devalued the currency of explicitly racist anti-Semitism, people continued to draw on the available pool of metaphors when characterizing a composer and his music as Jewish. As late as 1949, a critic skewered Copland with a veritable litany of codewords and code images:

> In American music, Aaron Copland is the great man for small deeds; a "shrewd investor of pennies," as Theodore Chandler describes him. A small, cool creative gift, but an ego of much frenetic drive, a devious personality with a feline *savoir faire*, with his fine commercial acumen and acute sense of the direction of today's wind, Aaron Copland is primarily a shrewd manager of *musique a succes*. He everlastingly changes his palette, his composing technique and his advertising technique. . . . His is a flagrant example of composer by propaganda. Quite early this alert, suave businessman of music began to sway his esthetics with the claims of the day.[38]

Copland is portrayed as "shrewd" and "devious," a man with great drive, acutely interested in money as the measure of success. He allegedly tunes his small talent to current fashion trends. He sells himself through "advertising" and "propaganda." The critic, incredibly, was music director at New York's prestigious Temple Emanu-El, Lazare Saminsky. Saminsky saw Copland as the most Jewish of American composers, one whose music represented "the well-known ghetto-type." Saminsky was simultaneously anti-Semitic and philo-Hebraic. Thus, while he attacked Copland the "ghetto" Jew, he also praised the "Hebrew soul such as flows in the gently, nobly warm and wistful melos of the slow movements in [Copland's] *Music for the Theatre*."[39] Jews and gentiles alike found their characterizations colored by tenacious, tendentious metaphors. Cultured in the ideological greenhouse of Europe, the stereotypes were transplanted to the landscape of American society. Jews were viewed as a clever, hedonistic, Oriental race. Perhaps, thought some, "the Jew" engineered the absurd success of jazzy modernism. If so, by what means did "the Jew" manipulate public taste?

Mason concluded that immigrant Jewish performers were primarily responsible for what he viewed as the undue attention bestowed upon Jewish and foreign music. Another writer later referred to the influx of these foreign musicians as the "second invasion" (considering the German influx of the 1840s as the first).[40] Composers such as Ernest Bloch, Darius Milhaud, Schoenberg, and Stravinsky came for increasingly long visits; eventually some decided to stay. (Stravinsky was not Jewish, though he got used to people's assuming that he was.)[41] Performers such as Koussevitsky, Stokowski, Rubinstein, Horowitz, Heifetz, and Piatagorsky strengthened the impression of a Russian Jewish invasion. And Jews seemed to be taking over the audience as well as the stage. A critic for the *New York Post*, in a scathing review of music by Ernest Bloch ("hot in the mouth with curry, ginger and cayenne"), reported that "Mr. Bloch got plenty of applause from a large audience, largely of the Oriental persuasion."[42] Jews did, in fact, constitute a sizable new concert audience. Of a Lewisohn Stadium all-Gershwin concert, attended almost exclusively by Jews, B. H. Haggin wrote that praise of Gershwin's classical efforts provided some patrons "with an excuse for enjoying popular music and for thinking that when they did so they were enjoying cultivated music."[43] Mason attacked the "highbrow," oversophisticated audiences who applaud whatever is fashionable. Of the newest parvenus, he wrote, "The luxurious classes become pampered and bored, and develop through [their] very vacuity a perverted taste for the unusual, the queer, the generally upside down and backside to."[44] A serious composer could scarcely reach out to the potential audience beyond the concert hall, when his small real audience was being dominated by an upwardly mobile but tasteless mob.

Some thought that the salvation of musical culture lay in exploitation of the new sound technologies; but when the media would not bend to the progressive will of Yankee classicism, they were branded tools of cosmopolitan Jewish manipulation. During the interwar years,

Serge Koussevitzky, Aaron Copland, and Leonard Bernstein (right to left) together formed three remarkable generations of mentors and disciples. *Courtesy Performing Arts Research Center, The New York Public Library at Lincoln Center.*

composers, critics, and educators pursued a nervous love affair with the nascent audio media, the phonograph and radio. Extravagant hopes were voiced that this "mechanical music" could be drafted to the progressive cause of bringing "good music" to the American people.[45] The emergence of commercial radio broadcasting in 1920 gave new vigor to the musical missionaries. Some of the arguments for and against the phonograph and radio had been rehearsed in prior disputes over the pianola, or mechanical piano player. Mason's mentor Arthur

Whiting had written a small-town scenario in which a newly arrived pianola kills folks' desire to play for themselves: "Its security puts all hand-playing to shame." Mason argued that mechanical music initially aggravated public indifference to classical music "by increasing access to rubbish and inattentiveness to everything." But eventually repetition renders "intolerable the conventionality, triviality, and emptiness of the popular,' [while] increasing understanding reveal[s] the permanent beauty of what is classic." Thus, for example, farmers requested "the radio companies to give them less jazz." A writer for the *Nation* waxed enthusiastic over the prospect of Walter Damrosch's conducting educational classical concerts over the air. David Sarnoff had hired Damrosch to oversee the direction of RCA's cultural commitment. Said Damrosch, "Give me the children and I will make a nation of music lovers." Another enthusiast wrote, "The greatest force of the talking machine is the democratising and educational influence."[46]

But all did not go as planned. Just as Tin Pan Alley found that it could not control the phonograph to its advantage, musical missionaries discovered that they could not do as they wished with the new media. It was true, as sociologists noted, that "mechanical inventions such as the phonograph and radio are bringing Middletown more contacts with more kinds of music than ever before." But Americans were insufficiently attentive to the classics to suit some people. Mason became discouraged that public inertia and the "commercialism" of radio and phonograph companies hindered the spread of musical literacy to all Americans. He thought that perhaps radio should be taken out of commercial hands. Others attacked the "Mass Media." From Norman, Oklahoma came the complaint: "Power complexes known as the radio industry are impoverishing the musical life of our regions by pre-empting the listening ear of every town, hamlet and farm home in the nation."[47]

Yet the large companies were not really ignoring classical music. As early as 1922 a complete concert of the New York Philharmonic was broadcast. Throughout the Depression, network commitment to classical music grew; and by the end of the decade all three major systems maintained a symphony orchestra. NBC devoted a third more airtime to classical music than the national average of all radio stations.[48] The real rub lay elsewhere.

Mason wrote to a friend in 1939 that he hoped to convince a major record company (probably Victor, where his former student Samuel

Chotzinoff wielded influence) to record some of his own music. The Yankee composer felt he was not getting adequate exposure. Why did his music go begging while Victor's recording of Gershwin's *Rhapsody in Blue* sold a million albums? New York and Hollywood were sucking the country's regions dry. Pointing to the prominence of Jews such as David Sarnoff in the new media, some Americans believed there existed a New York-Hollywood axis of Jewish cultural control.[49]

New York had been condemned for hollow brilliance, bigness, and business long before Jews played a significant role in its affairs. In 1744, a doctor from Annapolis denigrated fast-talking New Yorkers: "To talk bawdy and have a knack at punning passes among some there for good sterling wit." Urban historians note that "as early as the 1830's, New York had . . . acquired its reputation as the city of frenetic hustle and bustle." Foreign visitors, too, came to gawk at this "magnum opus of modern material civilization."[50] But by the mid-1920s, New York had become the geographical codeword for the mass media, for Jewishness, for jazz and the avant-garde, for the assorted urban ills of contemporary American civilization. Like the novelist Thomas Wolfe, many Americans were fascinated by New York, as they were fascinated by Jews. They didn't care to think where one left off and the other began.

Reporting on "The Attack on New York" in 1926, one writer noted that "the most fundamental charge being brought by its critics against New York is the charge that here is an 'alien' city, literally un-American and anti-American in its make-up." The journalist-historian Mark Sullivan suggested that "one is justified in doubting whether as much as ten per cent of New York's population is American in the sense of possessing, in the form of a heritage, old American ideals, prejudices, and characteristics." The country believed that New York lacked "American ideals as an inheritance from white American ancestry." The nativist author Madison Grant contended that "the man of the old stock is being crowded out of many country districts by these foreigners, just as he is today being literally driven off the streets of New York City by the swarms of Polish Jews." An Oregon anti-Semite complained about cities where "the Kikes are so thick that a white man can hardly find room to walk on the sidewalk." Reviewing John Tasker Howard's *Our American Music*, Oscar Thompson lamented that "the night club, not the great vault of the open sky . . . enlivens so many conceptions of what our music should be. It is the city composer who babbles most of capturing the spirit of the machine age." Ruggle's friend, the artist Thomas Hart Benton, grew increasingly restive about the influence of foreigners and Jews on American culture. He attacked the photographer Alfred Steiglitz as a symbol of decadent, foreign, effeminate, urban modernism. Some critics viewed the problem as that of conflicting localisms. There is "no American capital from which . . . [culture] naturally flows. . . . The nervous shriek of New York clamors stridently against the Anglicized Boston accent." Ultimately, "there is no cultural *modus vivendi*."⁵¹ By no means were critics of New York necessarily anti-Semites. But by general usage, the language with which people described New York grew to be coextensive with the images employed to describe American Jews.

Boosters and detractors of modern music equated it with the noise of cities like New York. Gershwin was pleased at the musical influence of the "machine age." He felt that "music is one of the arts which appeals directly through the emotions. Mechanism and feeling will have to go hand in hand, in the same way that a skyscraper is at the same time a triumph of the machine and a tremendous emotional experience, almost breathtaking." The city and the machine entered into many of Gershwin's inspirations. "It was on the train, with its steely rhythms, its rattle-ty-bang," that the construction of the *Rhapsody in Blue* came to him. "I heard it as a sort of kaleidoscope of America—of our vast melting pot, of our unduplicated national pep, of our blues, our metropolitan madness." His *Second Rhapsody* was originally titled *New York Rhapsody*, then *Rhapsody of Rivets*. As with *Rhapsody in Blue*, Gershwin was persuaded to substitute a more vaguely impressionistic title.⁵²

Just as genteel Yankees such as Mason and Ives escaped when they could from the "hell hole" of New York to their country retreats, their generation increasingly held to the conviction that art should provide an escape from the noise, bustle, and materialism of city life. It was one thing for Beethoven to include the sounds of country life in a symphony, quite another for composers to insert taxi horns, airplane propellers, typewriters, riveting guns, and train sounds into their music.⁵³ Noise was antimusic, or "anarchy" in Matthew Arnold's use of the term. As machines were not musical, New York was not America. "It is folly," wrote Mason, "to assume that art, which ought to be a relief from [modern civilization] . . . should reflect its defects, and madness to consent to such a debasement."

> This is the essential absurdity of all contemporary movements which try to model music on factories, locomotives, or skyscrapers, to bring art down to robots and morons. . . . One hardly knows whether to laugh or cry when, after travelling perhaps miles through a subway to reach a concert hall, breathing a sigh of relief and preparing to be lifted out of all this sordidness and confusion, the music at length begins, and proves to be only a poor imitation of more subway.[54]

While Mason complained in print, other Yankees protested with their feet. Ruggles set up shop in rural Vermont, where he fixed up an old one-room schoolhouse.

George Antheil's *Ballet Mecanique* focused attention on the avant-garde notion that noise and music need not be mutually exclusive, even if, or especially if, Matthew Arnold should turn in his grave. Antheil, a Polish-American composer, born in Trenton, New Jersey in 1900, set out to be outrageous. He built a career on dadaist-futurist naughtiness; he advertised himself as a musical Tom Sawyer. Antheil claimed to have invented many of the piano and percussion effects used in jazz. He, too, wrote a jazz opera. Since he was not Jewish, people searching for the ethnic roots of his avant-garde proclivities made do with his Polish ancestry. Even his boosters emphasized his Polish background over his American birth. Music critic Henrietta Straus pointedly called him a Slav:

> When he now seeks inspiration he no longer goes to the Negro orchestras, but to Morocco itself; and so he gives us the concentrated essence of what one might call the spirit of America, with all its terrific energy, its speed pressure, its machine rhythms, by the Slav out of Africa.[55]

Antheil had gone to the horse's mouth, as it were.

In "George Antheil and the Cantilena Critics," the poet William Carlos Williams questioned what it means when people reacted against modern music as Mason did:

> Here is Carnegie Hall. You have heard something of the great Beethoven and it has been charming, masterful in its power over the mind. We have been alleviated, strengthened against life—the enemy—by it. We go out of Carnegie into the subway and we can for a moment withstand the assault of the noise, failingly ! as the strength of the music dies. Such has been its strength to enclose us that we may even feel its benediction a week long.

> But as we came from Antheil's "Ballet Mecanique" a woman of our party, herself a musician, made this remark: "The subway seems sweet after that." "Good," I replied. . . . I felt that noise, the unrelated noise of life . . . had actually been mastered, subjugated.[56]

Williams saw in avant-garde music the opportunity to raise one's perceptions to a higher plateau after encountering the resistance of apparent ugliness. Art should be a means of overcoming, not of escape.[57]

But Mason coped with avant-garde modernism only reductively. To him, the triumph of modernism represented the triumph of New York, and threatened the final declension of New England. As Henry Gilbert said, with circumspection:

> Copland is a young man. He and I belong to different generations. We are poles apart as regards style of musical expression. Yet the principle which actuates us both is about the same. He also desires to write some music which, in its content, shall reflect and express American characteristics rather than European. But America to him, is New York.[58]

And through New York, noted Mason, there poured a torrent of influences. Yankee music could not make headway against the perceived Jewish menace because the New England strain was so "diluted and confused by a hundred other tendencies."[59]

The substance of Mason's social criticism, though not its tone, owed a great deal to the writings of the progressive sociologist Charles Horton Cooley. In a letter to Cooley (delivered after Cooley's death), Mason wrote that *Social Organization* was "almost the most revealing single treatment of what is the trouble with our American art that I know."[60] As an optimist who viewed art as communication, and communication as the panacea for social disequilibrium, Cooley expressed concern over the new immigration. "If they were wholly inferior, as we sometimes imagine, it would perhaps not matter much," he mused, "but the truth is that they contest every intellectual function with the older stock, and, in the universities for instance, are shortly found teaching our children their own history and literature." Though they do assimilate, the fusion is imperfect, "and in the northern United States, formerly dominated by New England influences, a revolution from this cause is well under way."

> It is as if a kettle of broth were cooking quietly on the fire, when some one should come in and add suddenly a great pailful of raw meats,

vegetables and spices—a rich combination, possibly, but likely to re-
quire much boiling. That fine English sentiment that came down to us
through the colonists more purely, perhaps, than to the English in the
old country, is passing away—as a distinct current, that is—lost in a
flood of cosmopolitan life.[61]

Agreeing with Cooley, Mason argued that from this "eclecticism,"
which resulted from tasting everything and digesting nothing, evolved
"the characteristic modern type—quick, sharp, and shallow."[62]

From time to time, Mason partially regained his old progressive
confidence. To his friend the philosopher Harry Overstreet, Mason
wrote that, along with John Powell and a few others, "I have up my
sleeve an idea no less brash than to try to insinuate gradually into our
music some expression of the English or Anglo-American qualities
that are nowadays completely choked under the modish cosmopolitanism and hard-boiled irony." But he found it truly like "crying in the
wilderness." He simply could not swallow Cooley's "kettle of broth."
"American music from 1914 to 1928 is the Music of Indigestion. Go to
a concert of any of the 'advanced' organizations of the day . . . and
listen to the rumblings and belchings of this indigestion."[63]

The struggle to shape the American self-imagination involved
duels fought with competing assimilation metaphors. Mason believed
that Yankee classicism would shape the metaphorical grammar of
American identity. But his mission was challenged by Jewish composers. Mason contended that Jews would try to displace Yankee classicism with a "falsehood of extremes." Melting pot, kettle of broth, the
music of indigestion, these were rhetorical metaphors, tactical
weapons in the larger war for control of the meta-metaphor of music
itself.[64] Who would compose the Great American Symphony?

In *The Melting Pot* (1909), Israel Zangwill popularized two
metaphors for a post-"New Immigration" America: America as the
melting pot, and America as a symphony. In Zangwill's play, David
Quixano, a young immigrant Jew, lives with his Old World grandmother and his uncle. David falls in love with a non-Jew, Vera Reven-
dal, who, it turns out, is the daughter of the Russian who oversaw the
slaughter of David's family during a pogrom. The struggle of their
love personifies the action of the American melting pot. "America is
God's Crucible," proclaims David, "the great Melting-Pot where all
the races of Europe are melting and re-forming! . . . A fig for your
feuds and vendettas! Germans and Frenchmen, Irishmen and En-

glishmen, Jews and Russians—into the Crucible with you all! God is making the American." David, an untutored genius composer, pours into his symphony hopes and idealism for a new nation among nations, higher and purer than the sordidness of Europe with its blood and diamonds. David creates America, for "the real American has not yet arrived. He is only in the Crucible, I tell you—he will be the fusion of all races, perhaps the coming superman. Ah, what a glorious Finale for my symphony—if I can only write it." Implicitly, Zangwill's assimilationist melting pot metaphor conflicts with his pluralist symphony metaphor.[65]

Assimilation or semitization, melting pot or potluck, Yankee partisans wanted nothing of the reality encompassed by these metaphors. Mason assumed that the ideal American type already had been blended, a hearty plain stock. In essence he was Uncle Sam, transcendental Yankee.[66] The Yankee composer, not some immigrant David Quixano, should create the terms of a harmonious, symphonic America. In Mason's opinion, the new immigrants were not smoothly blending into a new American type; they were a dissonant bellyache. Zangwill's play, like jazz and modernism, was itself a symptom of the problem: among the chunks of raw meats and vegetables thrown into the American pot, only a foreign Jew would have the temerity to write a play about a Jew composing the Great American Symphony. As Cooley implied, Jews dared to enter the hall of culture, the very pilothouse of the American ship.

Gentile fear of semitization fed on stereotypes of Jews as rudderless, cultureless eclectics; but paradoxically Jewish identification with the Yankee musical mission grew out of a Jewish sense of historical destiny, rooted in the "chosen people" concept.[67] Centennial composers had struggled to prove that they were destiny's chosen people, called to sing the American future. But immigrant Jews, drawing upon their own sense of historical sensibility, identified their ideals with the future of America.[68] Zangwill's decadent blue-blooded Yankee, Quincy Davenport, Jr., mocks David Quixano's identification with America: "*Your* America, forsooth, you Jew-immigrant! . . ." "Yes— Jew-immigrant!" replies David.

> But a Jew who knows that your Pilgrim Fathers came straight out of his Old Testament, and that our Jew-immigrants are a greater factor in the glory of this great commonwealth than some of you sons of the soil. It is

you freak-fashionables, who are undoing the work of Washington and
Lincoln.[69]

Zangwill's David identifies Yankee mission with Jewish mission.

The Jewish American theologian and philosopher Mordecai Kaplan gave this process of identification explicit form. The traditional
concept of the Jews as God's chosen people implicitly conflicts with
the imperatives of the democratic modern state, argued Kaplan: Jews
"realize intuitively that, if they were to persist in the literal acceptance
of that doctrine, they would have to exclude themselves from complete
self-identification with the state." Especially in the American context
it is necessary for Jews to evolve a "functional revaluation of that
belief," a kind of Jamesian moral equivalent to war. Kaplan proposed
to redefine the chosen people ideal in terms of awareness of the spiritual potentialities inherent in the concept of nationhood. "In sum, the
Jews must be prepared not only to foster their nationhood but to see in
nationhood as such, whether it be their own [Israel] or that of any
other people, the call of the spirit.[70]

There were high stakes in the symbolic battle to decide who
might compose the Great American Symphony, who might take on
the mantle of Emerson and Whitman to imagine the American dream.
Culture, the self-consciousness of the national imagination, drew
strength from the past to prophesy the future. But Mason feared that
his America could not survive the "rumblings and belchings" of an
eclectic musical culture which seemed intent on integrating all currents, including jazz, into some altogether new American symphony.
The only strand he could perceive running through this anarchy was
what he viewed as the temerity of Jews to meddle in things sacred.
Quite clearly, Yankees no longer monopolized a sense of national mission. In Kaplan's reconstruction of the chosen people concept, he
recalled the Jewish contribution to the notion of a progressive historiography. "If other peoples achieved a group *consciousness*, the Jews
achieved a group *self-consciousness*, that is, a consciousness in which
memory was long, and group imagination far-reaching. The individual
Jew lived and acted under the constant visualization of his people's
history." An important consequence of this self-consciousness "is
imagination or the power which enables a person to visualize himself
in some situation set up as a goal toward which he may strive."[71] Dared
the Jews slip into the American prophetic persona?

How could a Yankee such as Mason not quake to hear the closing lines of Zangwill's play: "Ah Vera," said David Quixano, "what is the glory of Rome and Jerusalem where all races and nations come to labour and look forward. (He raises his hands in benediction over the shining city.) Peace, peace, to all ye unborn millions, fated to fill this giant continent—the God of our *children* give you peace."[72]

Zangwill didn't really mean all nations and races. He intended to ally Jews with European-Americans. In an afterword to a revised edition of his play, Zangwill exposed his own prejudices against blacks. On just one occasion he allowed David, as an afterthought, to include Negroes in his melting pot; but Zangwill preferred that they stay in the South, or perhaps return to Africa. Yet he was not unaware of the ironies of American racial culture. He managed a bit of double-edged levity at the expense of white Christian Americans:

> Meanwhile, however scrupulously and justifiably America avoids physical intermarriage with the negro, the comic spirit cannot fail to note the spiritual miscegenation which, while clothing, commercialising, and Christianising the ex-African, has given "rag-time" and the sex-dances that go to it, first to white America and thence to the whole white world.
>
> The action of the crucible is thus not exclusively physical—a consideration particularly important as regards the Jew. The Jew may be Americanized and the American Judaized without any gamic interaction.[73]

This "spiritual miscegenation" was just what worked Mason up into such a stew.

In a case of life imitating art, Mason found himself reviewing a symphony, *America,* written by an immigrant Jew, which had won *Musical America* magazine's symphonic award for 1927. The composer, Ernest Bloch, had made the United States his home since 1916. As early as 1923, Bloch's name figured in commentary on the issue of musical "semitization":

> [Alfredo] Casella believes that, after the super-refinement of decadent European art, this nascent folk-music [of jazz] is resuscitating our frenzy and Dionysian force; he predicts that from it will spring, in turn, a 'new music' of artistic stamp. In Salzburg, at the 1922 festival, one critic seemed to find this frenzy and force in Ernest Bloch's Violin Sonata, in which he thought to recognize negro melodies. There are

those who will always see solid black, what is distinctly zebraic, if not Hebraic.[74]

Bloch's symphony *America* stirred people to question the propriety of an immigrant's taking it upon himself to express national sentiments. Critics questioned whether "a man who has only lately become American [can] fully grasp [the national vision]." Bloch set out to sing "the future credo of mankind." It was "the common purpose of widely diversified races ultimately to become one race, strong and great." In his symphony, Bloch tried to express the American experience in 1620, 1861–1865, and 1926. Jazz represents "Material 'prosperity'— Speed—Noise—'Man slave of the machines.'" The finale—the Future—"ends with an anthem, to be sung by a chorus and the audience, with the orchestra."[75]

Bloch's efforts made some Yankees nervous and angered others. John Tasker Howard, writing about "Our Contemporary Composers," decided that "if for no other motive than hospitality, we may place him here at the end of this chapter, separate from our other composers, and the reader may choose whether or not he will call him an American." "The creations of Jewish musicians in this country are Jewish music," wrote the critic W. J. Henderson. "Even Ernest Bloch's *America* sat down by the waters of Babylon."[76] Mason had warned Americans as early as 1920 that "our public taste is in danger of being permanently debauched, made lastingly insensitive to qualities most subtly and quintessentially our own, by the intoxication of what is, after all, an alien art":

> It was several years after these warnings had been written that Ernest Bloch, long the chief minister of that intoxication to our public, capped his dealings with us by the grim jest of presenting to us a long, brilliant, megalomaniac, and thoroughly Jewish symphony—entitled *America*. (In calling attention to this irony, it is hardly necessary to state that no 'anti-Jewish propaganda' is intended.)[77]

It struck Mason as a "grim jest" that Bloch dared to touch that which wasn't his.

The central irony of Mason's attack on Bloch is that Bloch himself aspired to communicate through his music many of the same sentiments which Mason held dear. Serious composers, wrote Bloch, "laboriously create their arbitrary and brain-begotten works, while the emotional element—the soul of art—is lost in the passion for me-

Ernest Bloch, attacked as a modernist Jew, here looks every bit the ancient Hebrew sage. *Courtesy New York Public Library, Lincoln Center.*

chanical perfection. Everywhere, virtuosity of means; everywhere, intellectualism exalted as the standard. This is the plague of our times, and the reason of its inevitable death." Though he would have subdued his praise of emotion, Mason might well have seconded Bloch's humanistic convictions had Bloch been a Yankee. In an apparently unanswered letter to Mason, Bloch wrote, "I do not know whether *you* feel as I do, a stranger in 'our time'—and, I must add, a stranger to most of the music written nowadays. . . . Thus I live already in the past, in the company of the great minds."[78]

The twenties were hard times for the centennial composers. They looked nostalgically forward to a morning star, presaging perhaps the sun arcing toward the West, to some young composer who could read the land. Who would speak for their past and their future? asked John Tasker Howard.

> In more recent years, jazz has come into our midst, and once again some of the nationalists thought they had found in it a panacea for all our ills. . . . Even though most of the jazz written today is a product of the sophisticated East, produced under commercial conditions, it nevertheless has its roots in the American soil. Originating with the Negroes, it has come to Broadway and Tin Pan Alley, and in a very real sense it has become a Jewish interpretation of the Negro. And what could be more American than such a combination, even though it does ignore those of us who have Puritan ancestors? The Mayflower must look elsewhere for a spokesman.[79]

At the end of the decade, Arthur Farwell Found his spirits down. Like the other Yankees, he wearied of battling in the urban wilderness. "In the last twenty years musical art has renounced melody, annihilated harmony, and courted the rhythms of the Hottentots," he wrote. Farwell thought it almost certain that "the next move will be towards some type of music that is recognizable as music. The pendulum of desperate dissonance, and clamorous cacaphony can scarcely swing farther than it has already gone." Was there hope, or would sensualism and mechanism drown the genuine voices of the representative Americans? "A childlike people, in both the good and the bad senses of the word, musically underdeveloped but promising," wrote Mason, "we find ourselves paralyzed on the very threshold of musical experience by the disillusionment, the cynicism, the blase striving after novelty, of a Europe old and in some ways effete."[80]

Yet even in the depths of his frightened and vicious polemics, Mason would reach back for the will to believe in the mission which his generation had undertaken. "One dares to hope that at last we are getting ready to outgrow our unmanly awe of Europe, preparing to look hopefully about us at our own life, and, interpreting it as it strikes our naive, unspoiled sentiment, make some music of our own."[81]

The Great White Hope

Americans looked to the West for their musical hero, for the one who would rescue the heritage of the Mayflower. John Tasker Howard recalled that mythical stature was bestowed upon Roy Harris from the beginning:

> When he first appeared on the scene, in the late 'twenties, he seemed the answer to all our prayers. Here was a genuine American, born in a log cabin in Oklahoma, like Lincoln, tall, lanky, rawboned, untouched by the artificial refinements of Europe or even the stultifying commercialism of cosmopolitan New York; a prophet from the Southwest who thought in terms of our raciest folk-tunes. Small wonder that we called him the white hope of American music.[82]

America needed not a clever arranger of musical misalliances but a big-boned, brawling fighter, a man who would put the jazzers in their place. Composers such as Mason and Farwell looked for a red-blooded man of the land to whom they could pass the torch of American culture, someone who would carry its flame high and unsullied. An infusion of fresh blood into the national soul must come from a man with a feeling for the rhythm of America's vitality. Mason eyed Howard Hanson (1896) and Douglas Moore (1893), a junior colleague at Columbia. He thought their music young, high-spirited, softhearted, energetic, and direct.[83] Ives inclined toward Henry Cowell, a Western original whose interests in new soundscapes and old folk tunes resonated with Ives's own enthusiasms. But their selections fell by the wayside as Roy Harris was chosen by acclamation in the early thirties.

Harris might have been a figment of an agent's fevered imagination, so perfect were his credentials. He was born in a log cabin in Lincoln County, Oklahoma, on Lincoln's birthday, 1898. His pioneer parents had settled just as the frontier was closing. To escape malaria, the family moved to a farm in California's San Gabriel Valley. At eight, Harris learned the rudiments of piano playing from his mother; and as a teenager, he picked up the clarinet for diversion. He bought his own farm at eighteen; but after service in World War I, he abandoned farming. At twenty-two, he enrolled as a special student at the University of California, where he studied philosophy, economics, and music, primarily with Arthur Farwell.

After training two years with Farwell, Harris decided to take on New York. His *Andante* beat out a "mass of manuscripts submitted to the New York Philharmonic Orchestra, and was introduced . . . at the Lewisohn Stadium in the summer of 1926." Following this triumph, he went to Paris to study with Boulanger, bolstered by successive Guggenheim Fellowships. Upon his return to the United States in

Against a rocky background, Roy Harris displays his farsighted, serious side. *Courtesy Performing Arts Research Center, The New York Public Library at Lincoln Center.*

1929, he composed the works that established him as a rising star. His *Symphony: 1933* had its premiere in Boston, "where Koussevitzky was launching Harris with the same steadfast persistence he had used for Copland." The *Symphony* was a knockout. Audiences and critics alike recognized in Harris a potential champion. "Commissions . . . came from the Boston Symphony, the League of Composers, the Westminster Choir, Columbia Records, Victor Records, Elizabeth Sprague Coolidge, and the Columbia Broadcasting System." Harris's *Third Symphony* became the first American symphony performed by Toscanini, an imprimatur of inestimable value. His music also garnered praise from Europeans. Alfredo Cassella wrote, "In producing a composer such as this master, America has placed herself in the front rank amongst those nations who are concerned with building a music for the future." As music chronicler David Ewen observed, Harris was "acclaimed as the white hope of American music."[84]

Critics compared the Americanness of New York and Oklahoma, of Copland and Harris, Jew and gentile. To Paul Rosenfeld, the feeling of Harris's music "was wider than Copland's, comprehensive of tragedy and eloquent of it in mournful accents and melodies. . . . The limitless feeling of the plains, the fierce impulses and frustrations of the American migrations, the long patience of the poor, often seem to sound in it."[85] Howard drew the contrast rather more pointedly:

> While racially Harris seems to derive definitely from the Scotch-Irish element of his ancestry, Aaron Copland embodies the Russian-Jewish element transplanted to American soil. Thus we find that while Harris reflects the prairies and vastness of the West, Copland brings us the sophistication of the cosmopolitan cities on the seaboard.[86]

The music critic Henry Taylor Parker praised Harris as "unmistakably American—American of the Far West," American in his "directness" and "unaffected roughness."[87] Few doubted that Harris reflected essential features of an American character.

Asked at a WPA composers' forum-laboratory, "Is there such a thing as 'American' music—of course, excluding Broadway jazz?" Lazare Saminsky replied that no doubt "America has outgrown the naive cultivation of the Negro and Indian songs which were supposed to lead . . . to the creation of American music. There are in American music clear characteristics, the same characteristics of the American people." The directness, humor, and verve of American character are, in "its broad, epic qualities . . . characteristic of the best American music. Among the best? . . . [To] my mind the most gifted, the strongest creative talent is Roy Harris." Saminsky then linked Harris's musical talent and his "racial" identity, as though one implied the other. "I think he is the most original, the most American of all, inasmuch as the main basic characteristic of the Anglo-Celtic strain is the source of American music." This Victorian leap from formal to national virtues runs through much praise of Harris. For example, Ewen argued that "Harris' best music is abstract, depending entirely on its musical logic for its appeal. Most important of all, it is intensely American. It is not easy, however, to put a finger on precisely what is American in [his instrumental pieces]. . . . And yet . . . we feel that we are in personal contact with American experiences."[88]

Writers depicted Harris as self-taught, as educated and inspired by the Western landscape. Almost never was he identified as a pupil of Boulanger in Paris. Ewen even slighted Harris's mother, intimating that the boy learned to play the piano "by himself." Farwell proudly announced his student to the world with the flourish: "Gentlemen, a genius—but keep your hats on!" As a canny booster, Farwell modestly stepped from the limelight: "If we would get at the melodic rationale of Harris, we must . . . follow him to his early life in the West. There are his teachers of melody—the broad horizon, the long undulations or the craggy lines of mountain contours, winding streams." Henry Parker argued that Harris's *Symphony: 1933* was American in its "uneven" and "propulsive" rhythms and melody, which "seem to derive from the West . . . from its air, its life, its impulses, even its gaits." Nicolas Slonimsky wrote that "Harris grew like an American primitive, and his talent was already well formed when he became exposed to the modern music of the 1920's."[89]

Whereas the popularity of Copland, Gershwin, and Bloch evinced ill-concealed anguish among Yankee partisans, Harris's wide acceptance caused open jubilation.[90] Harris courted America's assent to his music as a national norm. As others' music diverged from his ideal, to that extent was it less in touch with the lifeblood of the American self-imagination. Modernists and traditionalists, Jews and gentiles, Easterners and Westerners, musicians and laymen, rich and poor: people of every background experienced Harris's music as the incarnation of American ideals. After a performance of his *Third Symphony*, Harris received an encomium which Ives would have loved to get. The "manager of a baseball team wrote him: 'If I had pitchers who could pitch as strongly as you do in your Symphony, my worries would be over.'" Saminsky praised him as a "creator of works the appeal of which is practically universal."[91]

Farwell took care to launch his protege into the mainstream of the Yankee composers' tradition. "From old Anglo-Saxon stock, with Scotch and Irish ingredients, he arises not out of the mechanistic tumult of the times, but out of the broad metaphysical movement which gave birth to Emerson and Whitman." Drawing upon redemptive culture, Farwell portrayed Harris as the central figure in a rebirth of a deeply religious "time-spirit" from the rubble of postwar America's secular musical epoch, which was "messageless, direc- tionless, spiritually bankrupt." Farwell was convinced that Harris rep- resented "a deep rebellion of the general human soul, though more especially the Western American soul, and of purposeful and deter- mined thinking coupled with an emotional dynamism of possibilities not yet to be calculated." Yet Harris did not merely reflect these emergent aspirations; he was called to direct them:

> It may be that he will prove to be the protagonist of the time-spirit, by which I do not mean that passing phase which worships the machine . . . but of the new time-spirit which seeks the truer human values beneath the surface of present phenomena, and which must presently posit the deeper aspirations of the Twentieth Century. This is a large order, but frankly the one to which Mr. Harris has addressed himself from the beginning. It constitutes perhaps his chief claim to our atten- tion.[92]

Farwell was an enthusiastic student of Oswald Spengler, and rummaged through *The Decline of the West* to support his perception of the Yankee dilemma. Spengler seemed to illumine for Farwell America's dark drama of perilous transition. According to Spengler, the "idea of a Culture" is carried by a national spiritual will, by "race." For Spengler, "culture signified creativity, spontaneity, and spiri- tuality," writes Franklin Baumer. After its fulfillment, it ossified into civilization, which "spelled world-weariness, the oversophisticated in- tellect, and soullessness. The symbol of civilization was the megalopolis . . . dedicated to the cult of bigness, in the grip of machine organization, peopled by masses without roots."[93] Imaginatively read, Spengler could serve as an up-to-date Matthew Arnold, contrasting spiritual culture and materialist civilization. Farwell appropriated from Spengler such useful phrases as "time-spirit" to buttress redemp- tive culture.

As racial carrier of the American "time-spirit," Harris acquired a dual persona. He was the most earthy and natural of men and the most sensitively cultured. One side of him was sketched broadly in raw Bunyanesque strokes. This frontier hero strode into the public arena as American music's "white hope." Harris's "favorite dish," noted Ewen, "is steak and potatoes." But Farwell was nominating a hero of two facets. Harris was to be a fighter, but with the soul of a poet. His artistic nurture by America's broad landscape defined his genius as a composer. In Emersonian terms, he was to represent *the* American genius by realizing it: perceiving and completing it. Farwell cast Harris in the mold of Whitman's heroic bards: "Their President shall not be their / common referee so much as their / poets shall." He of Lincolnesque bearing, born in a log cabin, could be elected, if not president of the United States then Speaker of the House for America's "unacknowledged legislators," its musical artists. Raw genius defined his heroic dimension. A young man who "coupled farm work with the study of Greek philosophy" was obviously one of American music's "natural aristocracy."[94]

Ebulliently Harris accepted the nomination. He understood exactly the role he was expected to fulfill. He must grasp the torch of musical culture from the genteel Yankees, and inject some Western adrenalin back into the race to capture the imaginations of an American people waiting anxiously in the stands. Harris expressed clear awareness of the tensions within the Yankee aesthetic of identity:

> The creative impulse is a desire to capture and communicate feeling. . . . Always is it a lonesome hunger that gnaws within the human heart, forcing us to search for an understandable race-expression. The successful translation of creative impulses, objectifies, and records our gamut of possibilities.
>
> It is small wonder, then, that humanity regards the creative impulse as sacred. . . . [People regard] new translations of their own time-spirit with fear and trepidation. . . . [The artist] excels in sensitiveness, initiative, moral courage, power of coordination.[95]

Through an "auto-American-biographical strategy," Harris, like Emerson, accepted the role of "Americanus," the hero who reads the sacred text of the land itself to assert that America is "yet only at the cock-crowing and the morning star."[96] A musical "Americanus," Harris saw the essential dualism of America: a "nightmare of feverish struggling, a graveyard of suppressed human impulses." He asserted that "we have become so absorbed in material development that the intellectual and spiritual achievements by which all civilizations are eventually appraised are tolerated only if they serve an immediate commercial end." This American society was "spiritually naked." Harris contrasted society to the American land itself, the eternal

America. "America waits calmly between the Pacific and the Atlantic while the tide of the Mississippi rises and falls with the seasons." Harris would "translate" for society the "gamut of possibilities" writ in this "land of grandeur, dignity, and untold beauty." While Harris recognized the circularly symbiotic relationship between the artist and his national audience, he believed that ultimately the artist's genius helps the people realize itself. Carrying on the Yankee errand, Harris would communicate America to Americans.[97]

As Harris understood them, "the moods which seem particularly American to me are the noisy ribaldry, the sadness, a groping earnestness which amounts to suppliance towards those deepest spiritual yearnings within ourselves."[98] With great energy and enthusiasm, Harris composed a mountain of chamber, choral, and orchestral works, many of which he linked with themes of the American experience. He promoted himself as the ascendant star of the West, as one who could translate the land's contours into rugged, soaring lines of music. But by the late thirties, his star was already on the wane.

Increasingly, writers challenged Harris's musical qualifications to hold high public office. The potential of Harris's raw genius went unquestioned; but several critics emphasized its rawness. In his review of Harris's *Symphony for Voices*, on texts by Whitman, B. H. Haggin derided the composer's heroic status. "Roy Harris is everything a significant American composer should be: he was born in America, he loves America, he writes music to express the qualities and spirit of America as they appear to him." Haggin finds everything in order except for Harris's compositional skills. "His only deficiency is that he cannot write the music a significant American composer would write." Harris's advertisements for himself as America's musical spokesman tried the patience of even his admiring colleague Virgil Thomson. According to Thomson, "Harris's best works have a deeply meditative quality combined with exuberance." They "breathe an American air" and reflect "high artistic aims and a sophistication of thematic, harmonic, and instrumental usage."[99] But in 1940, Thomson was exasperated by the whole enterprise of Harris as culture hero:

> Mr. Harris's *American Creed* invites kidding, as all of his programmatically prefaced works do. . . . No composer in the world . . . makes such shameless use of patriotic feelings to advertise his product. One would think, to read his prefaces, that he had been awarded by God, or at least by popular vote, a monopolistic privilege of exposing our nation's

deepest ideals and highest aspirations. And when the piece so advertised turns out to be a mostly not very clearly orchestrated schoolish
counterpoint and a quite skimpy double fugue (neither of which has
any American connotation whatsoever), one is tempted to put the
whole thing down as insincere and a bad joke.[100]

Harris's reputation had begun to suffer the consequences of his role,
which demanded that his music be judged in terms of his programmatic nationalism.

Thomson's irritation with Harris foreshadowed the imminent collapse of the Yankee musical mission. Just as the Depression killed the
Harlem Renaissance, virtually overnight the Second World War cut
short discussions about a musical "white hope." Redemptive culture
seemed terribly important in 1930. Harris and his boosters even accommodated it to the social-realist rhetoric of the Depression era. But
in 1940, with a war disemboweling Europe, the "white hope" looked
like a pretentious shadow boxer, whose grandiloquence was only hot
air, signifying nothing.

The "white hope" was the last hope for the Yankee musical mission. A long, difficult pilgrimage had ended as a "fool's errand." Stoic-
ally New England's centennial composers had borne the stigmata of
their calling: to be artists and men, prophets and democrats. They had
conducted the Puritan errand in behalf of Matthew Arnold's
"sweetness and light." Yankees had voiced a theory of redemptive
culture that justified their classical music as a blueprint for the American self-imagination, a transcendental symbol of and for the essential
spirit behind the surface materialism of modern life. Burdened by self-
doubts, they applied their principles and their wits to master the long
night of the 1920s. Proponents of redemptive culture opposed the
devils of jazzy modernism and tried to wrest conceptual order from
formless anarchy. And when conniving false messiahs threatened an
inundation of sensualism and materialism, the mission was saved by a
son of the land. Down from the hills he strode to thwart the
moneychangers and to preach the one true gospel of America's spiritual destiny. He reached out beyond the present real audience. Touching the common souls of all potential publics, he strove to convert
them into one harmonious musical people. But then, in the fullness of
Harris's success, the world averted its eyes toward other concerns.
Like most Americans, Harris turned his energies to the war effort.
The Yankees' redemptive culture died in the war; but the struggle over
its principles would bear curious fruit decades later.

EPILOGUE

Americans were ambivalent as to whether Yankees were the symbolic group of repression or of sublimation. Critics such as Mencken and Van Vechten identified Yankees with a "Puritan" ethic that had spawned a heartless, capitalist civilization whose bloodless high culture was "all work and no play." Following Santayana, some writers portrayed Yankees as caretakers of a "genteel tradition" that set its repressive ethos against the ever-quickening tempo of modern life. Genteel Yankees would accept no blame for materialist modernity; nor would they assent to the suggestion that they were antiprogressive or impractical. Most cultural critics of the interwar years contrasted practical progressivism with bourgeois capitalism. Meanwhile, the mainstream of American opinion continued to honor Emerson and Thoreau as exemplars of a tradition in which ideal emotions were spiritually sublimated as authentic culture.

Having allied their errand with the humanist Victorian struggle against "anarchy," genteel Yankees such as Mason shifted the grounds of their chosenness from the future to the past. They clung to culture less as a tool for leadership than as an island of refuge. Boosters of redemptive culture increasingly associated its putative ethos with the claims of race and place as much as with the freedom of America's unbounded future. Americans have long cherished their myth of eternal youth; it is, as Oscar Wilde observed, "their oldest tradition." But even as Henry James celebrated the "innocence" of Hawthorne's Adamic America, he also articulated America's need for a heritage in which culture represented the accumulated layers of racial experience. James left the United States to mine the textured strata of Europe's heritage, while countrymen such as Van Wyck Brooks and Mason busily fabricated a ready-to-wear tradition—a "usable past." They turned New England into a museum, and called it a church.

"The Jazz Age" encompassed in musical metaphor the Arnoldian "anarchy" of postwar American life. Jazz symbolized sensuality or mechanism, or both. Its sensuality recalled its origin among Negroes. Its mechanistic elements reflected the hard, urban facade of contemporary existence. The popularity of jazz and its challenge to redemptive culture could be attributed to Jews. On these propositions, most parties to the war over jazzy modernism could agree.

As a symbolic group, Negroes allegedly exemplified the antitype of the repression and sublimation that seemed to characterize a Yankee ethos. Metaphorically regarded as but protohumans, Negroes hovered between beasts and children. As the creators of jazz, they were imagined alternately as a source of jungle primitiveness or of innocent spontaneity. Almost less than human, Negroes acted as perfect foils for New England's spiritual pretensions—ideal deviants. Deviants serve society by marking certain boundaries of behavior and belief, provided, of course, that they keep their place. If Yankees symbolized the intelligence and conscience of the North, Negroes epitomized the earthy hedonism of the South. But the widespread success of jazz called attention to the dissolution of this tidy symbolic geography.

Critics attributed the popularity of jazz among whites not to Negroes, deemed too dull to exploit their own essential characteristics, but to an intermediate symbolic group, the Jews. Dualistic stereotypes portraying Jews as coarse and sensual, yet cleverly ambitious, were resolved in the racial metaphor of the Jew-as-Oriental. Jews were thought to be rootless middlemen—neither black nor white—who combined in an ethos of consumption capitalism the bewildering intellectuality of technology and the preference for immediate gratification. In modern, jazzy classicism, Jews such as Gershwin and Copland seemed to have created a musical melting pot, metaphor for the "semitization" of the American sensibility. Jazz was the avant-garde of cultural anarchy, argued its critics. Boosters, however, praised these Jewish composers for reconstituting the generative American symbiosis between natural man and cultured man.

The Yankee composers' dreams for redemptive culture failed, but not completely. Their efforts helped to enunciate New England's claim for an enduring symbolic status. "The Yankee" continues to be valued by his countrymen as more than an oddball idealist, if less than the voice of America. As for classical composers, they exchanged the lonely barricades of redemptive culture for the relative security of college life. The postwar college boom provided numerous composers with the chance to hear their works performed before audiences increasingly eager not to be offended by abstruse culture. Although many "academic" composers espoused a strictly formalist aesthetic, their campus presence was justified on educational grounds: that as an essential part of a liberal education, familiarity with classical music is an elevating humanistic experience. It was devoutly hoped that this cultural sophistication would create a growing demand for the American composer's product.

Ironically, redemptive culture was resurrected in the 1960s, but in a new color: black, not white. Nominated to be art music by some white Americans and Europeans in the 1920s, jazz gradually gained in status among Negroes as well. Black intellectual pride in jazz rose inversely with the decline of jazz as a popular black music. As the ideological rationales for "Black Power" peaked in the late 1960s, jazz served increasingly as the cherished touchstone of self-worth for Negro intellectuals. No longer just entertainment, jazz was believed to express specifically Afro-American values. In the black aesthetic of identity, jazz possessed a uniquely organic beauty which drew inspiration from the sensual warmth—"soul"—of the Negro spirit. Black redemptive culture came full circle; some black writers, including Harold Cruse, voiced antiwhite and occasionally anti-Semitic racism. Still trapped by their oppression and by the metaphors of the old racial stereotypes, in pain and anger they acted out roles drawn from the music drama of the 1920s.

Study of the American self-imagination does not uncover solutions to problems of prejudice. Prejudice and preference interpenetrate. The critical faculty is manifold. It separates not only wheat from chaff but wines from wines, Bach from Telemann, them from us. If we are liberal, we teach our children to be discriminating but not to discriminate. We say that comparisons are odious, but we cannot live without them. "Solutions" for conflicts over taste and identity have a nasty tendency to slide toward brutality. Perhaps the best that we can do is to stand back and see in detail how we all habitually trade on the half-truths existence offers us. Through metaphor we shape our ambiguities into paradoxes. Metaphors are our handles on reality; they permit us to deal with our waking dreams and nightmares. But unexamined metaphors become mere tools of rhetoric, instruments with which we oppress others and ourselves.

NOTES

1. Thomas F. Gossett, *Race*, p. 83. Racial (or ethnic) thought is invariably stereotypical thinking. Where does the stereotype shade into the euphemistic (and value-neutral?) "generalization," or into the pejorative "prejudice?"

2. Writers characterized particular musical pieces, whole genres, even "music" in ways that reveal more about their cultural attitudes than about the music in question. The frequent ambiguity of these opinions may well dilute the specificity of *musical* knowledge for musicology, but such self-serving and musically diffuse commentaries provide useful data for the study of symbolic group dynamics.

3. The relative clarity of generational conflict in Europe was "embittered and muddied by ethnic considerations" in the United States. Victor Fell Yellin, "The Conflict of Generations in American Music—(A Yankee View)," p. 13.

4. The younger composers included William Grant Still (1895), Roger Sessions (1896), Howard Hanson (1896), Virgil Thomson (1896), Henry Cowell (1897), Roy Harris (1898), George Gershwin (1898), George Antheil (1900), and Aaron Copland (1900).

5. Yellin, p. 13.

6. The Puritans used music as one of the tools with which to build their New Jerusalem. The first important book printed in North America was the *Bay Psalm Book* (1640). Indeed, Puritans made the singing of psalms a civic and religious obligation; psalmody was central to the worship affirming their community in its holy enterprise.

7. Carl Engel, "Views and Reviews," *Musical Quarterly*, April 1925, p. 307. Burnet C. Tuthill, "Daniel Gregory Mason," *Musical Quarterly*, January 1948, p. 46.

8. Frank Rossiter, *Charles Ives and His America*, pp. 137–38.

9. Perry Miller, *Errand into the Wilderness*, pp. 9, 15; Sacvan Bercovitch, *The Puritan Origins of the American Self*, pp. 136, 157, 173–86; Sacvan Bercovitch, *The American Jeremiad*, pp. xi–30, 152, 180.

The phrase "practical idealism" served as an appropriately paradoxical motto for Americans' civil religion, linking instrumentality with ultimate meanings. See Henry F. May, *The End of American Innocence*, p. 14; Clifford Geertz, *The Interpretation of Cultures*, pp. 89–90.

10. Henry James, "Hawthorne," in Richard Ruland, ed., *A Storied Land*, pp. 56–57.

11. "In the postwar devotion to a serious and useful—above all, an ordered—art, Longfellow, Emerson, Holmes, Whittier, Lowell, and Charles Eliot Norton were both priests and deities. These men satisfied (and modified) the American need for objects of secular devotion." Jay Martin, *Harvests of Change*, p. 12.

12. For nonbelievers (Philistines), culture connoted the unproductive activities with which genteel people busied themselves, but to its devotees, it was potentially a civil religion. By the mid-nineteenth century, *culture* was used in English as a noun of process, referring to the development of intellectual and artistic potential. In *Culture and Anarchy* Matthew Arnold developed a theory of culture as a surrogate religion, the source of spiritual renewal, and the vehicle of traditional excellence. He opposed culture to "anarchy": materialist civilization in all its forms. Yet even as he missionized for culture, Arnold had to defend it against charges that it was merely the precious pseudoreligion of genteel people. Matthew Arnold, "Culture and Anarchy," in *The Portable Matthew Arnold*, pp. 491–92; Raymond Williams, *Keywords*, pp. 77, 81. Also see Raymond Williams, *Culture and Society, 1780–1950;* John Henry Raleigh, *Matthew Arnold and American Culture*, pp. 1–13, 80.

13. *Victorian* is commonly used to describe a postromantic lifestyle and world view associated with the middle class during the second half of the nineteenth century. Actually, Anglo-American Victorianism was divided against itself. Arrayed against the alleged normlessness of materialistic "Philistines" were the humanist Victorians, men such as Matthew Arnold, Charles Eliot Norton, and Daniel Gregory Mason. They shared a common alienation from the dominant business of making and getting. While they dared not reject the virtues of middle-class individualism or the objectivity of science, they emphatically denied that individualism and science provided the moral means for society to see itself whole. Instead they rallied around culture.

On Victorianism in the American context, see Daniel Walker Howe, "American Victorianism as a Culture"; Richard D. Brown, "Modernization: A Victorian Climax"; and David D. Hall, "The Victorian Connection." Raleigh, *Matthew Arnold*, pp. 47–49.

14. Van Wyck Brooks, "On Creating a Usable Past," *Source* (11 April 1918), pp. 337–41, in *Van Wyck Brooks*, p. 225.

15. Charles Horton Cooley, *Social Organization* (1909), with an introduction by Philip Rieff, p. 75.

16. The tie between American mission and racialism was established by the mid-nineteenth century (Gossett, *Race*, p. 179). George Mosse notes that racialism drew upon traditional Western ideals linking outer aesthetic grace with inner spiritual grace. George Mosse, *Toward the Final Solution*, pp. 11, 21–23.

17. Jackson Lears suggests that American Victorians were caught between ambivalent impulses toward autonomy and dependence. "At its most extreme," writes Lears, "withdrawal was animated by the desire to abandon autonomous selfhood and sink into a passive state of boundless union with all being, by the wish to experience what Freud called an 'oceanic feeling.'" That such a state was ideally entered via music was a common romantic conceit. Lears notes the attraction of "childlike" attributes associated with Oriental and medieval societies. He fails to emphasize the romantic origins of these exotic preoccupations. Nor does he develop the importance of black stereotypes in this connection; indeed, virtually no Negroes, real or imagined, exist in the America of T. J. Jackson Lears. Also see Lears on the therapeutic ideal. Jackson Lears, *No Place of Grace*, pp. 218, 141–42, 54.

1. THE NERVOUS BURDEN

1. Robert H. Wiebe, *The Search for Order, 1877–1920*.
2. David W. Noble, *The Progressive Mind, 1890–1917*, p. 53.

3. John Higham, *Writing American History*, p. 77.

4. Daniel Gregory Mason, *Music in My Time, and Other Reminiscences*, pp. 172–73, 202–204.

5. "There is a great Man living in this Country—a composer. He has solved the problem of how to preserve one's self and to learn. He responds to negligence by contempt. He is not forced to accept praise or blame. His name is Ives." Arnold Schoenberg, quoted in Henry Cowell and Sidney Cowell, *Charles Ives and His Music*, p. 114.

Although Ives had no patience to file or catalog his music, he meticulously collected and copied all reviews, promotional material, and correspondence. Bigalow Ives (nephew of Charles), in Vivian Perlis, ed., *Charles Ives Remembered*, p. 83. Ive's "reaction to the public reception of his composition is evidence that he desired to make musical contact with the masses." Frank Rossiter, *Charles Ives and His America*, p. 163.

6. J. W. DeForest, "The Great American Novel," in Richard Ruland, ed., *A Storied Land*, p. 29.

7. Henry Adams, *The Degradation of the Democratic Dogma*; Alan Simpson, *Puritanism in Old and New England*, p. 21; Barbara Miller Solomon, *Ancestors and Immigrants*, passim; David Hackett Fisher, *Historical Fallacies*, p. 139.

8. "One of the symptoms of decline was the prevalence among the gentry of more or less incapacitating nervous illness. The list of sufferers included the names of such prominent gentry leaders as Horace Bushnell, William Graham Sumner, William James, Octavius Brooks Frothingham, Charles Eliot Norton, and Edmund C. Stedman." Stow Persons, *The Decline of American Gentility*, p. 285. Also see Richard D. Altick, *Victorian People and Ideas*, p. 112; Noble, pp. 37–38.

9. George Santayana, "Genteel American Poetry," p. 94. "Most of the country, when it used the words *culture* or *tradition*, was likely to use another faintly comical word, *Boston*." Henry F. May, *The End of American Innocence*, p. 52; also pp. 30–51 passim. In the 1870s, J. W. DeForest urged a dialectic of local colors as the basis for a Great American Novel that would help develop an affective national unity. He reflected widespread ambivalence toward New England's role in this adventure of national self-creation. He applauded "that Yankeehood which goes abroad and leavens the character of the Republic," drawing on New England's "moral strength" and "keen intellect." But too often he found, as in the fiction of Oliver Wendell Holmes, a "Yankeehood . . . which stays in corners, speechless and impotent—a community of old maids, toothless doctors, small-souled lawyers, village poets, and shelved professors." Forty years before Santayana, DeForest attacked New England's gentility as "the coterie of an antique borough, amusing, queer and of no account." J. W. DeForest, "The Great American Novel," p. 28; John Tomsich, *A Genteel Endeavor*, pp. 1–26 passim.

10. John Tasker Howard, *Our American Music*, pp. 142–48, 286–94, 478–79; Sister Mary Justina Klein, "The Contribution of Daniel Gregory Mason to American Music" (Ph.D. dissertation), p. 14.

11. Rossiter, pp. 4, 6–12.

12. Ibid., p. 12. "George Ives lived an obscure life in Danbury, and its people treated him badly, both socially and musically." Ibid., p. 23.

13. Chester Ives, Dr. Charles Kauffman, Lehman Engel, John Kirkpatrick, all in Perlis, pp. 88, 112, 197, 225. "If a clear reaction to the social implications of George Ives's position as a musician is not to be found among his son's writings, a reaction to the *sexual* implications of that position is one of the most articulate themes in Charles Ives's life and work." Rossiter, pp. 23–24.

14. Mason, p. 7.

15. Klein, p. 18.

16. Mason, pp. 18, 40–42.

17. Ibid., pp. 34–35; Klein, pp. 14–15.

18. "Yet his New England blood and even the long association of his family with Harvard . . . were not for nothing. . . . Under all his meteoric brilliance there were a steadfast affection, an undemonstrative manliness, truly puritan in the best sense." Mason, pp. 33–34.

19. Rossiter, pp. 48, 72; Cowell and Cowell, p. 28; Mason, p. 372.

20. Mason, Hill, Carpenter, and (for a short time) Ruggles studied at Harvard. Ives and Smith were Yale men. Farwell studied at MIT. "A large majority of the creative composers born in our country is of Puritan New England stock. Of that blood are Chadwick, Gilbert, Parker, Whiting, Osgood, Foote, Carpenter, Converse, Atherton, Mason, Hill, Clapp, Fairchild, Ballantine, Thompson, and Sessions; and all but the first four are Harvard graduates." Walter Raymond Spalding, *Music at Harvard*, pp. 283–84.

21. Harold Osborne, *Aesthetics and Art Theory*, pp. 44–45.

22. Howard, pp. 319, 337; David Stanley Smith, "A Study of Horatio Parker," *Musical Quarterly*, April 1930, p. 158; Rossiter, p. 60.

23. Another imperious figure was Parker's teacher, the leonine George Whitefield Chadwick. Allan Langley, a violinist who studied at the New England Conservatory of Music, describes the impression Chadwick burned into his students: "Upon my presentation, he turned, or rather shot, an explosive and terrifying glance in my direction. (He habitually, as I afterwards observed, stared similarly at other newcomers, probably to establish in them a wholesome respect for both himself and what he stood for) . . . his initial fierceness was immediately tinctured with a sort of diabolical humor, which I was to learn was one of his chief characteristics." Allan Lincoln Langley, "Chadwick and the New England Conservatory of Music," *Musical Quarterly*, January 1934, p. 40.

24. Although Mason was among the intellectual elite at Harvard, there were odd gaps in his education. He gave up on German; he once placed Vienna in Iceland and George Washington in the Civil War. Mason, p. 39.

26. Ibid.; Charles Ives, *Memos*, p. 116. "After the first three weeks Parker asked the boy not to bring any more things of the sort into the classroom, and to stick to the work regularly assigned to the class." Cowell and Cowell, p. 32.

27. Cowell and Cowell, pp. 144–45.

28. Mason, pp. 35–36.

29. Rossiter, p. 82.

30. Mason, pp. 48, 50, 81–82; Klein, p. 16.

31. Mason, p. 102.

32. Mason, pp. 104–108, 110–13; Klein, p. 17; Frank Howes, *The English Musical Renaissance*, pp. 17–80, passim.

33. Mason, pp. 133–34.

34. Klein, p. 23.

35. Perlis, p. 31. Victor Fell Yellin, "Review of Records—Ives: The Celestial Country," p. 506.

36. Cowell and Cowell, pp. 38–39. Ives quoted, p. 59.

37. James Thomas Flexner, in Perlis, pp. 102–104. Also see George Grayson Tyler, ibid., p. 105 and pp. 10–11; Rossiter, pp. 88, 122.

38. Perlis, p. 31.

39. Anthony Lapine, in Perlis, p. 112; Julian Myrick, in ibid., p. 38; also see

ibid., p. 45.

40. Cowell and Cowell, p. 27; Jacques Barzun, *Music in American Life*, pp. 15–16.

41. Ives, pp. 130–31.

42. As Rossiter suggests, there is no reason to suppose that an insurance executive is necessarily closer to common folks than a professional composer. Ives, pp. 130–31; Rossiter, pp. 162–63; Ralph Waldo Emerson, "Conduct of Life: Wealth," in *The Complete Writings of Ralph Waldo Emerson*, p. 554.

43. Karl Muck was driven from his post at the height of the Germanophobia of World War I. His replacement, the estimable Pierre Monteux, did not pay off at the box office. He in turn was replaced by the larger-than-life figure of Serge Koussevitsky.

44. Mason, passim; David Ewen, *American Composers Today*, pp. 165–66; Claire Reis, *Composers in America*, pp. 176–77; Howard, pp. 634–35.

45. Cowell and Cowell, p. 67; Rossiter, p. 89.

46. Ives, pp. 70–71.

47. Summarizing material in Rossiter, pp. 197–99, 205–210, 224–26, 238–40, 278–82. Though conscientious enough to ask for scores of new works prior to hearing them, Gilman's actual review of the *Concord Sonata* seems to take off from Ives's own comments in his *Essays*. Gilman connects Ives's effort with Van Wyck Brooks's call for a "usable past." Ibid., p. 283.

48. Mason castigated Olin Downes, Irving Kolodin, and Philip Hale. Gilman was an exception. He was attentive to the works of both composers. Mason felt that Gilman was something of a fellow spirit, and tried to court his friendship. Daniel Gregory Mason to Lorraine Smith Resnik, 7 January 1939, to Henry Mason, 5 January 1939, to Lawrence Gilman, 29 November 1933, Daniel Gregory Mason Papers, Box 15, Columbia University Library, New York; Mason, *Music in My Time*, p. 175.

49. Ives, pp. 242–43. In Ives's case the penultimate critical insult came when, after very belated recognition, his music was taken to be derivative of contemporary European composers: Hindemith, Schoenberg, Stravinsky. Ives protested, first, that he didn't listen to any substantial amount of contemporary music, and second, that many of his pieces predated the works of the Europeans. He didn't even like their music. Ibid., pp. 27–29, 137–38.

50. Ibid., p. 41; Rossiter, p. 27; Mason, *Music in My Time*, pp. 312, 368, 398.

51. Cowell and Cowell, p. 106; Ives, quoted ibid., p. 44. Whether or not he was hurt by his burden, Ives remained a cheerful companion to his friends and loved ones. Ibid., p. 218.

52. Daniel Gregory Mason, "Our Orchestras and Our Money's Worth," p. 79.

53. Ibid., p. 75; Daniel Gregory Mason, "Our Public School Music," p. 705.

54. Daniel Gregory Mason, "The Depreciation of Music," pp. 13–15.

55. Daniel Gregory Mason, *The Dilemma of American Music, and Other Essays*, p. 51. Daniel Gregory Mason, *Tune In America*, pp. 10–11.

56. Daniel Gregory Mason to William Vaughn Moody, Daniel Gregory Mason Papers, Box 15, Columbia University Library, New York; Mason, *Music in My Time*, p. 99.

57. Ibid., p. 384.

58. Daniel Gregory Mason, "Democracy and Music," p. 652. On the links between Emerson and Arnold, see John Henry Raleigh, *Matthew Arnold and American Culture*, pp. 8–11.

59. The portrait of Emerson originated in an article Ives had submitted to the

Yale literary magazine. Unlike Mason's Thoreau article, Ives's effort was not printed. Cowell and Cowell, p. 36.

60. Charles Ives, *Essays before a Sonata, and Other Writings*, pp. 21–22, 24, 51.

61. Ibid., pp. 63, 65–66; Perlis, pp. 79, 103.

62. Mason and Ives turned neither to Chateaubriand nor to Byron, nor even to Whitman, to bolster their romantic stance of isolated artists; they turned to Emerson and Thoreau. In Whitman, a man seduced by grand opera, one finds just that combination of key romantic elements which Victorians tried to extirpate from culture: 1) "emotionalism," 2) "confusion between eroticism and religion," 3) "unredeemed *Weltschmerz.*" Surely, as Perry Miller noted, the Puritans were stretched between a hunger for mystical excitements and an ideal of control. Emerson brought the tension into literary consciousness, but he excluded its overtly sexual dimension. Joseph A. Mussulman, *Music in the Cultured Generation*, pp. 124–68; Warren Dwight Allen, *Philosophies of Music History* (1939), pp. 299, 303; Mason, *Music in My Time*, p. 101. On music and romanticism, see H. G. Schenk, *The Mind of the European Romantics*, p. 205. Perry Miller, *Errand into the Wilderness*, p. 192; Spalding, p. 144.

63. Henry Adams, *The Education of Henry Adams* (1918), vol. 2, pp. 123–24. Ives, *Memos*, pp. 133–34.

64. Carl Ruggles, born in 1876 in the sea town of Marion, Massachusetts, studied at Harvard briefly. He is well characterized in the following story: "Having gone to see him in Vermont," writes Virgil Thomson, "[Henry] Cowell arrived at the former schoolhouse that was Ruggles's studio and found him at the piano, playing the same chordal agglomerate over and over, as if to pound the very life out of it. After a time Cowell shouted, 'What on earth are you doing to that chord? You've been playing it for at least an hour.' Ruggles shouted back, 'I'm giving it the test of time.'" Henry Cowell, quoted in Virgil Thomson, *American Music since 1900*, p. 31. Ruggles, who radiated an aura of crusty self-reliance, had been supported by a wealthy woman patron for ten years when first he and Ives met in the late 1920s. Thomas Elliot Peterson, "The Music of Carl Ruggles" (Ph.D. dissertation), p. 7.

65. Rossiter, p. 57. Elliot Carter, in Perlis, p. 138; Carl Ruggles, in Perlis, p. 173; Ives, *Memos*, p. 73.

66. Flexner, Elliot Carter, in Perlis, p. 103.

67. David A. Hollinger, *Morris R. Cohen and the Scientific Ideal*, p. 27. Davidson was an influential progressive educator.

68. E. A. Baughan, quoted in Charles L. Graves, *Post-Victorian Music*, p. 250. Ibid., p. 254.

As male musicians struggled to assert their own masculinity and the masculine nature of "great" music, they developed a corresponding role for women in music. "Women are the great listeners, not only to eloquence, but also to music," wrote the Rev. Haweis. "The woman's temperament is naturally artistic, not in a creative, but in a receptive, sense. A woman seldom writes good music, never great music." American male musicians felt that women in the United States held too much power over their culture. "I do not think there has ever been a country whose musical development has been fostered so almost exclusively by women as America," wrote conductor Walter Damrosch. Speaking out of these prejudices, Ives and Mason periodically blasted the "philharmonic ladies" who, they felt, exerted excessive control over the policy affairs of major musical institutions. Rossiter, p. 27. Max Kaplan, "The Musician in America" (Ph.D. dissertation), pp. 207, 292. Rockefeller Panel Report, *The Performing Arts, Problems and Prospects*,

p. 28. John Henry Mueller, *The American Symphony Orchestra*, pp. vii–viii, 309–310. H. R. Haweis, *Music and Morals*, pp. 109–112.

69. Katherine Fullerton Gerould, "The Plight of the Genteel," p. 314; John Jay Chapman, "The Disappearance of the Educated Man," pp. 50, 86; Larzer Ziff, *The American 1890's*, pp. 242–49.

2. Redemptive Culture

1. The composer-as-critical-essayist was a product of the romantic composer's emerging relationship with new bourgeois audiences. E. T. A. Hoffmann, Hector Berlioz, Robert Schumann, and Richard Wagner established a new literary genre: music-criticism-as-visionary-tract. In his essays, the composer became a missionary for his music. Henry Raynor, *A Social History of Music*, p. 353; Max Graf, *Composer and Critic*, pp. 204–205.

2. *Communication* and *expression* are not mutually exclusive, of course. But in general, "communication" aesthetics avows a responsibility to some audience, while "expression" aesthetics emphasizes the sublimation through art of the artist's inner imperatives, regardless of the expectations or needs of any audience.

3. Sacvan Bercovitch, *The American Jeremiad*, pp. 64, 155. *Race*, prior to the Holocaust, loosely designated a group of any size. In a sense, race gives modern societies an ideological substitute for premodern kinship ties. Kinship networks provide premodern societies with principles of order and identity through metaphors of biological relationship (e.g., marriage, descent.) Racialism is metaphorically rooted in blood relationship. Muriel Dimen-Schein, *The Anthropological Imagination*, pp. 112–130n. The origins and metaphorical structure of racialism are discussed in part 2.

4. Religion, argued the sociologist Emile Durkheim, is society divinized. The religious distinction between untouchable concepts, activities, and things (the sacred) and the expediential (the profane) is the root relation from which all categories of thought follow. Emile Durkheim, *The Elementary Forms of the Religious Life*, pp. 37, 419.

The proliferation of metaphors throughout culture defines emergent worlds of meaning. (For a sociological analysis of root metaphors, analogic and iconic models, and rhetorical metaphors, see Richard H. Brown, *A Poetic for Sociology*, pp. 78, 85–89, 115, 125–26). The anthropologist Victor Turner suggests that "human social groups tend to find their openness to the future in the variety of their metaphors for what may be the good life and in the contest of their paradigms." Victor Turner, *Dramas, Fields, and Metaphors*, p. 14.

5. H. G. Schenk, *The Mind of the European Romantics*, p. 220; Walter E. Houghton, *The Victorian Frame of Mind, 1830–1870*, pp. 353–93 passim. Humanist Victorians tried to stop the dizzying dialectic of redefinition that charged the uniquely modernist engine of romanticism. Like E. T. A. Hoffmann's character the tormented musician Kreisler, romanticism fed on confusion: between worship of an organic, medieval Christian spirit and the pursuit of exotic sensations. Vibrating between organicism and expressionism, between spirit and sense, early German and French romanticism reveled in a flux of definitions that were "intentionally self-contradictory . . . deliberately inconsistent and unstable, fluid and expansive." Charles Rosen and Henri Zerner, "The Permanent Revolution," p. 23. Victorians, however, insisted upon spiritual order, first and last, and they grounded this belief in culture.

6. Leo N. Tolstoy, *What is Art?* (1896), pp. 49, 51, 133, 145.

7. Terminology is not uniform in the philosophy of art. For a discussion of the range of functionalist aesthetics, see Harold Osborne, *Aesthetics and Art History*, pp. 47–50. While Osborn uses the term *formalism* as we do here, Stephen Pepper prefers the subcategories *organistic*, *gestalt*, and *contextualist*. Yet another important version of conflict between formalism and functionalism appears in Marxist attacks on "mere formalism." *Encyclopedia Britannica*, 15th ed., s.v. "Aesthetics," by Stephen C. Pepper and Thomas Munro; Raymond Williams, *Keywoods*, pp. 113–15.

8. *Naturalism* is not used here in the sense literary critics prefer.

9. In practice the naturalistic metaphors of "window" or "mirror" often collapse into the "communication" imagery of functionalism, and vice versa.

10. In 1703 Leibniz dubbed music "occult arithmetic." John Hollander, *The Untuning of the Sky*, p. 12. Arthur Berger, introduction to D. W. Prall, *Aesthetic Analysis*, p. x. Neil Harris, *The Artist in American Society*, p. 185.

11. Arthur Schopenhauer, *The Philosophy of Schopenhauer*, p. 201; Margaret Fuller, quoted in Harris, pp. 175–76; Schenk, p. 29.

12. Lawrence Gilman, *Music and the Cultivated Man*, pp. 14–16.

13. W. J. Henderson, "The Function of Musical Criticism," *Musical Quarterly*, January 1915, p. 76.

14. Daniel Gregory Mason, *Music in My Own Time, and Other Reminiscences*, p. 15; Jay Martin, *Harvests of Change*, pp. 93–94; John Henry Raleigh, *Matthew Arnold and American Culture*, p. 125.

15. Sidney Lanier, quoted in Charles Ives, *Essays before a Sonata, and Other Writings*, p. 96.

16. Ibid., pp. 96, 100; Ralph Waldo Emerson, "Art," in *The Complete Writings of Ralph Waldo Emerson*, p. 234.

17. George Santayana, *The Sense of Beauty* (1896), p. 375.

18. Daniel Gregory Mason, "Two Tendencies in Modern Music. Tchaikowsky and Brahms," pp. 176, 178; Eduard Hanslick, *The Beautiful in Music*, pp. 11, 12, 166–67.

19. Mason, "Two Tendencies," p. 177.

20. Note Kant's view: "Now I say the beautiful is the symbol of the morally good, and that it is only in this respect . . . that it gives pleasure with a claim for the agreement of everyone else." (Immanuel Kant, *The Critique of Judgment*, p. 341). Unlike Kant, who subdivides the morally good into the intrinsic and the useful, Santayana defines the good as always utile, the beautiful as never utile. Santayana, p. 375.

21. Mason, "Two Tendencies," p. 184.

22. Ibid., p. 185; Mason, *Music in My Time*, p. 102n.

23. W. H. Hadow, *Studies in Modern Music*, pp. 9, 17–18; Sir Charles Hubert Hastings Parry, *The Art of Music*, p. 169; Warren Dwight Allen, *Philosophies of Music History*, pp. 297–303.

24. H. R. Haweis, *Music and Morals*, pp. 93–94. Haweis, in turn, was preceded by Anton Friedrich Justus Thibaut, a German jurist and amateur musician, whose *Über Reinheit der Tonkunst* (1825) became widely popular. A. F. Thibaut, *Purity in Music*.

25. Haweis, p. 39. It was characteristically Victorian to associate the worth of music with the morality of its composer. On these grounds, Mendelssohn was idolized by early Victorians in England and the United States. "In Mendelssohn, great art and a noble life were reconciled as in no other single individual. He was a conspicuously Cultured, Christian gentleman." Joseph A. Mussulman, *Music in the*

Cultured Generation, p. 62; also p. 59. Charles L. Graves, *Post-Victorian Music*, pp. 146–47.

26. Edmund Gurney, *The Power of Sound*, pp. 375, 379; Edgar Wind notes that Plato posed this issue of values with absolute clarity. "When a work of art is indicted in court for having a demoralizing effect, a not uncommon judicial procedure is to enquire whether it has any artistic merit; and if it can be established that it has, its innocence is regarded as proved. The practice . . . forgets that art intensifies what it transfigures, and that a great artist can do more harm than a little one. Plato was far more circumspect: 'And if any such man will come to us to show us his art, we shall kneel down before him and worship him as a rare and holy and wonderful being; but we shall not permit him to stay [in our city].'" The modern critic, suggests Wind, should keep his audience aware of the social dimensions which artworks possess. Edgar Wind, "The Critical Nature of a Work of Art," in Richard French, ed., *Music and Criticism*, pp. 67–69.

27. Daniel Gregory Mason, "Our Public School Music," p. 705; Daniel Gregory Mason, "Dissonance and Evil." Years later, in a letter to his friend Burnet Tuthill, Mason defended his own use of dissonance to create emotional tension rather than merely to create a sensuous effect. By this time (1947) Mason allowed himself the liberty of referring to "emotional tension" rather than "musical tension." Daniel Gregory Mason to Burnet Tuthill, 6 August 1947, Daniel Gregory Mason Papers, Box 15, Columbia University Library, New York.

Santayana argues that "while aesthetic judgments are mainly positive, that is, perceptions of good, moral judgments are mainly and fundamentally negative, or perceptions of evil." The former are also intrinsic judgments; the latter are instrumental. Mason views both categories of judgment as instrumental and sees both evil and dissonance as mere lacks of their positive counterparts. Santayana, p. 375.

28. Daniel Gregory Mason, *Music as an International Language*, p. 4.

29. Charles Ives, *Memos*, pp. 99, 123; Ives, *Essays*, pp. 83n., 84–85.

30. Ives, *Essays*, pp. 94–95; Brewster Ives, in Vivian Perlis, ed., *Charles Ives Remembered*, p. 79.

31. Ives, *Memos*, pp. 134–35; Mason, *Music in My Time*, p. 101; Ives, *Essays*, pp. 24–25, 39, 72–73, 82, 99.

32. Ives, *Essays*, pp. 3–4.

33. Ibid., pp. 8, 70–71.

34. Ibid., pp. 97–98.

35. Frank Rossiter, *Charles Ives and His America*, pp. 241–43.

36. Igor Stravinsky, quoted in Morroe Berger, "Jazz," p. xiii. B. H. Haggin, "Music and Common Sense—II," *Nation*, 19 January 1927, p. 72.

37. For example, the German critic Paul Schwers complained that Carl Ruggles's *Sun Treader* gave him "the impression of bowel constrictions in an atonal Tristanesque ecstasy." Schwers suggested the piece be renamed "Latrine-treader." Peter Yates, however, finds that Ruggles's work moves like "water-boiling in a pot—an expanding universe which is at the same time necessarily contracting, a motion without external limit." Eric Salzman describes the work in yet another vivid simile: "Short, reflective passages—marked 'Serene, *tempo rubato*'—alternate with great speaking, shouting dissonant prose, those jagged, striding, reaching lines that well up like the rocky contours of a giant landscape." Paul Schwers, *Allgemeine Musikzeitung* (Berlin, 18 March 1932), quoted in Nicolas Slonimsky, ed., *Lexicon of Musical Invective*, p. 146; Peter Yates, *Twentieth Century Music*, p. 280. Eric Salzman, liner notes to DGG 2530 048.

Beyond the problem of composer or critic communicating with a musically semiliterate public, the issue remains of whether, in any case, the quality of an artwork can be explained. Kant argued that "I must immediately feel pleasure in the representation of the object, and of that I can be persuaded by no grounds of proof whatever. Although, as Hume says, all critics can reason more plausibly than cooks, yet the same fate awaits them" (Kant, p. 308). A. J. Ayer, following G. E. Moore, identified this critical impotence as a form of the "naturalistic fallacy," the notion that any value judgment may be true or false in the scientific sense. *Encyclopedia Britannica*, 15th ed., s.v. "Aesthetics," p. 158.

38. Ives, *Essays*, p. 70.

39. Robert Schumann had felt it necessary to defend the composer's desire to give his audience literary clues as to his musical "meaning." "If a poet is licensed to explain the whole meaning of his poem by its title, why may not the composer do likewise?" Robert Schumann, quoted in Sam Morgenstern, *Composers on Music*, p. 150.

40. Rossiter, p. 283; Thompson, quoted ibid., p. 285.

41. Ives, *Essays*, p. 77. Francois Roussell-Despierres was the author of *L'ideal esthetique*, published in 1904.

42. Rosalie Sandra Perry, *Charles Ives and the American Mind*, pp. 8, 33–35; Hanslick, pp. 166–67.

43. Ives, too, used *romantic* and *classic*, but in an altogether different way. "Let us . . . say that a thing is classic if it is thought of in terms of the past and romantic if thought of in terms of the future." Ives, *Essays*, p. 26.

44. Ives, *Memos*, p. 95.

45. Van Wyck Brooks, "On Creating a Usable Past," *Source* (11 April 1918), pp. 337–41, in *Van Wyck Brooks*, p. 225; Claire Sprague, "Introduction," ibid., p. xiv; Bercovitch, p. 154.

46. Daniel Gregory Mason, *Artistic Ideals* (New York: W. W. Norton & Co., 1927), p. 183.

47. Daniel Gregory Mason, *Tune In America*, p. 159.

48. Clifford Geertz, *The Interpretation of Cultures*, p. 90; Mason, *Artistic Ideals*, pp. 174–75.

49. Ives, *Essays*, p. 26; Mason, *Music in My Time*, p. 4; Bigalow Ives, in Perlis, pp. 81–82; Rossiter, p. 96.

50. Rossiter, p. 163.

51. Some composers have denied this premise. Arnold Schoenberg, in a letter to Alexander von Zemlinsky (23 February 1918), reveals a deep despair with audiences. Schoenberg writes sourly that he has as little consideration for the listener as the listener has for him. "All I know is that he exists, and in so far as he isn't indispensable for acoustic reasons (since music doesn't sound well in an empty hall), he's only a nuisance." Schoenberg, quoted in Raynor, p. 9.

52. Mason, *Artistic Ideals*, pp. 165–68.

53. The phrasing of this summary of Cooley's interactionist perspective is drawn from Lewis Coser, "American Trends," in Tom Bottomore and Robert Nisbet, eds., in *A History of Sociological Analysis*, p. 308.

54. Mason, *Artistic Ideals*, pp. 169–70; Julian Huxley, quoted in Mason, *Tune In America*, p. 175; John Dewey, *Art as Experience*, pp. 336, 345–46; Charles Horton Cooley, *Human Nature & the Social Order* (1902), p. 92; Charles Horton Cooley, *Social Organization* (1909), pp. 80–81; Philip Rieff, "Introduction" to Cooley, *Social Organization*, p. xv.

55. Mason, *Artistic Ideals*, p. 187.
56. David W. Noble, *The Progressive Mind, 1890–1917*, pp. 133–34.

PART TWO: *Ethnic Dissonance*

1. Carl Engel, "Views and Reviews," *Musical Quarterly*, April 1925, p. 307.
2. Noah cursed Canaan, son of Ham, who had looked upon his father's nakedness, and condemned him to be a "servant of servants" to his brothers. By the seventeenth century Ham's curse became a stock European explanation for the blackness of Africans. Winthrop D. Jordan, *White over Black*, pp. 17–19, 36, 242, 416.

But blackness appears to have had powerful metaphorical overtones for Englishmen quite aside from any knowledge or concern that people's skin could be black. "Black," notes Jordan, "was an emotionally partisan color, the handmaid and symbol of baseness and evil, a sign of danger and repulsion." Ibid., p. 7.

3. Jordan, pp. 24–25, 32–37, 218–22, 229; Oscar Handlin, *Race and Nationality in American Life*, pp. 57–59. Linnaeus had, in Handlin's words, "spun a web in which generations of unhappy thinkers would be trapped." Ibid., p. 59.

4. Jordan, p. 229. Arthur O. Lovejoy points out that "the program of discovering the hitherto unobserved links in the chain played a part of especial importance in the beginnings of the science of anthropology." Arthur O. Lovejoy, *The Great Chain of Being*, pp. 233, 234, 236.

George M. Frederickson, *The Black Image in the White Mind*, p. 101. In 1799 an Englishman, Dr. Charles White, first outlined the theory that placed Negroes below whites on the Great Chain of Being. He viewed them as "an intermediate species between the white man and the ape." Thomas F. Gossett, *Race*, pp. 47–48.

Most religious slaveholders eschewed the blasphemous, if convenient, doctrine of polygenesis—the separate creation of blacks and whites. Gossett, pp. 65–66.

5. Frederickson, p. 253; Gossett, pp. 67–69, 144–49. Spencer outlined the doctrine portraying the Negro as a childlike example of incomplete evolution. The American Spencerian G. Stanley Hall argued that "primitive races . . . were in an early evolutionary stage, something like that of an arrested childhood." Ibid., pp. 149, 154.

Many white Americans were concerned about devolutionary breeding between races. Thomas Jefferson had already articulated the fear that "black men preferred white to black women 'as uniformly as is the preference of the Oran-utan for the black women over those of his own species.'" Jefferson quoted in Ronald Takaki, "The Black Child-Savage," in Gary B. Nash and Richard Weiss, eds., *The Great Fear*, p. 41.

6. Michael D. Biddis, *Father of Racist Ideology*, pp. 119–20.

7. Julien Freund, *The Sociology of Max Weber*, pp. 204–208. Not that Weber was wholly pleased at the Victorian world of materialism that had grown out of, and then overgrown, the Protestant ethic: "In the field of its highest development, in the United States, the pursuit of wealth, stripped of its religious and ethical meaning, tends to become associated with purely mundane passions, which often actually give it the character of sport.

"No one knows who will live in this cage in the future, or whether at the end of this tremendous development entirely new prophets will arise, or there will be a great rebirth of old ideas and ideals, or, if neither, mechanized petrification, embellished with a sort of convulsive self-importance. For of the last stage of this cultural development, it might well be said: 'Specialists without spirit, sensualists without heart; this nullity imagines that it has attained a level of civilization never before achieved.'" (Max Weber, *The Protestant Ethic and the Spirit of Capitalism*, p. 182.)

Freud found it difficult to disentangle sublimation and repression, sociologically considered. He was even less sanguine than Weber about the future of civilization. Sigmund Freud, *Civilization and Its Discontents*, pp. 26–30, 39–44, 92.

3. Jazz and the Asphalt Jungle

1. Even today jazz musicologists cannot agree on the character of jazz in the years prior to 1920. For all practical purposes, jazz history begins with jazz recordings. The prehistory of jazz must reconstruct the protean interactions of blues, marches, dances, and ragtime styles, as played in various social settings, in different regions.

2. Rudi Blesh and Harriet Janis, *They All Played Ragtime*, p. 4.

3. *Musical America*, 29 March 1913; *Metronome*, 20 May 1901; *American Federation of Musicians*, 1901: all quoted in Blesh and Janis, pp. 132, 134, 135.

4. Rupert Hughes, "A Eulogy of Ragtime," *Musical Record*, April 1899, quoted in Blesh and Janis, pp. 131–32.

5. Robert Dale Owen, *The Wrong of Slavery; the Right of Emancipation; and the Future of the African Race in the United States* (Philadelphia, 1864), quoted in Blesh and Janis, pp. 124–25; George M. Frederickson, *The Black Image in the White Mind*, pp. 101, 256–86.

6. H. Wiley Hitchcock, *Music in the United States*, pp. 107, 123; Robert C. Toll, *Blacking Up*, pp. 235–38, 243, 272.

7. Blesh and Janis, pp. 14, 17.

8. The key year was 1892: Patrick Gilmore, "the Columbus of the modern American Brass Band," died while performing at the St. Louis Exposition; and John Philip Sousa left the Marine Band to organize his own aggregation. Ibid., p. 73; Hitchcock, p. 118.

Both rags and marches are constructed on the basic plan of the rondo, ABACA-Coda. Furthermore, notes Gunther Schuller, "ragtime, like the march, has a duple time signature, and most of the rags, such as Joplin's *Maple Leaf Rag*, are marked 'tempo di marcia' or 'in slow march time.'" Schuller emphasizes that "many of the early rag compositions were called 'marches' outright." Gunther Schuller, *Early Jazz*, p. 33.

9. *New York Herald*, 13 January 1901, quoted in Blesh and Janis, p. 223; ibid., p. 75.

10. John Philip Sousa, *Marching Along*, quoted in Hitchcock, p. 120.

11. Antonin Dvořák, "Music in America," p. 433. Dvořák had been circulating his ideas since 1893.

12. Ibid. On this simile, cf. Emerson's "What is a weed? A plant whose virtues have not yet been discovered" (Ralph Waldo Emerson, "Fortune of the Republic," in *The Complete Writings of Ralph Waldo Emerson*, p. 1185); and, "One country's weeds may become in another country hothouse or ornamental plants, being cultivated there to greater or more prolific beauty, though they are not natural to the climate" (Peter Yates, *Twentieth Century Music*, p. 273). This recurring metaphor is the positive counterpart to the negative metaphor which suggests that foreign importations have no rootedness in the national soil, and hence cannot or should not survive.

13. *London Times*, quoted in Blesh and Janis, p. 134.

14. Edgar L. Kirk, "Toward American Music: A Study of the Life and Music of Arthur Farwell" (Ph.D. dissertation), pp. 1, 6, 10, 13–15; Arthur Farwell, "An Affirmation of American Music," *Musical World* 3, no. 1 (January 1903), in Gilbert Chase, ed., *The American Composer Speaks*, p. 93.

15. Farwell, in Chase, p. 93; Farwell's statement of purpose, quoted in Kirk, p. 16.

16. Charles Wakefield Cadman, in the *Musical Courier*, 12 August 1914, quoted in Blesh and Janis, p. 134; Hitchcock, p. 136; Edward Alexander MacDowell, *Critical and Historical Essays*, p. 146.

17. Charles E. Ives, *Memos*, pp. 39–40, 57; Hitchcock, pp. 73, 75.

18. Hiram K. Moderwell, "Ragtime," p. 284; Daniel Gregory Mason, "Concerning Ragtime," *New Music and Church Review* 17, no. 22 (March 1918), reprinted in Daniel Gregory Mason, *Contemporary Composers*, pp. 246–47; Charles E. Ives, *Essays before a Sonata, and Other Writings*, p. 94.

19. Edward Burlingame Hill, letter to Mason, quoted in Daniel Gregory Mason, *Music in My Time, and Other Reminiscences*, p. 36. A review in the *New York Times* of Hill's *Jazz Scherzo for Two Pianos and Orchestra* (probably using his "little Scherzino") suggested that "Hill . . . employs in a gentlemanly manner jazz rhythms. That is, in fact, the most polite jazz that we have heard—the guarded jest of a Cambridge drawing-room." Quoted by the *Boston Evening Transcript*, 7 January 1925, p. 10.

20. R. D. Darrell, "The Music of Henry F. Gilbert, John Powell, John Alden Carpenter, and Adolph Weiss," notes to New World Records, N.W. 228, pp. 2–3. Cadman, best known for his "Indian" compositions, published his *Dark Dances of the Mardi Gras* in 1932.

21. H. K. M. [Hiram Moderwell], "Gilbert and Cadman: Two American Pieces at the Metropolitan," *Boston Evening Transcript*, 25 March 1918, p. 13.

22. Karleton Hackett, "Mr. Gilbert and Ragtime," *Boston Evening Transcript*, 6 March 1918; picked up, reprinted from the *Evening Post;* Henry F. Gilbert, "Folk-Music in Art-Music—A Discussion and a Theory," *Musical Quarterly*, October 1917, p. 600; Henry Gilbert, quoted by Darrell, p. 2.

23. Mason, *Contemporary Composers*, p. 250.

24. Quoted by Robert S. Clark in his liner notes, Mercury SRI-75026; Ives, *Essays*, pp. 78–79.

25. Ives, *Essays*, p. 81.

26. Leonard Feather, *The New Edition of the Encyclopedia of Jazz*, p. 24. H. O. Brunn, *The Story of the Original Dixieland Jazz Band*, pp. 52–57. Neil Leonard, *Jazz and the White Americans*, p. 12. Rudi Blesh, *Shining Trumpets*, pp. 202–204.

27. Schuller, pp. 245–52. As black bands became popular with white audiences, Negroes felt nervous about the image their musicians projected among Whites. Both James Europe's all-Negro U.S. Infantry Hell Fighters Band and the "rough" jazz bands came under attack from image-conscious members of the black community. One of their musical spokesman in New York was Will Marion Cook, a violinist and successful composer of popular stage music. He intended his New York Syncopated Orchestra to be more "serious," less raucous than the jazz groups.

28. *New York Times*, 10 March 1919, p. 9.

29. Schuller, pp. 65–66, 68–70, 252–53; Daniel Gregory Mason, "The Jazz Invasion," p. 505.

30. Frederick Lewis Allen, *Only Yesterday*, pp. 32–34; Allen H. Spear, *Black Chicago*, pp. 12, 202, vii; Gilbert Osofsky, *Harlem*.

31. Quoted in Allen, p. 47. John Higham quotes a letter to the editor of the *New Republic* in 1924 which illustrates the extent to which the Klan touched a common chord among white, Protestant Americans. "The old Americans are getting a little panicky, and no wonder. . . . America, Americans and Americanism are being crowded out of America. It is inevitable that there should be silly forms of protest and rebellion. But the Ku Klux Klan and the hundred percenters are fundamentally right from the standpoint of an American unity and destiny." John Higham, *Strangers in the Land*, p. 264. Also see Thomas F. Gossett, *Race*, pp. 352–408.

32. H. E. Krehbiel, quoted in Leonard, p. 36.

33. The word *jazz* is of obscure origin, though theories abound. It may have grown out of a musician's nickname, or from a Creole version of the French word *jaser*, to chatter. It meant, in Chicago underworld slang, to fornicate, or, more loosely, to fool around. Before 1917 the word was generally spelled *jass*. New York notices for the ODJB altered *jass* to *jasz*, and a month later to *jazz*. Barry Ulanov, *Handbook of Jazz*, p. 100; Marshall Stearns, *The Story of Jazz*, p. 112; Brunn, pp. 30, 52, 57.

34. *New York Times*, 22 January 1921, p. 22; 4 February 1926, p. 4; 14 January 1926, p. 1. Morroe Berger, "Jazz: Resistance to the Diffusion of a Culture-Pattern," p. 464.

35. College students agreed with their parents that jazz was linked with cigarettes, alcohol, and sexuality. But for them it was an essential feature of generational rebellion. Paula Fass, *The Damned and the Beautiful*, pp. 303–306.

36. J. Hartley Manners, *The National Anthem*, pp. 27–28.

37. Ibid., p. 28.

38. Ibid.; John R. McMahon, "Back to Pre-War Morals," *Ladies' Home Journal*, November 1921, quoted in Leonard, p. 32; Laurette Taylor, quoted in untraced newspaper clipping, quoted in Leonard, p. 38.

39. Dixon, quoted in Frederickson, pp. 280–81; also see pp. 325–27; Madison Grant's *The Passing of the White Race* (1916) and Lothrop Stoddard's *The Rising Tide of Color* (1920) also provided intellectual fuel for "the resurgent racism of the early twenties." Higham, pp. 271–72.

40. Dixon, quoted in Frederickson, p. 281.

41. For a concise discussion of the dynamics of racial and sexual disequilibrium, see Peter Loewenberg, "The Psychology of Racism," in Gary B. Nash and Richard Weiss, eds., *The Great Fear*, pp. 186–201.

42. H. L. Mencken, *H. L. Mencken on Music*, pp. 186, 188.

43. Buster Bailey, quoted in Leonard, p. 39.

44. Ibid.

45. Berger, p. 463; White, quoted in Leonard, p. 40.

46. Fritz Laubenstein, "Jazz-Debit and Credit," *Musical Quarterly*, October 1929, p. 615; quoted in Berger, p. 263; John Gould Fletcher, "A Jazz Critic," *Dial*, 23 August 1919, p. 156.

47. Robert Cole, "Conspiracy of Silence against Jazz," *New York Times*, 21 September 1919, sec. 7, p. 6; *New York Times*, 30 December 1920, p. 3; 26 September 1926, p. 26.

48. Quoted in Leonard, pp. 43–45.

49. Mason, "Jazz Invasion," p. 505.

50. Burnet C. Tuthill, "David Stanley Smith," *Musical Quarterly*, January 1942, pp. 63–65; David Stanley Smith, "A Study of Horatio Parker," *Musical Quarterly*, April 1930, p. 153; John Tasker Howard, *Our American Music*, p. 484; David Stanley Smith, "Putting Jazz in Its Place," pp. 31–32.

51. David Ewen, *American Composers Today*, pp. 91-92; Kirk, pp. 14-22; Arthur Farwell, "The Zero Hour in Musical Evolution," *Musical Quarterly*, January 1927, p. 91.

52. Albert Nelson Marquis, ed., *Who's Who in America*, vol. 16, p. 1981.

53. Richard H. Pells, *Radical Visions and American Dreams: Culture and Social Thought in the Depression Years* (New York: Harper Torchbooks, 1973), pp. 34-35.

54. Robert Kimbal, "Shuffle Along," program notes to New World Records' recreation of Sissle and Blake's review-show, N.W. 260, pp. 1-4; Gilbert Seldes, *The Seven Lively Arts* (1924), pp. 154, 158.

55. Gilbert Seldes, "Toujours Jazz," *Dial*, August 1923, pp. 151-58, 160, 163.

56. Virgil Thomson, "Jazz," *American Mercury*, August 1924, pp. 465, 467.

57. The Drifter, "In the Driftway," *Nation*, 20 August 1924, pp. 190-91.

58. Philip Curtiss, "Amos 'N' Andy 'N' Art," *Harper's Magazine*, May 1931, pp. 633-36. Music critic B. H. Haggin was unimpressed with the new technical assessments of jazz. He labeled these efforts pedantry, whatever their ultimate verdicts. It is impossible to translate technique and beauty, one into another, he argued. No technical analysis can prove either works by d'Indy or jazz works to be beautiful or not. A writer such as Seldes tried to vindicate his pleasure in jazz by reference to technical features of jazz, using musical terms which his readers might not understand. Others, like Mason, disliked jazz, and tried to prove the inferiority of jazz by references to its "primitive technique." Both arguments are pedantic and false, according to Haggin. B. H. Haggin, "The Pedant Looks at Jazz," *Nation*, 9 December 1925, pp. 685-88.

59. Bruce Kellner, *Carl Van Vechten and the Irreverent Decades*, pp. 8, 17. Van Vechten quoted, pp. 3, 35.

60. Nathan Irvin Huggins, *Harlem Renaissance*, p. 94.

61. *Time*, quoted in Kellner, p. 195.

62. Edward Lueders, "Mr. Van Vechten of New York City," p. 36.

63. Carl Van Vechten, "George Gershwin: An American Composer Who Is Writing Notable Music in the Jazz Idiom," p. 40; and "The Black Blues: Negro Songs of Disappointment in Love:—Their Pathos Hardened with Laughter," pp. 57, 92.

64. Carl Van Vechten, "Prescription for the Negro Theatre," p. 92.

65. Carl Van Vechten, "Moanin' wid a Sword in Ma Han'," pp. 100, 102.

66. W. E. B. DuBois, "Review of *Nigger Heaven*," *Crisis*, December 1926, quoted as a preface in Carl Van Vechten, *Nigger Heaven* (1926), pp. vii, viii; Langston Hughes, *The Big Sea* (New York: Hill and Wang, Inc., 1940), quoted as a preface in Van Vechten, *Nigger Heaven*, p. xvii.

67. Huggins, pp. 85, 199. This use of *civility* is explained in my analysis of John Murray Cuddihy, *The Ordeal of Civility*.

68. Alain Locke, ed., *The New Negro* (1925), p. xvii; James Weldon Johnson, "Race Prejudice and the Negro Artist," *Harper's Magazine*, November 1928, p. 776; W. E. B. DuBois, "Criteria of Negro Art," *Crisis*, October 1926, p. 297, in W. E. B. DuBois, *The Seventh Son*, vol. 2, p. 321; Osofsky, p. 186.

69. It also contained the germ of an antiwhite "radical racial primitivism." Huggins, pp. 125-26.

70. Johnson, p. 775; Van Vechten, *Nigger Heaven*, p. 90; J. A. Rogers, "Jazz at Home," in Locke, p. 217.

71. Langston Hughes, "Nude Young Dancer," in Locke, p. 227.

72. The search for the roots of the black artistic soul occasionally led to naive

enthusiasm for ersatz African art. Art scholar Thomas Munro wrote: "The Blon-
diau African Collection now being shown . . . at the New Art Circle in New York
. . . deserves, as a whole, neither the word 'primitive,' nor "African,' nor 'art.' The
objects . . . are in large part modern imitations . . . by unskilled African natives
who are trying in vain to recapture the art of their ancestors." Thomas Munro,
"Good and Bad Negro Art," *Nation*, 2 March 1927, pp. 212–13.

73. Quoted in Jim Haskins, *The Cotton Club*, p. 73.
74. John Hammond, with Irving Townsend, *John Hammond On Record*, p. 28.
75. Ibid., pp. 29–30, 37, 60–61, 89, 91.
76. Irving Kolodin, "Number One Swing Man," *Harper's Magazine*, September
1939, pp. 431–35; B. H. Haggin, "Music," *Nation*, 14 October 1939, pp. 420–21;
Hammond, p. 73; John Hammond, letter to the editor, "John Hammond on B.
H. H.," *Nation*, 4 November 1939, p. 508.
77. Barry Ulanov, *Duke Ellington*, pp. 103–105; Hammond, *On Record*, pp. 136–
37.
78. Haskins, p. 53; Ulanov, *Ellington*, p. 95.
79. Stearns, p. 133.
80. Quoted in Haskins, p. 24.
81. The whole issue became serious enough to invite a little joshing:

> The Jazzer toils not, neither doth he spin,
>   But gambles, smokes, and drinks and bets on horses.
> 'Tis Jazz that leads the feet to paths of sin;
>   It breaks up homes, it stimulates divorces,
> It wrecks the nerves, it makes a horrid din,
>   Impairs both taste and health and wastes resources;
> It tempts our boys from virtue and the farm,
> And that is why we view it with alarm. . . .
> In every age before some Moloch-shrine
>   A fickle, shameless generation grovels.
>   . . . wherefore, as
> We must be damned for something, make it Jazz!

Arthur Guiterman, "Jazz," *Harper's Monthly Magazine*, October 1923, p. 716.
82. It would be as foolish to brand James Weldon Johnson, Langston Hughes,
or John Hammond "racists" as it would be to deny that even these men were
tethered by "racialist" generalizations.
83. Mason, "Jazz Invasion," p. 506; Daniel Gregory Mason, "Jazz for the Illiterate."
84. Mason, "Jazz Invasion," p. 506.
85. Raymond Williams, *Culture and Society, 1780–1950*, pp. 42–48, 56–70.
86. Mason, "Jazz Invasion," pp. 502–503. Or, as Fritz Laubenstein wrote,
"Good taste or great art then, is not the monopoly of the snobbish few, but of the
disciplined few who prove themselves worthy of it. And in such as democracy a
ours, absence of the 'will to power' is the only let to the attainment of this
privileged position. To say that the test of art is its appeal to the great masses of
humanity, therefore, is not at all equivalent to saying that all that has popular
approval or appeal is the best art—the standard by which jazz hopes to justify itself
as an art and to commend itself to the painstakers." Laubenstein, pp. 616–617.
87. Mason, "Jazz Invasion," pp. 505–507.
88. Sacvan Bercovitch, *The Puritan Origins of the American Self*, p. 169.

89. Basil Willey, *Nineteenth Century Studies*, pp. 1–26; H. Stuart Hughes, *Consciousness and Society*, pp. 33–39; Daniel Gregory Mason, "Artistic Ideals: IV, Originality," p. 4; Mason, "Jazz Invasion," p. 507.

90. Moderwell was writing about ragtime, but Mason replied as though Moderwell had been discussing jazz. Mason, "Jazz Invasion," p. 505; Moderwell, p. 286.

91. Virgil Thomson saw jazz as "the temporary urban aspect of . . . [America's 'vast and explosive musical energy.'] Virgil Thomson, "The Cult of Jazz," p. 118; Mencken, p. 186.

4. THE DISTORTED MIRROR

1. Perry Miller, *Errand into the Wilderness*, pp. 12–13.

2. The phrase "custodians of culture" has been borrowed from Henry F. May, *The End of American Innocence*, pp. 30ff.

3. Quoted in Hugh Honour, *The New Golden Land*, p. 119.

4. Images of America as an ever-new, prebiblical utopia mingled with images of New World jungled filled with exotic, scary creatures. According to Howard Mumford Jones, this dualism was firmly fixed in the European imagination prior to the English colonizations. Both myths fed into the European view of America as breeder of revolutionary trends. Since the American Revolution, the United States has been often regarded as an exporter of the dangerously new, of "Americanism." See Howard Mumford Jones, *O Strange New World: American Culture: The Formative Years* (New York: The Viking Press, 1964), pp. 69–70, 273, 311.

5. Darius Milhaud, "The Jazz Band and Negro Music," p. 169; T. R. Ybarra, "'Jazz 'er Up!' Broadway's Conquest of Europe," *New York Times*, 18 December 1921, sec. 3, p. 1; *New York Times*, 14 January 1923, p. 12; 28 July 1922, p. 3; 25 February 1924, p. 1; 29 January 1926, p. 10; 3 April 1927, p. 23; 20 November 1927, p. 2; 12 October 1927, p. 27; 8 January 1928, p. 8; 19 February 1928, p. 8; 15 April 1928, p. 2.

6. Milhaud, p. 169; M. Robert Rogers, "Jazz Influence on French Music," *Musical Quarterly*, January 1935, p. 60; Honour, p. 259; Max Jones and John Chilton, *The Louis Armstrong Story, 1900–1971*, p. 129; H. O. Brunn, *The Story of the Original Dixieland Jazz Band*, pp. xvi, 131; Jones and Chilton, p. 129.

7. Jones and Chilton, p. 130.

8. Barry Ulanov, *Duke Ellington*, pp. 130, 132, 134, 136.

9. Quoted in Stanley Dance, *The World of Duke Ellington*, pp. 77–78; Ellington quoted in Ulanov, p. 151; Ulanov paraphrasing Hughes, Ulanov, p. 140; see also Ulanov, p. 139; Morroe Berger, "Jazz: Resistance to the Diffusion of a Culture-Pattern," pp. 466–67, 480–81; Chadwick Hansen, "Social Influences on Jazz Style: Chicago, 1920–1930," p. 501; Dance, pp. 74–75, 88–89, 120, 122.

10. Quoted in Ulanov, pp. 142–44.

11. Ibid., pp. 149–50; quoted by Rogers, p. 60; Carl Engel, "Views and Reviews," *Musical Quarterly*, October 1932, p. 651.

12. Rogers, pp. 36, 57.

13. Ernest Ansermet, in *La revue romande*, 15 October 1919, quoted in Louis Harap, "The Case for Hot Jazz," *Musical Quarterly*, January 1941, p. 53.

14. *New York Times*, 11 July 1926, cited in Rogers, pp. 61, 64.

15. William Bolcom, notes to Nonesuch H-71281; Darius Milhaud, *Notes without Music*, p. 102; Milhaud, "Jazz Band," pp. 169–70.

16. Milhaud, "Jazz Band," pp. 171–73.

17. Quoted in Sam Morgenstern, ed., *Composers on Music*, p. 359.

18. Milhaud, *Notes*, p. 164; quoted in Rogers, p. 66.

19. Jones and Chilton, p. 130.

20. W. J. Henderson, "Ragtime, Jazz, and High Art," p. 203.

21. Ibid. "For my own part," wrote Mason, "I confess that my joy in the use of beautiful simple tunes like *Deep River* in . . . the Quartet on *Negro Themes*, was partly due to their giving me a chance to indulge my own naivete without a sense of inferiority. . . . [Yet there was] a lack of complete correspondence between the temperament of the composer and the material of the composition. The material was scarcely complex enough for me, or I was scarcely simple enough for it—put it either way you choose." Daniel Gregory Mason, *Music in My Time, and Other Reminiscences*, p. 366.

22. Carl Engel, "Views and Reviews," *Musical Quarterly*, October 1923, p. 586.

23. Charles Horton Cooley, *Human Nature & the Social Order*, p. 184.

24. J. A. Rogers, "Jazz at Home," in Alain Locke, ed., *The New Negro* (1923), p. 218; F. Scott Fitzgerald, "Echoes of the Jazz Age," in *The Crack Up*, p. 15; Sigmund Spaeth, *The Art of Enjoying Music*, p. 316.

25. Percy Grainger, "The Impress of Personality in Unwritten Music," *Musical Quarterly*, July 1915, pp. 416–35; *Boston Evening Transcript*, 2 January 1925, p. 11.

26. *Philadelphia North American*, 4 March 1922, in Nicolas Slonimsky, ed., *Lexicon of Musical Invective*, p. 200.

27. Hale, *Boston Herald*, 27 January 1924, ibid.; Downes, *New York Times*, 16 March 1924, ibid., p. 202; Igor Stravinsky, quoted in the *Boston Evening Transcript*, 7 January 1925, p. 10.

28. Daniel Gregory Mason, *The Dilemma of American Music, and Other Essays*, pp. 46, 115, 123.

29. Taylor, *Dial*, September 1920, in Slonimsky, p. 198; Rosenfeld, *Dial*, February 1921, ibid.; Mason, *Dilemma*, p. 117.

30. R. D. Darrell, "The Music of Henry F. Gilbert, John Powell, John Alden Carpenter, and Adolph Weiss," notes to New World Records, N.W. 228, p. 4.

31. Program notes to Desto DST-6407. Critics perceive what they wish to perceive. The critic Paul Rosenfeld suggested that *Skyscrapers* was an out-of-date paean to idealized Workers, Skyscrapers, and the Jazz Age, all of which were passé. Rosenfeld interpreted Carpenter's effort as "a ballet of Workers, blinking traffic signals, acetylene burners, steel girders, jazz, Magic Cities, and choruses of strong, gaunt, big-wristed plain-haired operators soulfully aspiring to the painful purple dawn." Paul Rosenfeld, "Musical Chronicle," *Dial*, May 1926, p. 440.

32. Quoted in Thomas Claude Pierson, "The Life and Music of John Alden Carpenter" (Ph.D. dissertation), pp. 16–17.

33. Emile Nolde, "Primitive Art," in Victor H. Meisel, ed., *Voices of German Expressionism*, p. 35. Nolde's infatuation with "blood-and-soil" ideals eventually led him, unsuccessfully, to seek Nazi approval of his paintings. Other expressionists viewed their movement as a beginning for a socialist attack on the middle classes. Meisel, p. 30; Klaus Berger, "The Heritage of Expressionism," ibid., pp. 204–205.

34. Paul Gauguin, letter to his wife Mette, in Herschel B. Chipp, ed., *Theories of Modern Art*, p. 79.

35. Irving Howe, ed., *The Idea of the Modern in Literature and the Arts*, p. 12; see also Philip Rahv, quoted in Richard Chase, "The Fate of the Avant-Garde," ibid., p. 146.

36. Renato Poggioli, *The Theory of the Avant-Garde*, p. 218.

37. Ibid., p. 217; Honour, pp. 248-49.

38. F. T. Martinetti, "The Foundation and Manifesto of Futurism" (1908), in Chipp, pp. 286-87.

39. Honour, p. 254.

40. Howe, pp. 23-25, 29-30. For example, love of the machine did not necessarily imply a nihilist abandonment to the dynamic of contemporary civilization. The precisionism of Charles Demuth and the early William Carlos Williams exalted the machine for the formal organicism, the self-sufficiency of its integrated parts. James Guimond, *The Art of William Carlos Williams*, pp. 41-53. Stravinsky's fascination with mechanical things was precisionist, as his aesthetic was formalist. Joan Peyser, *The New Music*, pp. 101, 108, 111. His characterization of Ravel as a Swiss watchmaker reflects equally on his own outlook. Yet these observations, caveats really, do not alter the fact that as a whole the European avant-garde did associate either expressionist primitivism or mechanistic dynamism with "Americanism."

41. Suggesting that aesthetically we may have seen "The End of the Renaissance," Leonard Meyer contrasts antiteleological and existential avant-garde art with teleological art (i.e., traditionalist art in which artist and audience engage in a formalized courtship of expectations deferred and ultimately consummated). The antiteleological artist seeks a return to the "primitive" enjoyment of media as nature—sound, light, or words, without grammar and syntax. Meyer distinguishes antiteleological avant-gardism ("radical empiricism") from existential avant-gardism. While the former seeks to dissolve choice in nature, the latter seeks to enthrone socially untrammeled individual choice. Meyer himself tentatively equates antiteleological avant-gardism with Americanism. Leonard B. Meyer, *Music, the Arts, and Ideas*, pp. 68-76.

42. Honour, p. 256.

43. "The Art of Noises" amplified themes broached a year earlier by Ballila Pratella. Their views were later consolidated by Enrico Prampolini, a figure who bridged the futurist and dadaist movements: "The elements and the plastic symbols of the Machine are inevitably as much symbols as a god Pan, the taking down from the Cross, of the Assumption of the Virgin, etc." Prampolini cautioned that it was not the "exterior reality" of the Machine to which he referred but "the plastic-mechanical analogy that the Machine suggests to us in connection with various spiritual realities." Enrico Prampolini, "The Aesthetic of the Machine and Mechanical Introspection in Art," in Lucy R. Lippard, ed., *Dadas on Art*, pp. 118-19.

44. Basically Varèse attacked the futurists as mere collectors of undigested noises. "Italian Futurists," wrote Varèse in a Poggioli-like passage, "why do you merely reproduce the vibrations of our daily life only in their superficial and distressing aspects? My dream is of instruments that will obey my thought." Varèse quoted in Fernand Ouelette, *Edgard Varèse*, p. 39.

45. Edgard Varèse, quoted on Vanguard SRV-274SD.

46. Varèse did not care to associate his New World avant-gardism with jazz; most critics, with notable exceptions such as Lawrence Gilman and Paul Rosenfeld, did not care to associate it with music at all. Stokowski presented the premiere of *Ameriques* in Philadelphia in 1926. A performance in New York was followed by one in Paris—then nothing, no performances until it was recorded in the mid-1960s. Slonimsky, pp. 213-17; Ouelette, pp. 75, 77-79, 88-89.

47. Tom Carlson, "Ernst Křenek: Jonny Spielt Auf," notes for Mace MXX 9094. The opera summary is drawn from Carlson.

48. Ibid.

49. Lawrence Adler, "'Jonny' and 'Manon,'" *Nation*, 27 February 1929, p. 264.

50. Lotte Lenya, "Lotte Lenya Remembers Mahagonny," and H. H. Stuckenschmidt, "City of Nets," both notes for Columbia K3L 243, pp. 6–9, 11–13; V. Gorodinsky, *Music of Spiritual Poverty* (Moscow, 1950), in Slonimsky, p. 110.

51. Witchhunts against the "formalist" heresy in the USSR simply obscure the fact that Soviet critics, as much as Western "Marxists" such as Theodore Adorno, speak not for the proletariat but for an alienated, intellectual minority. See Peter K. Etzkorn, ed., *Music and Society*, pp. 18–23. "Much of the 'Marxist' writing of the 'thirties,'" notes Raymond Williams, "was in fact the old Romantic protest that there was no place in contemporary society for the artist and the intellectual, with the subsidiary clause that the workers were about to end the old system and establish Socialism, which would then provide such a place." Raymond Williams, *Culture and Society, 1780–1950*, p. 271.

5. PASSING THE TORCH

1. Sacvan Bercovitch, *The Puritan Origins of the American Self*, pp. 179, 182; Henry David Thoreau, *Walden, or, Life in the Woods*, title page.

2. Charles Schwartz, *Gershwin*, pp. 48–52.

3. Frank R. Rossiter, *Charles Ives and His America*, pp. 217, 270, 281.

4. Arthur Hertzberg (with more emphasis than his evidence can support) has singled out Voltaire as the pivotal figure in the transition from religious to secular Jewish stereotypes. (Arthur Herzberg, *The French Enlightenment and the Jews*, pp. 300, 303.) Thomas Gossett points out that early anti-Semitism did have a racial dimension. Thomas Gossett, *Race*, pp. 9–12.

5. Hannah Arendt, *The Origins of Totalitarianism*, pp. 172–73; Raymond Williams, *Culture and Society, 1780–1950*, pp. 70–85; Michael D. Biddis, *Father of Racist Ideology*, pp. 124, 254–55; Morris Ginsburg, "Antisemitism" (1943), in his *Essays in Sociology and Social Philosophy*, p. 190; Oscar Handlin, *Race and Nationality in American Life*, p. 67; Thomas F. Pettigrew, *Racially Separate or Together?*, pp. 178–92.

Eighteenth-century European race theory distinguished Europeans from others, principally by color. Amateur anthropologists such as Sir William Lawrence introduced "the idea of superior and inferior races into Europe itself," an idea whose germ was already present in Voltaire's condemnations of the Jews. (Quote from Gossett, *Race*, pp. 56–57). Racial anti-Semitism characterized Jews by analogy to non-European races of color, hence the Jew as "Oriental," as carrier of "dark" blood. English and German racial theory developed in the context of nationalism (ibid., p. 122). Anti-Semitism excluded Jews from the identity of race and nation.

In the American context, however, where there was a present, visible colored race, the idea that Jews existed between black and white categories seemed concretely plausible to many people. The Negro presence in the United States had led to a distinctive history of racialism, shaped by the experience of slavery (e.g., Americans had a prolonged affair with polygenist theories). Antiimmigrant racialism, and specifically the stereotypes of Eastern European Jews, marked a synthesis of two fairly separate streams of racial thinking. Thus, although Europeans analogized between Jews and foreigners of color, in the United States color-labeling strategies derived from actual black-white interaction were applied to Jews. For example, in the 1920s a white gentile might say of an acceptable Jew, as he might say of an acceptable Negro, "He's white."

6. Andre Coeuroy, "The Musical Aesthetics of the Comte de Gobineau," *Musical Quarterly*, July 1930, pp. 305–13. It is in this spirit that Gilbert Seldes wrote, "To anyone who inherits several thousand centuries of civilization [*sic!*], none of these things the negro offers can matter unless they are apprehended by the mind as well as by the body and the spirit. . . . So far . . . [Negroes] have shown comparatively little evidence of the functioning of their intelligence." Gilbert Seldes, "Toujours Jazz," *Dial*, August 1923, p. 160.

7. Lazare Saminsky, *Music of the Ghetto and the Bible*, p. 69; Lazare Saminsky, *Essentials and Prophecies* (1932), enlarged edition, pp. 48–49, 82–83, 118. Although today the designation of Jews as "Oriental Semites" is generally considered anti-Semitic, such was not the case prior to the Holocaust. Thus in the 1930s even the renowned Jewish philosopher Mordecai Kaplan could, without irony, refer to the "Jewish mind which has retained its oriental cast down to our own day" (Mordecai M. Kaplan, *Judaism as a Civilization* [1934], p. 257). In a narrowly defined linguistic context, it is still acceptable to call Hebrew an Oriental language. But it is not acceptable to derive racial categories from linguistic categories.

8. John Murray Cuddihy, *The Ordeal of Civility*, pp. 4–10.
Cuddihy follows the standard historiography of "modernization" sociology. For example, C. E. Black identifies modernization as the third and most dynamic of the great revolutions in human experience, superseding the changes from "prehuman to human life and from primitive to civilized societies." Jews participated in the second revolution (one of seven groups). Negroes are not mentioned, though the reader is left to surmise that they made it through the first revolution. This type of Weberian sociology tends to be a rationalization, shall we say, of history-as-the-rise-of-the-West. Cyril E. Black, *The Dynamics of Modernization*, pp. 1–5.
Cuddihy's analysis places Jews on the fringes of "modernization." Cuddihy ambiguously admires Jews as the most important force of "demodernization" in Western civilization; the Jewish struggle against the steamroller of progress makes an interesting spectacle. Three problems recur in his study: (1) the confused assumption that *modernism* and *modernization* refer to the same features of Western civilization; (2) the misperception that "Protestant" society as a whole has adapted to "modernization"; (3) the tendentious suggestion that Jews are either irrelevant or obstructive to the march of Western "progress." A humanist Victorian like Mason would agree with the first and last views; however, the second assertion would seem patently false to any of the genteel Yankee composers. Cuddihy's confusions are quite as mischievous, potentially, as Mason's.

9. John Higham, *Send These to Me*, p. 194.
Higham's analysis is paralleled by the view of Lewis Erenberg in his recent study of New York nightlife from 1890 to 1930. Erenberg attempts to explain "the transformation of the image and reality of male and female character and the Protestant approach to passion in public life." He writes that "the Jews broke the back of the Protestant-dominated [film] companies" and fed middle-class audiences hungering "for urban, consumption-oriented dramas featuring visions of a new life." They brought "class to formerly forbidden pleasures." Thus movies could "purvey to all classes the themes of urban life: experience, indulgence in exciting but safe amusements, new roles for men and women, and a redefinition of success as consumption." Neither Henry Ford nor Daniel Gregory Mason would have felt the need to change a word of Erenberg's analysis; though surely Erenberg does not view "the" restless, rootless, successful Jew of his portrayal as evil. Lewis A. Erenberg, *Steppin' Out*, pp. xiii, 72.

10. The image of "the Jew" as an unnatural member of Western society has had many incarnations: stranger, gadfly, middleman, disease, roadblock, parasite.

11. Quoting Irving Greenberg, in Edna Bonacich, "A Theory of Middleman Minorities," p. 195. Contrast Cuddihy and Higham on the Jewish ethos with Cuddihy on American Protestant civil religion: "The Protestant ethic deferred consumption. The Protestant esthetic defers ostentation. The Protestant etiquette—or, bourgeois civility—defers community." John Murray Cuddihy, *No Offense*, p. 211. Cuddihy sees the Protestant ethos as triumphant; Higham isn't so sure.

Actually, the asceticism of the Puritan Protestant ethic had fallen away rapidly as capitalism expanded on its own steam. Many seventeenth- and eighteenth-century New England merchants cannot be pegged as men called to an ascetic errand. After the Civil War, when consumer capitalism began to spread throughout the United States, the loudest cries against materialistic civilization came from the humanist Victorians. Expostulators of the "Plight of the Genteel" perfected the technique of milking their status displacement as a form of cultural one-upmanship. Bernard Bailyn, *The New England Merchants in the Seventeenth Century*, p. 139; David M. Potter, *People of Plenty*, pp. 166–72.

12. Sacvan Bercovitch, *The American Jeremiad*, p. 76.

13. Barbara Miller Solomon, *Ancestors and Immigrants;* pp. 2, 17–19, 21, 38–40, 42, 176, 187.

14. Olga Samaroff Stokowsky, *An American Musician's Story*, p. 36. Of course, in opera one would want an Italian name. Thus in *A Quiet Lodging*, by George Whitefield Chadwick, a character becomes "Signor Yayelli" to have an opportunity to perform in the United States. Victor Fell Yellin, "Chadwick, American Realist," p. 88.

15. David Ewen, *George Gershwin*, pp. 3–5. On his birth certificate he is listed as Jacob Gershwine, apparently a misspelling of the family name Gershvin, itself a partial anglicization of Gershovitz. Schwartz, p. 4.

16. Quoted in Ewen, pp. 70–71. Note that Isaac Goldberg quotes the first line as "Sentimental Oriental Gentlemen are we." Isaac Goldberg, *George Gershwin*, p. 16.

17. Ewen, pp. 3–5, 13–15, 20–21, 32, 53–57.

18. Ibid., pp. 58–59, 67–68. Gershwin studied with Wallingford Riegger briefly in the twenties, with Cowell intermittently toward the end of the decade. Schwartz, p. 56.

19. Ewen, pp. 74–75, 77.

20. Ibid., pp. 80, 82–83.

21. Ibid., pp. 80–81.

22. Henrietta Straus, "Jazz and 'The Rhapsody in Blue,'" *Nation*, 5 March 1924, p. 263.

23. Carl Engel, "Views and Reviews," *Musical Quarterly*, April 1926, p. 304; Henry O. Osgood, *So This Is Jazz*, p. 180.

24. Aaron Copland, "Composer From Brooklyn: An Autobiographical Sketch," in Gilbert Chase, ed., *The American Composer Speaks*, pp. 168–70.

25. Ibid., pp. 172, 174–75.

26. Rossiter, p. 223. Marion Bauer and Claire R. Reis, "Twenty-Five Years with the League of Composers," *Musical Quarterly*, January 1948, pp. 1–3.

27. Arnold Dobrin, *Aaron Copland*, pp. 81–82; Copland, p. 175; Julia Smith, *Aaron Copland*, p. 60.

28. Paul Rosenfeld, "Musical Chronicle," *Dial*, February 1926, pp. 174–75.

29. Isaac Goldberg, "Aaron Copland and his Jazz," *American Mercury*, September 1927, pp. 63–64.

30. John Tasker Howard, *Our Contemporary Composers*, p. 149; Hale and Chotzinoff, quoted in Nicolas Slonimsky, ed., *Lexicon of Musical Invective*, p. 86; Goldberg, p. 65.

31. Paul Fritz Laubenstein, "Race Values in Aframerican Music," *Musical Quarterly*, July 1930, p. 396; Paul Rosenfeld, "Musical Chronical," *Dial*, May 1926, p. 442; *Jewish Influences in American Life, vol. III: International Jew: The World's Foremost Problem* (reprints from the *Dearborn Independent*, 1921), pp. 65, 70, 75, 78.

32. Gilbert Seldes, "The Negro's Songs," *Dial*, March 1926, p. 249.

33. Daniel Gregory Mason, *The Dilemma of American Music, and Other Essays*, pp. 51, 102.

34. Daniel Gregory Mason, *Tune In America*, p. 160.

35. Ibid., pp. 162–64; *Jewish Influences*, p. 81.

36. *Jewish Influences*, p. 68. In the European context, Nazis wrote much the same things about Jews and culture. "The Jewish people, with all its apparent intellectual qualities, is nevertheless without any true culture. . . . What he achieves in the field of art is either bowdlerization or intellectual theft." Adolf Hitler, *Mein Kampf*, quoted in George L. Mosse, ed., *Nazi Culture*, p. 7. On Richard Eichenaur's Nazi polemic *Music and Race*, see Arthur Mendel, "The Subversive Jews," *Nation*, 19 April 1933, p. 454.

37. Mason, *Tune In America*, pp. 17–35 passim. In a letter to Randall Thompson, Mason refers with bitter frustration to Copland's mentor Serge Koussevitsky: "I should be unwilling to kiss him even if he played something of mine. To kiss him before the fact is unthinkable." Daniel Gregory Mason, letter to Randall Thompson, 1 December 1935, Daniel Gregory Mason Papers, Box 15, Columbia University Library, New York.

It seems odd that after attacking in print modernism, jazz, Jews, and Copland, Mason should have been so annoyed (or even surprised) when Copland said nothing to either him or Thompson at an American music festival after performances of their works. "When one remembers the demeanor of Copland at Rochester," Mason wrote to Thompson, "one feels as if one were living in a monkey cage instead of a civilization" (Mason, letter to Thompson; Mason, *Music in My Time*, p. 393). To place Mason's tirade in perspective, most people have found Copland to be characteristically "sober, cheerful, considerate . . . direct and at the same time tactful." Virgil Thomson, *American Music since 1900*, p. 49.

38. Lazare Saminsky, *Living Music of the Americas* (1949), quoted in Slonimsky, p. 87. Note that Saminsky misquotes Chandler, entirely reversing his actual meaning. See Theodore Chandler, "Aaron Copland," in Henry Cowell, ed., in *American Composers on American Music*, p. 49.

39. Saminsky, *Essentials*, pp. 152–54.

40. Mason, *Tune In America*, pp. 17–35, passim; Paul S. Carpenter, *Music*, p. 97.

41. Telling about one of his hospitalizations, Stravinsky related how, as a matter of course, the nurses took him for a Jew even though his medical chart listed his "religious preference" as "Russian Orthodox Church." Igor Stravinsky, *Themes and Conclusions*, p. 156.

42. Quoted in Slonimsky, pp. 66–67.

43. B. H. Haggin, "Gershwin and Our Music," *Nation*, 5 October 1932, p. 309. Haggin surely intended no slur by his comments.

44. Daniel Gregory Mason, "Democracy and Music," p. 650.

45. Born a toy, the phonograph first served, then overshadowed, America's popular music industry. In the 1890s technical advancements made the phonograph commercially feasible. Tin Pan Alley picked up the machine as an advertising aid to song plugging. After the turn of the century, public phonograph sales exploded as a result of the synergistic effects of improved fidelity, lower costs, and aggressive advertising by Eldridge Johnson, founder of Victor Talking Machines. In short order the "toy" was usurping business from song publishers. Victor's management saw the advertising benefits of tying their name to a "cultured" image. They signed and recorded the great opera stars of the world, including Caruso. Victor charged a premium for its classical "Red Seal" records and used its classical connection to create the impression of Victor as an elite, quality-conscious company. An architect of the progressive education music movement, Francis Elliot Clark, was hired to promote Victor's goods in schools, colleges, and universities. Roland Gelatt, *The Fabulous Phonograph*, pp. 49–55, 58–68, 73, 97–98, 115, 131, 141, 194, 271, 667; Margaret Grant and Herman S. Hettinger, *America's Symphony Orchestras*, p. 51; John Tasker Howard and George Kent Bellows, *A Short History of Music in America*, p. 200.

46. Arthur Whiting, "The Mechanical Player," *Yale Review*, July 1919, quoted in Mason, *Dilemma*, p. 36; Mason, *Tune In*, p. 11; Blanche Bloch, "Music on the Air," *Nation*, 5 June 1929, p. 671; T. Carl Whitmer, "The Energy of American Crowd Music," *Musical Quarterly*, January 1918, p. 102.

47. Robert S. Lynd and Helen Merrell Lynd, *Middletown*, p. 244; Daniel Gregory Mason, "The Jazz Invasion," pp. 510–11; Carpenter, *Music*, p. 4.

48. Dickson Skinner, "Music Goes into Mass Production," *Harper's Magazine*, April 1939, p. 487.

49. Daniel Gregory Mason, letter to Leo Lewis, 10 March 1939, Daniel Gregory Mason Papers, Box 15, Columbia University Library, New York; Carpenter, pp. 4–5; Editors of *Fortune, Jews in America*, pp. 55, 58–62.

50. Samuel Eliot Morison, *The Oxford History of the American People*, p. 146; Charles N. Glaab and A. Theodore Brown, *A History of Urban America* pp. 84, 108.

51. Charles Merz, "The Attack on New York," *Harper's Monthly Magazine*, June 1926, pp. 81–82; Sullivan, quoted ibid., p. 82; Madison Grant, *The Passing of the Great Race* (1916), quoted in William E. Leuchtenburg, *The Perils of Prosperity, 1914–32*, p. 206; quoted in John Higham, *Strangers in the Land*, p. 286; Oscar Thompson, quoted in Saminsky, *Essentials*, p. 148; Barbara Rose, *American Art since 1900*, pp. 116–19; Babette Deutsch, "America in the Arts," *Musical Quarterly*, July 1921, p. 305.

52. George Gershwin, "The Composer in the Machine Age," in Chase, p. 141; Gershwin, quoted in Goldberg, p. 139; Ewen, p. 180.

53. Gershwin, "Composer," p. 141.

54. Mason, "Jazz Invasion," pp. 506–507.

55. Henrietta Straus, "American Music via Europe," *Nation*, 10 September 1924, p. 268.

56. William Carlos Williams, *Selected Essays of William Carlos Williams*, pp. 60–61.

57. Williams—a second-generation American, a poet, and a middle-class doctor not committed to a Victorian ethos—tried to grasp the meaning of America by immersing himself in the sensual texture of American life, past *and* present. Yet Williams, like most of the centennial composers, had no use for what he

called the "secondary culture" of the big cities: a culture which waxes as the national "primary culture" wanes. "With the approach of the city, international character began to enter the innocent river and pervert it." Ibid., p. 147; William Carlos Williams, *I Wanted to Write a Poem*, p. 79. On the "Oriental" Jew, see Williams, *Selected Essays*, p. 216.

58. Henry F. Gilbert, "Notes on a Trip to Frankfurt in the Summer of 1927: With Some Thoughts on Modern Music," *Musical Quarterly*, January 1930, pp. 26–27.

59. Daniel Gregory Mason, "Is American Music Growing Up? Our Emancipation from Alien Influences," p. 16.

60. Daniel Gregory Mason, letter to Charles Horton Cooley, 20 April 1929, Daniel Gregory Mason Papers, Box 15, Columbia University Library, New York.

61. Charles Horton Cooley, *Social Organization* (1909), p. 170. Opponents of Spencer and Sumner, such as Ward and Cooley, were "comfortable in the midst of race theorizing" in spite of their progressive liberalism. Gossett notes that their racialism was linked to their concern with the effects of the new immigration (Gossett, *Race*, pp. 167, 174).

62. Mason, "Democracy," p. 650.

63. Daniel Gregory Mason, letter to Harry Overstreet, 6 January 1935, Daniel Gregory Mason Papers, Box 15, Columbia University Library, New York; Mason, *Dilemma*, p. 12.

64. See Victor Turner, *Dramas, Fields, and Metaphors*, pp. 14, 17; Richard H. Brown, *A Poetic for Sociology*, pp. 107–113; Hugh Dalziel Duncan, *Communication and Social Order*, pp. 121–43, 169–70, 190–95, passim.

65. Israel Zangwill, *The Melting Pot* (1909), pp. 33–35. Horace Kallen, in "Democracy versus the Melting Pot," develops the pluralist implications of the symphony metaphor. His article was reprinted in Horace M. Kallen, *Culture and Democracy in the United States*.

66. Actually, Uncle Sam was created by the British as a derisive caricature of Lincoln. By the end of the nineteenth century Uncle Sam had aged considerably in externals, and was generally recognized as a Yankee type. Hugh Honour, *The New Golden Land*, p. 200.

67. Horace Kallen came to this awareness stimulated by Barrett Wendell, with whom Kallen studied at Harvard. Wendell entertained the quaint notion that Puritans not only thought of their America as a new Israel, they were actually descended from Jews. Higham, *Send These to Me*, p. 205.

68. For a related interpretation, see Neil Shumsky, "Zangwill's *The Melting Pot*: Ethnic Tensions on Stage."

69. Zangwill, pp. 86–87.

70. Kaplan, p. 23.

71. Ibid., pp. 261–63; emphasis in the original.

72. Zangwill, p. 185; emphasis in the original.

73. Ibid., p. 207.

74. Carl Engel, "Views and Reviews," *Musical Quarterly*, January 1923, p. 150.

75. Lawrence Adler, "Bloch's America," *Nation*, 30 January 1929, pp. 141–42; Bloch, as cited by John Tasker Howard, *Our American Music*, p. 517.

76. W. J. Henderson, quoted in Saminsky, *Music of the Ghetto*, p. 8; Howard, p. 514.

77. Mason, *Tune In America*, p. 162.

78. Ernest Bloch, "Man and Music," *Musical Quarterly*, October 1933, p. 375;

Ernest Bloch, letter to Daniel Gregory Mason, 6 June 1946, Daniel Gregory Mason Papers, Box 15, Columbia University Library, New York.

79. Howard, p. 6.

80. Arthur Farwell, Michigan *State Journal*, 1 January 1930, quoted in Edgar L. Kirk, "Toward American Music: A Study of the Life and Music of Arthur Farwell" (Ph.D. dissertation), p. 72; Mason, *Tune In America*, p. 167.

81. Mason, *Tune In America*, p. 169.

82. Howard, p. 133.

83. Ibid., pp. 168–69.

84. David Ewen, *American Composers Today*, pp. 118–19; Thomson, *American Music*, p. 50.

85. Paul Rosenfeld, "Current Chronicle: Copland-Harris-Schuman." *Musical Quarterly*, July 1939, p. 377. During the Depression, critics naturally emphasized that great democratic artists communicated a deep concern for the heroic struggles of the ordinary American.

86. Howard, p. 145.

87. Henry Taylor Parker, "Manifold, Abundant, Individual," p. 4.

88. Saminsky, quoted in Ashley Pettis, "The WPA and the American Composer," *Musical Quarterly*, January 1940, pp. 101–102; Ewen, *American Composers*, p. 119.

89. Arthur Farwell, "Roy Harris," *Musical Quarterly*, January 1932, pp. 18, 25; Ewen, *American Composers*, p. 118; Parker, "Symphony of Roy Harris," p. 4; Nicolas Slonimsky, "Roy Harris," *Musical Quarterly*, January 1947, p. 25.

90. Bloch, from 1925 to 1930, and Copland, from 1945 to 1950, were the American composers most performed by American orchestras on a national average. On a local average, orchestras favored local composers. John Henry Mueller, *The American Symphony Orchestra*, p. 279.

91. Slonimsky, "Harris," p. 33; Saminsky, *Essentials*, pp. 178–79.

92. Farwell, "Zero Hour," p. 95, and "Harris," pp. 19, 31.

93. Oswald Spengler, *The Decline of the West* (New York: Alfred A. Knopf, Inc., 1928), in Ronald H. Nash, ed., *Ideas of History*, vol. 1, p. 152; Bruce Mazlish, *The Riddle of History*, p. 337; Franklin L. Baumer, *Modern European Thought*, p. 508.

94. Walt Whitman, *Leaves of Grass*, 1860 text, p. 115; Ewen, *American Composers*, pp. 118, 120.

95. Roy Harris, "The Growth of a Composer," *Musical Quarterly*, April 1934, p. 188.

96. Bercovitch, *Puritan Origins*, pp. 177, 179.

97. Roy Harris, "Problems of American Composers," in Henry Cowell, ed., *American Composers on American Music*, pp. 149, 156, 165. Though he did not mention names, Harris clearly meant to separate himself from composers who grew up cut off from the American land. Such men "can never absorb the pregnant silences which yield peace, reverence, aspiration, grandeur, and dignity." Ibid., p. 164.

98. Harris, quoted in Slonimsky, "Harris," p. 23.

99. B. H. Haggin, "Records," *Nation*, 2 April 1938, p. 396; Thomson, *American Music*, p. 149.

100. Virgil Thomson, *New York Herald Tribune*, 21 November 1940, in Slonimsky, p. 107.

BIBLIOGRAPHY

MANUSCRIPT COLLECTIONS

New York. Columbia University Library. Daniel Gregory Mason Papers.

NEWSPAPERS AND PERIODICALS

General Listings:
American Mercury. 1924, 1927, 1935.
Atlantic. 1919–1930.
Boston Evening Transcript. 1918–1925.
Dial. 1919–1929.
Harper's Magazine. 1919–1940.
Musical Quarterly. 1915–1949.
Nation. 1919–1939.
New York Times. 1918–1942.

Specific Citations:
Berger, Morroe. "Jazz: Resistance to the Diffusion of a Culture-Pattern." *Journal of Negro History* 32 (1947): 462–92.
Bonacich, Edna. "A Theory of Middleman Minorities." *American Sociological Review* 38 (October 1973):583–94.
Brown, Richard D. "Modernization: A Victorian Climax." *American Quarterly* 27 (December 1975):533–48.
Chapman, John Jay. "The Disappearance of the Educated Man: Our Colleges Tend to Turn Out Successful Executives Rather Than Cultivated Men." *Vanity Fair,* July 1925, pp. 50, 86.
De Forest, J. W. "The Great American Novel." *Nation,* 9 January 1868, pp. 27–29.
Dvořák, Antonin. "Music in America." *Harper's,* February 1895, pp. 428–34.
Gerould, Katherine Fullerton. "The Plight of the Genteel." *Harper's Magazine,* February 1926, pp. 312–14.
Hall, David D. "The Victorian Connection." *American Quarterly* 27 (December 1975):561–74.
Hansen, Chadwick. "Social Influences on Jazz Style: Chicago, 1920–1930." *American Quarterly* 12 (Winter 1960): 493–506.
Henderson, W. J. "Ragtime, Jazz, and High Art." *Scribner's Magazine,* February 1925, pp. 200–203.
Howe, Daniel Walker. "American Victorianism as a Culture." *American Quarterly* 27 (December 1975):507–32.

Lueders, Edward. "Mr. Van Vechten of New York City." *New Republic*, 16 May 1955, pp. 36–37.

Mason, Daniel Gregory. "Artistic Ideals: IV, Originality." *Musical Quarterly*, January 1927, pp. 1–13.

———. "Democracy and Music." *Musical Quarterly*, October 1917, pp. 641–54.

———. "The Depreciation of Music." *Musical Quarterly*, January 1929, pp. 6–15.

———. "Dissonance and Evil." *Atlantic Monthly*, August 1904, pp. 226–32.

———. "Is American Music Growing Up? Our Emancipation from Alien Influences." *Arts and Decoration*, November 1920, p. 16.

———. "Jazz for the Illiterate." *American Mercury*, December 1943, p. 761.

———. "Our Orchestras and Our Money's Worth." *Harper's Magazine*, June 1928, pp. 75–80.

———. "Our Public School Music." *Outlook*, 19 March 1904, pp. 701–706.

———. "Two Tendencies in Modern Music. Tchaikowsky and Brahms." *Atlantic Monthly*, February 1902, pp. 175–84.

Milhaud, Darius. "The Jazz Band and Negro Music." *Littell's Living Age*, 18 October 1924, pp. 169–73.

Moderwell, Hiram K. "Ragtime." *New Republic*, 16 October 1915, pp. 284–86.

Parker, Henry Taylor. "Manifold, Abundant, Individual: The Symphony of Roy Harris Is Absorbing, Impressive American Work." *Boston Evening Transcript*, 27 January 1934, p. 4.

Rosen, Charles, and Zerner, Henri. "The Permanent Revolution." *New York Review of Books*, 22 November 1979, pp. 23–30.

Santayana, George. "Genteel American Poetry." *New Republic*, 29 May 1915, pp. 94–95.

Shumsky, Neil. "Zangwill's *The Melting Pot*: Ethnic Tensions on Stage." *American Quarterly* 27 (March 1975):29–41.

Smith, David Stanley. "Putting Jazz in Its Place." *Literary Digest*, 5 July 1924, pp. 31–32.

Thomson, Virgil. "The Cult of Jazz." *Vanity Fair*, June 1925, pp. 54, 118.

Van Vechten, Carl. "The Black Blues: Negro Songs of Dissappointment in Love:—Their Pathos Hardened with Laughter." *Vanity Fair*, August 1925, pp. 57, 86, 92.

———. "George Gershwin: An American Composer Who Is Writing Notable Music in the Jazz Idiom." *Vanity Fair*, March 1925, pp. 40, 78, 84.

———. "Moanin' wid a Sword in Ma Han'." *Vanity Fair*, February 1926, pp. 60, 100, 102.

———. "Prescription for the Negro Theatre." *Vanity Fair*, October 1925, pp. 46, 92, 98.

Yellin, Victor Fell. "Chadwick, American Realist." *Musical Quarterly* 61 (January 1975):77–97.

———. "The Conflict of Generations in American Music—(A Yankee View)." *Arts and Sciences* 1 (Winter 1962–63):13–16.

———. "Review of Records—Ives: The Celestial Country." *Musical Quarterly*, July 1974, pp. 500–508.

DISSERTATIONS

Kaplan, Max. "The Musician in America: A Study in His Social Roles (Introduction to a Sociology of Music)." Ph.D. dissertation, University of Illinois, 1951.

Kirk, Edgar Lee. "Toward American Music: A Study of the Life and Music of Arthur George Farwell." Ph.D. dissertation, Eastman School of Music, 1958.

Klein, Sister Mary Justina. "The Contribution of Daniel Gregory Mason to American Music." Ph.D. dissertation, the Catholic University of America, 1957.

Peterson, Thomas Elliot. "The Music of Carl Ruggles." Ph.D. dissertation, University of Washington, 1967.

Pierson, Thomas Claude. "The Life and Music of John Alden Carpenter." Ph.D. dissertation, University of Rochester, 1954.

BOOKS

Adams, Henry. *The Degradation of the Democratic Dogma.* Introduction by Brooks Adams. New York: Macmillan Co., 1920.

————. *The Education of Henry Adams.* 2 vols. New York: Time Incorporated, 1946.

Allen, Frederick Lewis. *Only Yesterday.* New York: Bantam Books, 1931.

Allen, Warren Dwight. *Philosophies of Music History: A Study of General Histories of Music, 1600–1960.* New York: Dover Publications, 1962.

Arendt, Hannah. *The Origins of Totalitarianism.* Cleveland: Meridian Books, 1951.

Arnold, Matthew. *The Portable Matthew Arnold.* Edited by Lionel Trilling. New York: Viking Press, 1949.

Altick, Richard D. *Victorian People and Ideas.* New York: W. W. Norton & Co., 1973.

Bailyn, Bernard. *The New England Merchants in the Seventeenth Century.* New York: Harper Torchbooks, 1955.

Barzun, Jacques. *Music in American Life.* Bloomington: Indiana University Press, 1956.

Baumer, Franklin L. *Modern European Thought: Continuity and Change in Ideas, 1600–1950.* New York: Macmillan Co., 1977.

Bercovitch, Sacvan. *The American Jeremiad.* Madison: University of Wisconsin Press, 1978.

————. *The Puritan Origins of the American Self.* New York: Yale University Press, 1975.

Biddis, Michael D. *Father of Racist Ideology: The Social and Political Thought of Count Gobineau.* New York: Weybright & Talley, 1970.

Black, Cyril E. *The Dynamics of Modernization: A Study in Comparative History.* New York: Harper & Row, 1966.

Blesh, Rudi. *Shining Trumpets: A History of Jazz.* New York: Da Capo Press, 1976.

————, and Janis, Harriet. *They All Played Ragtime.* New York: Oak Publications, 1971.

Bottomore, Tom, and Nisbet, Robert, eds. *A History of Sociological Analysis.* New York: Basic Books, 1978.

Brooks, Van Wyck. *Van Wyck Brooks: The Early Years.* Edited by Claire Sprague. New York: Harper Torchbooks, 1968.

Brown, Richard H. *A Poetic for Sociology: Toward a Logic of Discovery for the Human Sciences.* Cambridge: Cambridge University Press, 1977.

Brunn, H. O. *The Story of the Original Dixieland Jazz Band.* Louisiana State University Press, 1960.

Carpenter, Paul S. *Music: An Art and a Business.* Norman: University of Oklahoma Press, 1950.

Chase, Gilbert, ed. *The American Composer Speaks*. Louisiana State University Press, 1966.

Chipp, Herschel B., ed. *Theories of Modern Art*. Berkeley: University of California Press, 1968.

Chotzinoff, Samuel. *Day's at Morn*. New York: Harper & Row, 1964.

Cooley, Charles Horton. *Human Nature & the Social Order*. New York: Schocken Books, 1964.

———. *Social Organization*. New York: Schocken Books, 1962.

Cowell, Henry, ed. *American Composers on American Music*. New York: Frederick Ungar Publishing Co., 1933.

———, and Cowell, Sidney. *Charles Ives and His Music*. New York: Oxford University Press, 1959.

Crunden, Robert M. *Ministers of Reform: The Progressives' Achievement in American Civilization, 1889–1920*. New York: Basic Books, 1982.

Cuddihy, John Murray. *No Offense: Civil Religion and Protestant Taste*. New York: Seabury Press, 1978.

———. *The Ordeal of Civility: Freud, Marx, Levi-Strauss, and the Jewish Struggle with Modernity*. New York: Basic Books, 1974.

Dance, Stanley. *The World of Duke Ellington*. New York: Charles Scribner's Sons, 1970.

Dewey, John. *Art as Experience*. New York: Capricorn Books, 1934.

Dimen-Schein, Muriel. *The Anthropological Imagination*. New York: McGraw-Hill Book Co., 1977.

Dobrin, Arnold. *Aaron Copland: His Life and Times*. New York: Thomas Y. Crowell Co., 1967.

DuBois, W. E. B. *The Seventh Son: The Thought and Writings of W. E. B. DuBois*. 2 vols. Edited by Julius Lester. New York: Vintage Books, 1971.

Duncan, Hugh Dalziel. *Communication and Social Order*. London: Oxford University Press, 1962.

Durkheim, Emile. *The Elementary Forms of the Religious Life: A Study in Religious Sociology*. Translated by Joseph Ward Swain. New York: Free Press, 1965.

Editors of *Fortune*. *Jews in America*. New York: Random House, 1936.

Emerson, Ralph Waldo. *The Complete Writings of Ralph Waldo Emerson*. New York: Wm. H. Wise & Co., 1929.

Encyclopedia Britannica. 15th ed. s.v. "Aesthetics," by Stephen C. Pepper and Thomas Munro.

Erenberg, Lewis A. *Steppin' Out: New York Nightlife and the Transformation of American Culture, 1890–1930*. Westport, Connecticut: Greenwood Press, 1981.

Erikson, Kai T. *Wayward Puritans: A Study in the Sociology of Deviance*. New York: John Wiley & Sons, 1966.

Etzkorn, Peter K., ed. *Music and Society: The Later Writings of Paul Honingsheim*. New York: John Wiley & Sons, 1973.

Ewen, David. *American Composers Today*. New York: H. W. Wilson Co., 1949.

———. *George Gershwin: His Journey to Greatness*. Englewood Cliffs: Prentice-Hall, 1970.

Fass, Paula. *The Damned and the Beautiful: American Youth in the 1920's*. New York: Oxford University Press, 1977.

Feather, Leonard. *The New Edition of the Encyclopedia of Jazz*. New York: Bonanza Books, 1960.

Fischer, David Hackett. *Historical Fallacies: Toward a Logic of Historical Thought*. New York: Harper Torchbooks, 1970.

Fitzgerald, F. Scott. *The Crack Up*. Edited by Edmund Wilson. New York: New Directions, 1945.

Frederickson, George M. *The Black Image in the White Mind*. New York: Harper Torchbooks, 1971.

French, Richard, ed. *Music and Criticism*. Cambridge: Harvard University Press, 1948.

Freud, Sigmund. *Civilization and Its Discontents*. Translated by James Strachey. New York: W. W. Norton & Co., 1961.

Freund, Julien. *The Sociology of Max Weber*. Translated by Mary Ilford. New York: Vintage Books, 1968.

Geertz, Clifford. *The Interpretation of Cultures*. New York: Basic Books, 1973.

Gelatt, Roland. *The Fabulous Phonograph: From Edison to Stereo*. New York: Appleton-Century, 1965.

Gilman, Lawrence. *Music and the Cultivated Man*. New York: W. E. Rudge, 1929.

Ginsburg, Morris. *Essays in Sociology and Social Philosophy*. Baltimore: Penguin Books, 1968.

Glaab, Charles N., and Brown, A. Theodore. *A History of Urban America*. New York: Macmillan Co., 1967.

Goldberg, Isaac. *George Gershwin: A Study in American Music*. New York: Frederick Ungar Publishing Co., 1958.

Gossett, Thomas F. *Race: The History of an Idea in America*. Dallas: Southern Methodist University Press, 1963.

Graf, Max. *Composer and Critic: Two Hundred Years of Music Criticism*. New York: W. W. Norton & Co., 1946.

Grant, Margaret, and Hettinger, Herman S. *America's Symphony Orchestras: And How They Are Supported*. New York: W. W. Norton & Co., 1940.

Graves, Charles L. *Post-Victorian Music*. London: Macmillan & Co., 1911.

Guimond, James. *The Art of William Carlos Williams*. Urbana: University of Illinois Press, 1968.

Gurney, Edmund. *The Power of Sound*. London: Smith, Elder & Co., 1880.

Hadow, W. H. *Studies in Modern Music*. First Series. London: Seeley, Service & Co., 1892.

Hammond, John, with Townsend, Irving. *John Hammond On Record: An Autobiography*. New York: Summit Books, 1977.

Handlin, Oscar. *Race and Nationality in American Life*. Garden City: Doubleday Anchor Books, 1957.

Hanslick, Eduard. *The Beautiful in Music*. Translated by Gustav Cohen. London: Novello, Ewer & Co., 1891.

Harris, Neil. *The Artist in American Society: The Formative Years, 1790–1860*. New York: Simon & Schuster, 1966.

Haskins, Jim. *The Cotton Club*. New York: Random House, 1977.

Haweis, H. R. *Music and Morals*. London: W. H. Allen & Co., 1892.

Herzberg, Arthur. *The French Enlightenment and the Jews*. New York: Columbia University Press, 1968.

Higham, John. *Send These to Me: Jews and Other Immigrants in Urban America*. New York: Atheneum, 1975.

———. *Strangers in the Land: Patterns of American Nativism, 1860–1925*. New York: Atheneum, 1970.

———. *Writing American History: Essays on Modern Scholarship*. Bloomington: Indiana University Press, 1970.

Hitchcock, H. Wiley. *Music in the United States.* Englewood Cliffs: Prentice-Hall, 1974.

Holbrooke, Joseph. *Contemporary British Composers.* London: Cecil Palmer, 1925.

Hollander, John. *The Untuning of the Sky: Ideas of Music in English Poetry, 1500–1700.* New York: W. W. Norton & Company, 1970.

Hollinger, David A. *Morris R. Cohen and the Scientific Ideal.* Cambridge, Massachusetts: MIT Press, 1975.

Honour, Hugh. *The New Golden Land: European Images of America from the Discoveries to the Present.* New York: Pantheon Books, 1975.

Houghton, Walter E. *The Victorian Frame of Mind, 1830–1870.* New Haven: Yale University Press, 1957.

Howard, John Tasker. *Our American Music: Three Hundred Years of It.* New York: Thomas Y. Crowell Co., 1929.

————. *Our Contemporary Composers.* New York: Thomas Y. Crowell Co., 1941.

————, and Bellows, George Kent. *A Short History of Music in America.* New York: Thomas Y. Crowell Co., 1957.

Howe, Irving, ed. *The Idea of the Modern in Literature and the Arts.* New York: Horizon Press, 1967.

Howes, Frank. *The English Musical Renaissance.* London: Secker & Warburg, 1966.

Huggins, Nathan Irvin. *Harlem Renaissance.* New York: Oxford University Press, 1971.

Hughes, H. Stuart. *Consciousness and Society: The Reorientation of European Social Thought, 1890–1930.* New York: Vintage Books, 1958.

Ives, Charles. *Essays before a Sonata, and Other Writings.* Edited by Howard Boatwright. New York: W. W. Norton & Co., 1962.

————. *Memos.* Edited by John Kirkpatrick. New York: W. W. Norton & Co., 1972.

Jewish Influences in American Life. Vol. 3: *The International Jew: The World's Foremost Problem* (reprints from *The Dearborn Independent,* 1921).

Jones, Howard Mumford. *The Age of Energy: Varieties of American Experience, 1865–1915.* New York: Viking Press, 1971.

————. *O Strange New World: American Culture: The Formative Years.* New York: Viking Press, 1964.

Jones, Max, and Chilton, John. *The Louis Armstrong Story, 1900–1971.* Boston: Little, Brown & Co., 1971.

Jordan, Winthrop D. *White over Black: American Attitudes toward the Negro, 1550–1812.* Baltimore: Penguin Books, 1968.

Kallen, Horace M. *Culture and Democracy in the United States: Studies in the Group Psychology of the American Peoples.* New York: Coni & Liveright, 1924.

Kant, Immanuel. *The Critique of Judgment.* Translated by J. H. Bernard. In *Philosophies of Art and Beauty,* edited by Alvert Hofstadter and Richard Kuhns, pp. 280–343. New York: Modern Library, 1964.

Kaplan, Mordecai M. *Judaism as a Civilization.* New York: Schocken Books, 1967.

Kellner, Bruce. *Carl Van Vechten and the Irreverent Decades.* Norman: University of Oklahoma Press, 1968.

Lears, T. J. Jackson. *No Place of Grace: Antimodernism and the Transformation of American Culture, 1880–1920.* New York: Pantheon Books, 1981.

Leonard, Neil. *Jazz and the White Americans.* Chicago: University of Chicago Press, 1962.

Leuchtenburg, William E. *The Perils of Prosperity, 1914–32*. Chicago: University of Chicago Press, 1958.

Lippard, Lucy R., ed. *Dadas on Art*. Englewood Cliffs: Prentice-Hall, 1971.

Locke, Alain, ed. *The New Negro*. New York: Atheneum, 1968.

Lovejoy, Arthur O. *The Great Chain of Being*. New York: Harper Torchbooks, 1936.

Lynd, Robert S., and Lynd, Helen Merrell. *Middletown: A Study in Modern American Culture*. New York: Harcourt, Brace & World, 1929.

————. *Middletown in Transition: A Study in Cultural Conflicts*. New York: Harcourt, Brace & World, 1937.

MacDowell, Edward Alexander. *Critical and Historical Essays*. Boston: Arthur P. Schmidt, 1912.

Manners, J. Hartley. *The National Anthem*. New York: George H. Doran Co., 1922.

Maretzek, Max. *Revelations of an Opera Manager in Nineteenth Century America*. New York: Dover Publications, 1968.

Marquis, Albert Nelson, ed. *Who's Who In America*. Vol. 16. Chicago: A. N. Marquis Co., 1930.

Martin, Jay. *Harvests of Change: American Literature, 1865–1914*. Englewood Cliffs: Prentice-Hall, 1967.

Mason, Daniel Gregory. *Contemporary Composers*. New York: Macmillan Co., 1918.

————. *The Dilemma of American Music, and Other Essays*. New York: Macmillan Co., 1928.

————. "The Jazz Invasion." In *Behold America!* edited by Samuel D. Schmalhausen, pp. 499–513. New York: Farrar & Rinehart, 1931.

————. *Music as an International Language*. New York: American Association for International Conciliation, 1913.

————. *Music in My Time, and Other Reminiscences*. New York: Macmillan Co., 1938.

————. *Tune In America*. New York: Alfred A. Knopf, 1930.

May, Henry F. *The End of American Innocence*. Chicago: Quadrangle Books, 1959.

Mazlish, Bruce. *The Riddle of History: The Great Speculators from Vico to Freud*. Minerva Press, 1966.

Meisel, Victor H., ed. *Voices of German Expressionism*. Englewood Cliffs: Prentice-Hall, 1970.

Mencken, H. L. *H. L. Mencken on Music*. Edited by Louis Cheslock. New York: Shirmer Books, 1955.

Meyer, Leonard B. *Music, the Arts, and Ideas*. Chicago: University of Chicago Press, 1967.

Meyers, Marvin. *The Jacksonian Persuasion*. New York: Vintage Books, 1957.

Milhaud, Darius. *Notes Without Music*. New York: Alfred A. Knopf, 1953.

Miller, Perry. *Errand into the Wilderness*. New York: Harper Torchbooks, 1956.

Morgenstern, Sam, ed. *Composers on Music: An Anthology of Composers' Writings from Palestrina to Copland*. New York: Pantheon Books, 1956.

Morison, Samuel Eliot. *The Oxford History of the American People*. New York: Oxford University Press, 1965.

Mosse, George L., ed. *Nazi Culture*. New York: Grosset & Dunlap, 1966.

————. *Toward the Final Solution: A History of European Racism*. New York: Howard Fertig, 1978.

Mueller, John Henry. *The American Symphony Orchestra: A Social History of Musical Taste*. Bloomington: Indiana University Press, 1951.

Mussulman, Joseph A. *Music in the Cultured Generation: A Social History of Music in America, 1870–1900*. Evanston, Illinois: Northwestern University Press, 1971.

Nash, Gary B., and Weiss, Richard, eds. *The Great Fear: Race in the Mind of America*. New York: Holt, Rinehart & Winston, 1970.

Nash, Ronald H., ed. *Ideas of History*. 2 vols. New York: E. P. Dutton & Co., 1969.

Newman, Ernest. *The Life of Richard Wagner*. 4 vols. New York: Alfred Knopf, 1933–1946.

Noble, David W. *The Progressive Mind, 1890–1917*. Chicago: Rand McNally & Co., 1970.

Osborne, Harold. *Aesthetics and Art History: An Historical Introduction*. New York: E. P. Dutton & Co., 1970.

Osgood, Henry O. *So This Is Jazz*. Boston: Little, Brown & Co., 1926.

Osofsky, Gilbert. *Harlem: The Making of a Ghetto, Negro New York, 1890–1930*. New York: Harper Torchbooks, 1966.

Ouelette, Fernand. *Edgard Varèse*. Translated by Derek Coltman. New York: Orion Press, 1968.

Parry, Sir Charles Hubert Hastings. *The Art of Music*. London: Kegan Paul, 1893.

Perlis, Vivian, ed. *Charles Ives Remembered: An Oral History*. New York: W. W. Norton & Co., 1974.

Perry, Rosalie Sandra. *Charles Ives and the American Mind*. Kent, Ohio: Kent State University Press, 1974.

Persons, Stow. *The Decline of American Gentility*. New York: Columbia University Press, 1973.

Pettigrew, Thomas F. *Racially Separate or Together?* New York: McGraw-Hill Book Co., 1971.

Peyser, Joan. *The New Music*. New York: Dell Publishing Co., 1971.

Poggioli, Renato. *The Theory of the Avant-Garde*. Translated by Gerald Fitzgerald. New York: Harper & Row, 1968.

Potter, David M. *People of Plenty: Economic Abundance and the American Character*. Chicago: University of Chicago Press, 1954.

Prall, D. W. *Aesthetic Analysis*. Introduction by Arthur Berger. New York: Thomas Y. Crowell Co., 1964.

Raleigh, John Henry. *Matthew Arnold and American Culture*. Berkeley: University of California Press, 1961.

Raynor, Henry. *A Social History of Music: From the Middle Ages to Beethoven*. London: Barrie & Jenkins, 1972.

Reis, Claire. *Composers in America*. New York: Macmillan Co., 1938.

Richey, Russell E., and Jones, Donald G., eds. *American Civil Religion*. New York: Harper & Row, 1974.

Rockefeller Panel Report. *The Performing Arts, Problems and Prospects*. New York: McGraw-Hill Book Co., 1965.

Rose, Barbara. *American Art since 1900: A Critical History*. New York: Frederick A. Praeger, 1967.

Rossiter, Frank. *Charles Ives and His America*. New York: Liveright, 1975.

Ruland, Richard, ed. *A Storied Land: Theories of American Literature*. New York: E. P. Dutton & Co., 1976.

Saminsky, Lazare. *Essentials and Prophecies*. New York: Thomas Y. Crowell Co., 1939.

——. *Music of the Ghetto and the Bible*. New York: Bloch Publishing Co., 1934.

Samuels, Maurice. *Jews on Approval*. New York: Liveright, 1932.

Santayana, George. *The Sense of Beauty*. New York: Charles Scribner's Sons, 1969.

——. *Winds of Doctrine: Studies in Contemporary Opinion*. New York: Charles Scribner's Sons, 1926.

Schenk, H. G. *The Mind of the European Romantics: An Essay in Cultural History*. Garden City: Anchor Books, 1969.

Schopenhauer, Arthur. *The Philosophy of Schopenhauer*. Edited by Irwin Edman. New York: Modern Library, 1928.

Schuller, Gunther. *Early Jazz*. New York: Oxford University Press, 1968.

Schwartz, Charles. *Gershwin: His Life and Music*. New York: Bobbs-Merrill Co., 1973.

Seldes, Gilbert. *The Seven Lively Arts*. New York: Sagamore Press, 1957.

Simpson, Alan. *Puritanism in Old and New England*. Chicago: University of Chicago Press, 1955.

Slonimsky, Nicolas, ed. *Lexicon of Musical Invective*. New York: Coleman-Ross Co., 1953.

Smith, Julia. *Aaron Copland*. New York: E. P. Dutton & Co., 1955.

Solomon, Barbara Miller. *Ancestors and Immigrants: A Changing New England Tradition*. New York: John Wiley & Sons, 1956.

Sousa, John Philip. *Marching Along*. Boston: Hale, Cushman & Flint, 1928.

Spaeth, Sigmund. *The Art of Enjoying Music*. New York: McGraw-Hill Book Co., 1933.

Spalding, Walter Raymond. *Music at Harvard*. New York: Coward-McCann, 1935.

Spear, Allen H. *Black Chicago: The Making of a Ghetto, 1890–1920*. Chicago: University of Chicago Press, 1967.

Stearns, Marshall. *The Story of Jazz*. New York: A Mentor Book, 1956.

Stokowski, Olga Samaroff. *An American Musician's Story*. New York: W. W. Norton & Co., 1939.

Stravinsky, Igor. *Themes and Conclusions*. London: Faber & Faber, 1972.

Thibaut, A. F. *Purity in Music*. Translated by John Broadhouse. London: W. Reeves, 1882.

Thomson, Virgil. *American Music since 1900*. New York: Holt, Rinehart & Winston, 1971.

Thoreau, Henry David. *Walden, or, Life in the Woods*. New York: Holt, Rinehart & Winston, 1961.

Toll, Robert C. *Blacking Up: The Minstrel Show in Nineteenth-Century America*. London: Oxford University Press, 1974.

Tolstoy, Leo N. *What is Art?* Translated by Aylmer Maude. Indianapolis: Bobbs-Merrill Co., 1960.

Tomsich, John. *A Genteel Endeavor: American Culture and Politics in the Gilded Age*. Stanford: Stanford University Press, 1971.

Turner, Victor. *Dramas, Fields, and Metaphors: Symbolic Action in Human Society*. Ithaca: Cornell University Press, 1974.

Ulanov, Barry. *Duke Ellington*. London: Musician's Press Limited, 1946.

——. *Handbook of Jazz*. New York: Viking Press, 1960.

Van Vechten, Carl. *Nigger Heaven*. New York: Harper Colophon Books, 1971.

Walzel, Oskar. *German Romanticism*. Translated by Alma Elise Lussky. New York: Capricorn Books, 1932.

Weber, Max. *The Protestant Ethic and the Spirit of Capitalism*. Translated by Talcott Parsons. New York: Charles Scribner's Sons, 1958.

Whitman, Walt. *Leaves of Grass*. Ithaca: Cornell University Press, 1961.

Wiebe, Robert H. *The Search for Order: 1877–1920*. New York: Hill & Wang, 1967.

Willey, Basil. *Nineteenth Century Studies: Coleridge to Matthew Arnold*. New York: Harper Torchbooks, 1949.

Williams, Raymond. *Culture and Society, 1780–1950*. New York: Harper Torchbooks, 1958.

———. *Keywords: A Vocabulary of Culture and Society*. Oxford University Press, 1976.

Williams, William Carlos. *I Wanted to Write a Poem*. Boston: Beacon Press, 1958.

———. *Selected Essays of William Carlos Williams*. New York: New Directions Books, 1954.

Yates, Peter. *Twentieth Century Music*. New York: Funk & Wagnalls, 1967.

Zangwill, Israel. *The Melting Pot*. New York: Macmillan Co., 1926.

Ziff, Larzer. *The American 1890's, The Life and Times of a Lost Generation*. New York: Viking Press, 1966.

Zuck, Barbara. *A History of Musical Americanism*. Ann Arbor, Michigan: UMI Research Press, 1980.

MISCELLANEOUS SOURCES CITED

Bolcom, William. Liner notes to Nonesuch H-71281.

Carlson, Tom. "Ernst Krenek: Jonny Spielt Auf." Liner notes to Mace MXX 9094.

Clark, Robert S. Liner notes to Mercury SRI-75026.

Darrell, R. D. "The Music of Henry F. Gilbert, John Powell, John Alden Carpenter, and Adolph Weiss." Liner notes to New World Records, N.W. 228, pp. 2–3.

Kimbal, Robert. "Shuffle Along." Liner notes to New World Records, N.W. 260, pp. 1–4.

Lenya, Lotte. "Lotte Lenya Remembers Mahagonny." Liner notes to Columbia K3L 243, p. 609.

Liner notes to Desto DST-6407.

Liner notes to Vanguard SRV-274SD.

Salzman, Eric. Liner notes to DGG 2530 048.

Stuckenschmidt, H. H. "City of Nets." Liner notes to Columbia K3L 243, pp. 11–13.

INDEX

Adams, Brooks, 14
Adams, Henry, 14, 39, 134
Adler, Lawrence: quoted, 126–27
Aesthetic of identity: and Yankee composers, 7–8, 108
Aldrich, Richard, 96
America: debate over essential identity of, 3, 14, 65–72, 78, 79–80, 81, 92, 94, 104, 108, 109–11, 118, 124, 139, 153–68, 169–71; and the Jews, 145–46
Americanism: and the avant-garde, 125–27; and Yankee composers, 6
Ansermet, Ernest, 115
Antheil, George, 130, 152–53
Anti-Semitism: and aesthetics, 6, 150–51; and Copland, 146–47; and Henry Ford, 143–46; and jazz, 131–34, 140, 171, 192n7
Armstrong, Louis, 69, 112, 113
Arnold, Billy, 112, 116
Arnold, Matthew: and Mason, 36, 37, 38, 106–107, 108, 173n12; and Yankee composers, 3, 4, 7, 44; mentioned, 42, 43, 49, 132, 152
Art: as communication, 45, 47; and the masses, 36; as representational, 48; as a sacred activity, 2, 16, 48. *See also* Musical culture
Audience: attitudes of composers toward, 13–14, 181n51
Auric, 116
"Auto-American biography," 6
Avant-garde, 66, 69–70, 110, 119, 123–27, 152–53, 190n41

Bach, 51, 52, 54, 55, 112, 115
Bailey, Buster, 88
Baker, Josephine, 93
Band music: and ragtime, 76–77. *See also* Ives, George
Barbirolli, Sir John, 33
Barzun, Jacques, 31
Basie, Count, 102

Bauer, Marion, 115
Baugh, E. A., 40
Baumer, Franklin: quoted, 165
Beach, Mrs. H. H. A., 4
Bechet, Sidney, 111, 115
Beethoven, 51, 52, 54, 55
Belfrage, Cedric, 112
Bell, Clive, 93–94
Bellamann, Henry, 33–34
Bellini, 136
Benton, Thomas Hart, 151
Bercovitch, Sacvan, 6, 45, 107, 133–34
Berlin, Irving, 94, 98, 137
Bernstein, Leonard, 148
Billings, William, 4
Blake, Eubie, 93
Blesh, Rudi, 76
Bloch, Ernest, 70–71, 130, 133, 137, 143, 147, 164; *America*, 131, 157–59
Boston Symphony, 32–33, 80, 140, 141, 162, 176n43
Boulanger, Nadia, 130, 140, 161, 164
Brahms, 27, 50–58 *passim*
Brillant, Maurice, 115
British empiricism, 47–48, 50
Brooks, Van Wyck, 7–8, 37, 43, 59, 169–70
Brown, Lawrence, 103
Brownell, William, 49–50
Burleigh, Harry T., 83
Butler, Nicholas Murray, 28

Cable, George Washington, 80
Cadman, Charles Wakefield, 78, 80
Carney, Harry, 112
Carpenter, Edward: on Mason's articles, 27
Carpenter, John Alden, 4, 5, 91, 122, 189n31
Carter, Elliot, 40
Casella, Alfredo, 120–21, 157, 163
Centennial composers: defined, 3–4; education of, 19, 21–22; mission of, 6–7, 8–9; and vernacular music, 80–81. *See also* Redemptive culture, Yankee composers

[208]

Chadwick, George, 4, 78, 79, 175*n*23
Chapman, John Jay, 42
Cheatle, John, 113
Chotzinoff, Samuel, 143, 149–50
Civil religion. *See* Art; Musical culture
Classical versus vernacular music, 11–12, 22, 23. *See also* Vernacular music
Classicism. *See* Romanticism and classicism
Cocteau, Jean, 115
Cole, Bob, 93
Cole, Robert, 90
Coleridge, 108, 132
Confry, Zes, 94
Conscience collective of Yankee composers, 9, 10
Cook, Will Marion, 83, 84, 184*n*27
Cooley, Charles Horton, 8, 45–46, 61–62, 118, 153–54, 155
Coolidge, Elizabeth Sprague, 54, 162
Copland, Aaron, 70–71, 130–33 *passim*, 139–43, 146, 148, 163; mentioned, 164, 170
Cotton Club, 101, 103–104, 105, 141
Cowell, Henry, 23, 31, 129–30, 140, 161
Cowell, Sidney, 23, 31
Critics. *See* Music critics
Cruse, Harold, 171
Cuddihy, John Murray, 132, 133, 192*n*8
Culture. *See* Art; Musical culture
"Collective representations": defined, 2. *See also* Metaphors
Curtiss, Philip, 95

Damrosch, Walter, 137, 140, 149
Davidson, Thomas, 40
Debussy, 55, 88, 111
Delaunay, Charles, 115
Delius, Frederick, 112
Dewey, John, 45–46, 61–62
Dexter, Dave, 102
Diaghilev, 122
D'Indy, 55
Dissonance: attitudes of Ives and Mason toward, 11–12, 21–22, 40, 53–54, 180*n*27; George Ives on, 23; and jazz, 129
Dixon, Thomas, 86–87
Dobrin, Arnold, 141
Dodge, Mabel Evans, 96
Downes, Olin, 34, 120
Dreiser, Theodore, 95
DuBois, W. E. B., 98, 99, 100
Dudley, Bessie, 105
Durey, 116
Durkheim, Emile, 2, 178*n*4
Dvořák, 27, 69, 73–74, 77, 81–82, 98
Dyson, George, 121

Education: Mason and, 13, 35–37; as a progressive era panacea, 10–11
Effeminacy in music: Ives's fear of, 5, 6, 13–14, 31–32, 39–40, 42. *See also* Manliness
Elgar, 55, 137
Eliot, Charles W., 134
Ellington, Duke, 69, 103, 112–15, 117
Elman, Mischa, 137
Emerson, Ralph Waldo, 6, 7, 13, 14, 32, 37–39, 60, 72, 107, 169
Engel, Carl, 115, 118, 139
Entertainment: music as, 77
Ethnicity: defined, 2, 132. *See also* Race
Europe, James Reese, 83, 93, 111, 184*n*27
Ewen, David, 163–64, 165

Farwell, Arthur, 4, 5, 9, 74, 77–78, 91, 130; promoter of Roy Harris, 160–66 *passim*
Fellowship of the future, 45–46, 61–63
Ferroud, P. O., 115
Fiedler, Arthur, 77
Finck, Henry T., 139, 140
Fisher, David Hacket, 14
Fitzgerald, F. Scott, 119
Fletcher, John Gould, 89–90
Flexner, James Thomas, 29
Foote, Arthur, 4, 78
Ford, Henry, 36, 143–46
Formalism and functionalism, 44–45, 46–48; and Ives and Mason, 7, 58; Stravinsky and, 56. *See also* Naturalism
Franck, Cesar, 27, 55
Frederickson, George M., 75
Freud, Sigmund, 68, 173*n*17
Fuller, Margaret: quoted, 49

Gabrilowitsch, Ossip, 26, 32
Gauthier, Eva, 136
Geertz, Clifford, 60
Gentility: and aesthetics, 11–12; and Santayana, 15–16, 43; and the Yankee composers, 25, 40, 42, 169
German idealism, 48, 50
Gershwin, George, 70–71, 94, 96, 98, 130, 131, 134, 135–39, 141, 143, 147, 150, 151, 164, 170
Gershwin, Ira, 135
Gilbert, Gama, 101–102
Gilbert, Henry, 78, 80–81, 153
Gilman, Lawrence, 34, 49, 57, 139
Gobineau, Count Arthur de: on race, 67–68, 131–32
Godowsky, 137
Goetschius, Percy, 27, 129
Goffin, Robert, 115

Goldberg, 141, 143
Goldmark, Rubin, 136, 140
Goodman, Benny, 101, 102
Goosens, Eugene, 34
Grainger, Percy, 112, 120
"Great White Hope": Roy Harris as, 72, 161–68
Greenough, Horatio, 57, 58
Grieg, 27, 54
Griffith, D. W.: *Birth of a Nation*, 87
Grofe, Ferde, 137
Gurney, Edmund, 53

Hadow, W. H., 27, 49, 52
Haggin, B. H., 56, 101–103, 147, 167
Hale, Philip, 120, 143
Hambitzer, Charles, 136
Hammond, John, 68, 92, 101–104, 109, 115
Handy, W. C., 83, 84
Hanslick, Edward, 51, 52, 55, 57–58
Hanson, Howard, 129, 161
Hardin, Lil, 112
Harlem Renaissance, 68–69, 95, 96, 99, 100, 101
Harris, Neil, 48
Harris, Roy, 72, 130, 161–68
Haweis, The Reverend H. R., 52–53, 54
Hawthorne, Nathaniel, 7, 38, 57, 169
Heifetz, Jascha, 137, 147
Henderson, Fletcher, 84
Henderson, W. J., 49, 117–18, 158
Herbert, Victor, 137
Higham, John: quoted, 22, 132, 133
Hill, Edward Burlingame, 4, 19, 24, 65, 80, 128
Hines, Earl, 102
Hogan, Ernest, 93
Hollinger, David, 40
Honegger, 116
Horowitz, 147
Howard, John Tasker, 21, 71, 141, 143, 150, 158, 160–61
Howe, Irving, 123
Hughes, H. Stuart, 107
Hughes, Langston, 99, 100
Hughes, Rupert: on ragtime, 75
Hughes, Spike, 103, 112
Humes, Helen, 102
Humperdinck, Engelbert, 78
Huxley, Julian, 62

Indian music, 9, 73–74, 77, 78, 79, 91, 163. *See also* Vernacular music
Ingalls, Jeremiah, 4
Ives, Brewster, 54, 61
Ives, Charles: aesthetic ideas of, 9, 46–47,

49–50, 54–59, 82, 88; attitude of public toward, 10, 33–35; career, 5–6, 7, 12–14, 28–32, 42–43; and Cowell, 130, 161; early life, 4, 17, 19, 31; education, 11–12, 19–24; photographs, 20, 30; and ragtime, 79–80; and redemptive culture, 44–46, 60–63; and Thoreau, 38–39; *Charlie Rutlage*, 56; *Concord Sonata*, 33–34, 38, 54, 56–57; *Essays before a Sonata*, 38, 54, 55, 56–57; First Piano Sonata, 79; Fourth Symphony, 34; *Holiday Quick Step*, 31; *In Flanders Field*, 56; "In the Inn," 79; *Memos*, 31–32; "Ode to a Music Critic," 34; *Ragtime Pieces*, 79; "Three Page Sonata," 79; *Three Pieces in New England*, 34; Violin Sonatas, 33, 34; *Washington's Birthday*, 55–56
Ives, Edith, 29, 30
Ives, George, 17, 19, 21–22, 23, 77, 174n13
Ives, Harmony Twitchell, 29, 35, 40

James, Henry: on Hawthorne, 7, 169
James, William, 18, 62
Janis, Harriet, 76
Jazz, 66–72, 73–108, 186n58; European reaction to, 69–70, 109–18, 188n4; and Jews, 130–60; as sensual and mechanistic, 69, 106, 107–108, 119, 121–23, 151–52, 170–71
Jazz Age, 66, 119, 170
Jefferson, Thomas, 132, 182n5
Jews: as an ethnic group, 66, 68, 70–71, 170, 193n10, 194n36; and jazz, 130–60, 192n9
Johnson, F. Rosamond, 83
Johnson, Hall, 93
Johnson, James Weldon, 99, 100
Johnson, Kenneth, 105
Jolson, Al, 126, 136
Joplin, Scott, 76

Kant, 45, 48, 50, 179n20, 181n37
Kaplan, Mordecai, 156, 192n7
Kelley, Edgar Stillman, 78
Keppard, Freddie, 83
Kern, 136
Kilenyi, Edward, 136
Kirkpatrick, John, 34
Kneisel Quartet, 32, 40
Kolodin, Irving, 101–102
Koussevitsky, Serge, 32–33, 115, 140–41, 147, 148, 162
Krehbiel, H. E., 85
Kreisler, Fritz, 137
Křenek, Ernst: *Jonny spielt auf*, 70, 126–27
Ku Klux Klan, 85, 87, 185n31

Lamb, Joseph, 76
Lambert, Constant, 113–15
Lanier, Sidney, 49, 50
Lapine, Anthony, friend of Ives, 31
Laubenstein, Fritz, 89, 143, 187n86
Law, Andrew, 4
Lewis, Sinclair, 95
Linnaeus, Carolus: on race, 67
Liszt, 55, 77, 135
Locke, Alain, 99, 100, 110
Lodge, Henry Cabot, 14
Loeffler, 78
Lombardo, Guy, 112
Lowell, James Russell, 134

McCormack, John, 137
MacDowell, Edward, 4, 74, 78, 79, 81–82
McKay, Claude, 99
Manliness in music, 13–14, 17, 24, 39–40, 55. See also Effeminacy in music
Manner versus substance: Ives and, 57–59, 82, 88
Manners, J. Hartley: The National Anthem, 86, 96
Martin, Jay, 49
Martinetti, F. T., 124
Mason, Daniel Gregory: aesthetic ideas, 46–47, 49–54, 57–59, 60–63, 79, 81–82, 88, 119, 149–50, 151–52; career, 5, 7, 8, 9, 12–14, 26–28, 42–43; and critics, 34–35; early life, 16–18; education, 11, 18–24, 25; and jazz, 84, 90, 106–108, 110, 118, 120–22, 145–49 passim; and Jews, 71, 133–34, 194n37; and the masses, 35–38, 42; and redemptive culture, 10, 44, 46, 65–66, 128–29, 153–61, 169–70; Artistic Ideals, 61; Chanticleer Overture, 33, 128; Contemporary Composers, 54, 79; Dilemma of American Music, The, 120–21; "Dissonance and Evil," 53–54; From Grieg to Brahms, 54; "Idealistic Basis of Thoreau's Genius, The," 37; Music and Morals, 52–53; Music as an International Language, 54, 62; "Our Public School Music," 53; Quartet for Piano and Strings, 32; Quartet on Negro Themes, 33; Symphony No. 1, 32; Symphony No. 2, 33; Symphony No. 3, Lincoln, 33; "Two Tendencies in Modern Music," 50
Mason, Mary Taintor, 28
Mason, Dr. William, uncle of D. G. Mason, 26
Masses, the: and aesthetic culture, 49; education of, 11, 13, 35–38; Ives and, 32
Materialism, 49, 169; and the avant-garde,

124–25; and jazz, 69, 106–108. See also Gentility
Mengelberg, Willem, 137
Mencken, H. L., 88, 108, 169
Metaphors: and jazz, 119; and Jews, 131, 147; and Negroes, 67–68, 87, 182n2; and symbolic groups, 2, 3, 171, 178n4
Milhaud, Darius, 110, 111, 116–17, 136, 139, 147
Miller, Perry: quoted, 109
Mills, Florence, 93
Modernism: and Charles Ives, 5–6; and Jewish composers, 71, 110–11, 119, 122–24, 153
Moderwell, Hiram, 79, 80–81, 108
Monteux, Pierre, 32
Moody, William Vaughn, 18, 37
Moore, Douglas, 161
Morgan, Justin, 4
Morrison, George, 84
Muck, Karl, 52, 80
Music criticism, 3, 56; and Ives and Mason, 34–35, 44; and jazz, 69, 115
Musical culture: as an activity for gentlemen, 21; as civil religion, 3, 7, 8, 10, 11, 44–45; and Mason, 43; and morality, 51–59; as a spiritual art, 48–50. See also Education; Mason, Daniel Gregory
Myrick, Julian, Ives's business partner, 29, 31

Nanton, Trick Sam, 112
Nationalism, 59, 68, 81–82. See also America
Naturalism, 44–45, 46–48, 59
Negro music: influence of, 33, 69, 70, 73–74, 77, 78, 80, 118, 163, 189n21
Negroes: and jazz, 116; and Jews, 141, 143–44; migration of, to cities, 85; and racial stereotypes, 66, 67, 68–69, 71, 75, 87–89, 94, 100–101, 104, 110, 170–71, 182n4
Nelson, Stanley, 113
"Nervous burden," 9, 10–43 passim, 174n8
New England school of composers, 4. See also Yankee composers
New York: stereotypic view of, 150–53, 163
Newman, Ernest, 90
Noble, David, 10–11, 63
Nolde, Emil, 123
Norris, Homer, 78
Norton, Charles Eliot, 18, 134

Original Dixieland Jazz Band, 83, 84, 111
Ornstein, Leo, 120
Osborn, 78
Osgood, H. O., 137, 139
Overstreet, Harry, 154

Owen, Robert Dale, 75

Paderewski, 26, 135
Paine, John Knowles, teacher of D. G. Mason, 4, 21, 22–23
Panassie, Hughes, 115
Parker, Henry Taylor, 163, 164
Parker, Horatio, teacher of Ives, 21, 22–23, 57, 58, 91
Parker, Theodore, 4, 54
Parry, Sir Hubert, 27, 52
Parsons, Talcott, 132
Perlis, Vivian: quoted, 31
Perry, Rosalie Sandra, 57
Pfitzner, Hans, 78
Philadelphia Orchestra, 32, 120
Phonograph, 147–48, 195n45
Piatagorsky, 147
Picasso, 120, 125
Pierne, 117
Plato, 2, 48, 49
Poggioli, Renato, 124
Porter, Cole, 94
Poulenc, 115
Powell, John, 154
Programmaticism, 81; Ives and, 55–59, 168. See also Harris, Roy
Progressivism: described, 10–11; and redemptive culture, 45–46, 134. See also Education; Redemptive culture
Prokofieff, 121
Protestant ethic, 68, 89, 132–33, 193n11
Prunieres, Henry, 115
Purcell, 136
Puritans: as antecedents of the centennial composers, 6, 9, 14, 45, 63, 109, 168, 169, 172n6, 175n20, 177n62

Race: and the Jews, 131–34; in the United States, 1–2, 8, 178n3, 191n5, 196n61; and the Yankee composers, 45, 59, 67–68, 82–83
Rachmaninoff, Sergei, 137
Racialism and racism, 2, 173n16; and aesthetics, 66, 67–68; and the Jews, 71, 171; and Negroes, 75, 85–89. See also Ethnicity; Race
Ragtime, 66, 67, 69, 73, 74–82, 83, 111, 183n8
Ravel, Maurice, 55, 115–16
Read, Daniel, 4
Redemptive culture, 3, 6–8, 10, 13, 14–15, 168; and jazz, 68, 70–72, 83, 88, 89, 119, 123; music as, 44–46, 110–11; and ragtime, 79–80; and the Yankee composers, 60–63, 65–66, 106–107, 128–29, 169–71
Reiner, Fritz, 33

Reisman, Leo, 116
Remick, Jerome H., 136
Rieff, Philip, 62
Robeson, Paul, 93
Robinson, Edward Arlington, 28
Romanticism and classicism, 48, 50, 51–52, 55, 58, 125, 178n5
Romantics, 7, 47, 48–49
Roosevelt, Theodore, 40, 42
Rosenfeld, Paul, 56, 121, 140, 141, 143, 163, 189n31
Rosenthal, Moritz, 137
Rossiter, Frank, 17, 56
Roussel, Albert, 115
Roussell-Despierres, 57
Royce, Josiah, teacher of Mason, 18, 26
Rubinstein, 147
Ruggles, Carl, 4, 9, 91, 140, 151, 152, 177n64, 180n37; and Ives, 35, 40; photograph of, 41
Russolo, Luigi, 125

Saint-Saëns, 27
Salt, Henry S., 37
Saminsky, Lazare, 132, 146–47, 163
Santayana, 15–16, 18, 43, 50, 174n9, 179n20, 180n27
Sargeant, Winthrop, 101–102
Sarnoff, David, 149–50
Satie, 111, 117, 125
Savage, Philip Henry, 18
Schenk, H. G., 49
Schmitz, E. Robert, 34
Schoenberg, Arnold, 13, 136, 147
Schopenhauer, 27, 45, 48, 49, 51
Schuller, Gunther, 84
Schumann, Robert, 26, 52, 58
Scott, James, 76
Scriabin, 120, 140, 143
"Search for order": progressive mission as, 10
Seldes, Gilbert, 68, 92–95, 104, 109, 115, 136, 137, 144–45
Sessions, Roger, 129
Sissle, Noble, 93
Slavs: glamorous image of, 135–36
Slonimsky, Nicholas, 34, 164
Smith, Bessie, 104
Smith, David Stanley, 4, 5, 65, 90–91, 128
Solomon, Barbara, 134
Sousa, John Philip, 76–77, 137
Spaeth, Sigmund, 119
Spencer, Herbert, 52, 67–68, 107–108
Spengler, Oswald, 91, 92, 165
Spirituals, 69, 76, 82, 83, 98
Sprague, Claire, 59
Stanford, Charles Villiers, 27
Stearns, Harold, 106

Stearns, Marshall, 103–104
Steiglitz, Alfred, 151
Still, William Grant, 93, 129
Stock, Frederick, 33
Stokowski, Leopold, 32, 100, 137, 147
Stokowski, Olga Samaroff, 135
Stowell, Edgar, 54
Straus, Henrietta, 139, 152
Stravinsky, Igor, 111, 137, 139, 147; Ives on, 55, 88; Mason on, 36, 119, 120–22; program and, 56; *Rite of Spring*, 69, 110, 120, 121, 137
Sullivan, Louis, 57, 58
Sullivan, Mark, 150
Symbolic groups: importance of, 1–3; and Negroes, 170; and race, 2–3, 68. *See also* Jews; Negroes; Race

Tailleferre, 116
Taylor, Bayard, 50
Taylor, Deems, 106, 121, 136, 137
Taylor, Laurette, 86
Tchaikowsky, 27, 50, 51, 52, 53, 58, 77; Ives on, 55, 88
Thayer, Abbott H., 27
Thibaut, Jacques, 115
Thomas, Theodore, 27, 36, 77
Thomas, W. I., 1
Thompson, Oscar, 57, 150–51
Thomson, Virgil, 94–95, 129, 130, 167–68
Thoreau, 13, 37–39, 42, 57, 60, 128, 169
Toll, Robert, 76
Tolstoy, Leo, 47, 53, 57
Toscanini, Arturo, 162–63
Tradition: as lifeline of culture, 7–8, 45; in tension between myth and history, 59, 61
Transcendentalists, 9, 38. *See also under names of particular individuals*
Tryon, Winthrop, 34
Turpin, Tom, 76
Twain, Mark, 29
Twitchell, Joseph, 29

Ulanov, Barry, 103, 112
Untermeyer, Louis, 89

"Usable past," 7–8, 45, 59, 169–70

Van Vechten, Carl, 68, 92, 95–100, 101, 104, 109, 115, 136, 169
Varèse, Edgard, 125–26, 130, 140, 190n44, n46
Vernacular music, 9, 22, 23, 32, 43, 73–74, 77, 81–82, 120. *See also* Indian music; Negro music
Victorian manliness, 21, 40; and musicians, 177n68
Victorian vision of art, 179–80n25; and Seldes, 93; and the Yankee composers, 3, 4, 6, 7, 44, 45, 46–49, 53, 58, 173n13

Wagner, 51, 52, 55, 77
Walker, George W., 93, 111
Walter, Bruno, 33
Weber, Max, 68, 132, 182–83n7
Weill, Kurt, 70, 126–27
Weiss, Adolf, 140
White, Mrs. Elise F., 89
Whiteman, Paul, 94, 116, 136–37
Whiting, Arthur, 4, 26, 27, 148–49
Whitman, Walt, 72, 106, 124, 166, 167
Wiebe, Robert, 10
Wilde, Oscar, 169
Williams, Bert, 111
Williams, William Carlos, 152–53, 190n40, 195–96n57
Wolfe, Thomas, 150
Wolfsohn, Henry, 135
Woods, Harriet, 45
Worthington, Harvey, 78

Yankee composers, 3–9; and attitudes of the public, 14–16; and the avant-garde, 127; and jazz, 66, 69, 70, 91–92; and the Jews, 145, 147, 153, 155; and redemptive culture, 128–29, 168, 169–70; schools of, 4. *See also* Centennial composers
Yellin, Victor, 28

Zangwill, Israel: *The Melting Pot*, 154–56, 157